Latin Grammar

Latin Grammar

Dirk Panhuis

THE UNIVERSITY OF MICHIGAN PRESS Ann Arbor

First paperback edition 2009
English translation copyright © by the University of Michigan 2006
English translation/adaption by Dirk Panhuis and Gertrud Champe
Originally published in Dutch as Latijnse grammatica by Garant,
Antwerp (B.)-Apeldorn (Ne.) © Dirk Panhuis and Garant 1998, 2005
Published in the United States of America by
The University of Michigan Press
Manufactured in the United States of America
♾ Printed on acid-free paper

2012 2011 2010 2009   4 3 2 1

A CIP catalog record for this book is available from the British Library.

Library of Congress Cataloging-in-Publication Data

Panhuis, Dirk G. J.
    [Latijnse grammatica. English]
    Latin grammar / Dirk Panhuis.
        p. cm.
    Includes index.
    ISBN-13: 978-0-472-11542-6 (cloth : alk paper)
    ISBN-10: 0-472-11542-1 (cloth : alk paper)
    1. Latin language—Grammar.   I. Title.
PA2087.P275   2006
478.2'421—dc22   2006045668

ISBN 978-0-472-03373-7 (pbk. : alk. paper)

Preface

A Latin grammar is an indispensable tool for Latin students who pursue study of the language past the introductory course. As soon as they start reading texts for the sake of the texts and of Roman culture, they should always have a reference work at hand to check and expand their knowledge of grammar. Beginning students can use the morphology section of this book from the start, as well as the synopsis of the use of the cases (end of chap. 9) and the introductory section on sentence structure (chap. 10).

Many of the examples are taken from texts that are frequently read in a Latin curriculum. Rereading those sentences will refresh the student's memory of that text and the Roman history and culture it embodies. The meaningful context provided by such a sentence will be a good stimulus for a correct understanding of the grammatical phenomenon.

Syntax and semantics of the sentence have become the central area of linguistics during the last half century. Sentence phenomena therefore have to be seen as such and should no longer be viewed as applied morphology. Particular emphasis is placed on the central role of the predicate in the structure of the sentence. Moreover, many constructions are to be explained not on the sentence level but on the higher level of the context. Several of them have been known for a very long time, but for the last three decades, they have been treated in a more systematic way, under the heading *textlinguistics* or *discourse studies*. In this book too, they are explicitly dealt with as supra-sentential phenomena.

Much attention has been given to a scientifically justified organization of this book based on the levels in the grammatical hierarchy and particularly on the structure of the sentence. Concepts have been explained and definitions formulated with great care; morphological, syntactic, semantic, and supra-sentential concepts have been clearly labeled as such. However, occasionally a balance had to be sought between a correct linguistic definition and current educational practice.

Presenting language structures in tables appears to be beneficial for a firm understanding. Here, scientific and didactic clarity go hand in hand. Furthermore, the user of this book will find numerous suggestions for translations whenever the English language requires a different turn for typical Latin structures.

This English edition is a slightly corrected adaptation of the original publication in Dutch. A glossary has been added in this English edition.

It is my pleasure to thank again the many Flemish high school students who forced me to make abstract concepts clear to them. Also, some

Belgian and Dutch Latinists deserve my thanks for their discussions and remarks during the preparation of the first and second editions of the original publication: Dr. H. Pinkster, Dr. M. Bolkenstein, Dr. R. Risselada, J. de Jong, Dr. M. Lavency, T. Brabants, M. Hoefmans, J. Piolon, and R. Vermeersh.

Last but not least, this American edition would have been impossible without the help of Dr. Gertrud Champe (PhD in comparative literature, University of Iowa, specializing in translation and teaching German and Latin to graduate students in the humanities). Her comments, queries, English language corrections, and guidance through American educational practice have been invaluable. But nobody other than myself is to be held accountable for weaknesses or errors.

It is to be hoped that the use of this grammar will provide as much pleasure to others as the writing of it provided to me.

Dr. Dirk Panhuis
Louvain, Belgium

Contents

The Pronunciation of Length and Stress

The Length of the Syllables

a) A syllable bearing a macron on the vowel is long (e.g., the last two syllables in *magnitūdō*).
b) A syllable containing a diphthong is long (e.g., the first syllable in *causa*).
c) A syllable containing a vowel followed by two or more consonants (including the double consonant *x*, but not an *h*) is long by position (e.g., in *rex*, the first syllable in *magnitūdō*, and all three syllables in *respondent*), unless indicated otherwise with the sign for a short vowel (e.g., the first syllable in *pătris*).
d) Other syllables are short (e.g., both syllables in *rosa*, the last syllable in *causa*, and the second syllable in *magnitūdō*).

Some disyllabic words, such as *mihi* and *ubi*, bear no length mark because the last syllable is sometimes long and sometimes short.

Stress (Word Accent)

In the word *respondēret*, the penultimate syllable is long (as indicated by the macron); the stress thus falls on the (here underlined) penultimate.

In *iustitia*, the penultimate syllable is short. (A vowel preceding another vowel is short.) Therefore the stress falls on the (here underlined) antepenultimate.

Disyllabic words bear the stress on the first syllable, irrespective of the length of that syllable.

In the paradigms of the declensions and conjugations, the vowel of the stressed syllable is sometimes underlined to indicate the shift in stress as a consequence of the changing number of syllables of a word (e.g., nom./voc. pl. *rosae*, gen. *rosārum*).

PART 1

Alphabet and Phonology

1

Alphabet and Phonology

Alphabet

1. The Latin alphabet is derived, through Greek, from the Phoenician alphabet. As a consequence of this borrowing, some letters are superfluous for the Latin phonological system (e.g., the three letters *c, k,* and *q* stand for the one sound [k][1]), and other letters are ambiguous (e.g., there is only one letter *a* for the long and short vowels [a:] and [a]). Nevertheless, Latin can manage with the letters of the imported alphabet. By means of twenty-three letters, the thirty-seven meaningful sounds, or phonemes, of Latin can be rendered.

2. The **twenty-three letters** of the Latin alphabet and their **pronunciation** are as follows:

A   Short [a] as in *cup* and in the first syllable of *aha,* or long [a:] as in *father.*

B   Voiced [b] as in *barba* 'beard', but voiceless [p] before *t* or *s* as in *urbs* [urps].

C   Voiceless [k], irrespective of the following sound, as in *Caesar* [Kaisar]. Note: the abbreviation *C.* represents (in the archaic spelling) the voiced [g] of *Gāius.*

D   Voiced stop [d].

E   Short [e] as in *let,* or long [e:] as in *prey* (without the final diphthongal element) or as in German *See* or French *été.*

F   Voiceless fricative [f].

G   Voiced stop as in *get,* but never as in *germ.* Note: before *n* the letter *g* is pronounced as the allophone [ŋ] as in *hangnail.* Thus, *signum* is pronounced [siŋnum], not as *signal; agnus* is pronounced [aŋnus], not as in church Latin or in French *agneau.*

H   Voiceless fricative [h]. A very weak consonant (§ 7b).

I   Short vowel [i] as in *dip,* or long vowel [i:] as in *deep.* Semi-consonant before or between vowels (sometimes written as *j*) as in *you.*

K   Voiceless stop [k]. Extremely rare.

L   Lateral liquid [l].

M   Labial nasal consonant [m]. Very weak at the end of a word (§ 376, 468).

---

1. Symbols between square brackets in this chapter are those of the International Phonetic Alphabet.

N   Dental nasal consonant [n]. Before a velar (*g, c, ch*) or labiovelar (*qu*) (§ 4), the *n* is pronounced as the allophone [ŋ] as in *ancora* 'anchor' and *lingua* 'language'.

O   Short [o] as in *pot*, or long [o:] as in *bone* (without the final diphthongal element), German *Sohn*, or French *beau*.

P   Voiceless stop [p].

Q   [k]. This letter only occurs in combination with *u* to indicate the simultaneous lip rounding. So the two letters (digraph) *qu* indicate one labiovelar sound [kʷ] (§ 4, 7b).

R   Trilled or rolled liquid [r] as in Scottish.

S   Voiceless fricative [s] as in *sing* and *lesson*, but never as in *roses*.

T   Voiceless stop [t].

U/V Short vowel [u] as in *put*, or long vowel [u:] as in *boot*. Also semi-consonant [w] as in Latin *uentus, uīnum* and English *wind* and *wine*. This semi-consonant is often written as *v* (*ventus, vīnum*). The Romans only wrote capital letters (VENTVS, VINVM). In Latin *an-tī-quus*, the first *u* is part of the labiovelar consonant [kʷ]; the second *u* is a vowel. But *vacuus* [wa-ku-us] contains two successive vowels and therefore three syllables total.

X   One letter for two consonants: [ks].

Y   Short [y], or long [y:] as in French *lune* and German *Tür*. Together with the next letter, *y* was added to the end of the Latin alphabet in the first century B.C. in order to spell Greek loanwords, such as *nympha, Olympia, Lȳdia,* and *gȳrus* 'circle'.

Z   Voiced fricative [z] at the beginning of a word, or double consonant [zz] in the middle of a word. This consonant only occurs in Greek loanwords, such as *Zephyrus* and *Amāzōn*.

3. **Double consonants** should be pronounced **double** or **long**. This is required not only by the weight or quantity of the syllables (§ 7) but also by difference in meaning: compare *ager* 'field' and *agger* 'rampart'; *anus, -ūs* 'old woman' or *ānus, -i* 'arse' and *annus, -i* 'year'; *cārus* 'dear' and *carrus* 'cart'; *adit* '(he) visits' and *addit* '(he) adds'; *erāmus* 'we were' and *errāmus* 'we err'.

Phonological system

4. The **system of consonants** consists of nineteen consonants (and two semi-consonants). When consonants are pronounced, the air-stream from the lungs is transformed by the following factors:

   a) If the vocal cords in the glottis of the larynx vibrate, a **voiced consonant** is produced; if not, the consonant remains **voiceless**. If, after a stop (§ 4c), air escapes through the glottis before the next vowel or consonant is pronounced, an **aspirated stop** occurs.

b) A consonant occurs when the air-stream is more or less interrupted somewhere in the mouth. The interruption can be located at
  – both lips (or for [f], the lower lip and upper teeth) for **labial** consonants;
  – the teeth for **dental** consonants;
  – the alveolar ridge just after the teeth for **alveolar** consonants;
  – the hard palate for **palatal** consonants;
  – the velum or soft palate for **velar** consonants;
  – the velum but with simultaneous lip rounding for **labiovelar** consonants;
  – the glottis in the larynx for a **glottal fricative [h]**.

c) The **degree** or **manner** of the interruption of the air-stream can vary, including
  – **stops** or **occlusives** (*ob-claudere*): the air-stream is completely interrupted;
  – **nasals**: the air-stream in the mouth is closed, but the breath escapes through the nose;
  – **fricatives**: some air whirls through a narrow passage in the mouth;
  – **liquids**: the air passes at the side of the tongue [l] or during the vibration of the tongue [r]. A liquid is a sonant, that is, it is less consonant than a stop or a fricative. This explains exception 2 in § 7b.
  – **semi-consonants** or **approximants**: there is little interruption of the air-stream, so that semi-consonants resemble vowels. The difference is that semi-consonants stand at the margin of a syllable (as in *iam* and *vī-num*), the vowels at the nucleus of the syllable (as in *vī-num*) (§ 2, U/V).

		Labial	Dental / Alveolar	Palatal	Velar	Labiovelar	Glottal
Nasal		m	n				
Stop							
	Voiced	b	d		g	gu [gʷ]	
	Voiceless	p	t		c / k	qu [kʷ]	
	Voiceless aspirated	ph*	th*		ch*		
Fricative							
	Voiced		z				
	Voiceless	f	s				h
Liquid							
	Lateral		l				
	Trill		r				
Semi-consonants				i [j]		u [w]	

*The voiceless aspirated stops *ph, th,* and *ch* were pronounced as, respectively, [pʰ] in emphatic "pig!", [tʰ] in emphatic "terrible!" (not interdental [θ] as in "theater"), and [kʰ] in emphatic "You cat!"

5. **The vowel system** contains eleven vowels, ten Latin and one Greek (*y*). **Vowels** are classified according to whether they are pronounced with the tongue high in the mouth (**high** or **closed vowels**) or low (**low** or **open vowels**). The *i* [i:], a **front vowel**, is pronounced with the tongue near the palate, the *u* [u], a **back vowel**, with the tongue near the velum or soft palate (§ 4). When pronouncing the *a*, the tongue lies **low** in the mouth. Back vowels and the *y* [y] are pronounced **with lip rounding**, the front vowels, except the *y*, **without lip rounding**.

	Front	Back
Closed vowels	y ī ĭ ŭ ū	
Half-closed vowels	ē ō	
Half-open vowels	ĕ ŏ	
Open vowels	ă ā	

6. **Diphthongs** start with a vowel and end with a higher (more closed) semi-vowel/semi-consonant [i/j] or [u/w]. Only diphthongs beginning with an *a* occur frequently. Diphthongs were pronounced in cultivated speech and literary Latin well into imperial times but occurred as mid-monophthongs in popular speech from an early date (§ 376).

   ae: [aʲ]: *Rōmae* (old spelling *Romai*), *praetor.* Popular pronunciation: [e].

   au: [aʷ]: *Claudius, auris.* In popular pronunciation, *Clōdius, ōriculum* (cf. French *oreille*) (§ 376).

   ei: [eʲ] as in *day*, though with a rather more open starting point. It occurs only in a few instances of synizesis in poetry: *deinde* (besides *de-in-de*), *au-reis* (otherwise *au-re-īs*). But *dē-i-ci-ō.*

   eu: [eʷ]: only in the words *neu, seu,* and *heu(s)* and in Greek loanwords, such as *Orpheus.*

   oe: [oʲ] as in *boy: poena, proelium.* Also *proin-de* in poetry, in addition to *pro-in-de.*

   ou: [oʷ] as in *go:* only in *prout*, in addition to disyllabic *pro-ut.*

   ui: [uʲ] as in French *oui: cuī, huīc.*

Quantity of syllables

7. **A syllable is heavy** or **long** in the following cases:

   a) **Heavy or long by nature:**
   – a syllable containing a **long vowel** or **diphthong**: *ha-bē-re, clau-sus, ro-sae;*
   – a final *-i, -o, -u: servī, legō, mōtū;*

– an ablative singular ending with *-a, -o, -i, -u, -e* (but not in the consonant declension): *rosā, servō, marī, fructū, rē* (but *rēge*);
– accusative plural masculine and feminine endings in all declensions: *rosās, servōs, lēgēs, fructūs, rēs;*
– dative and ablative plural endings in *-īs: rosīs, servīs;*
– imperative singular active in the a- or e-conjugation: *amā, habē;*
– final *-ē* of the adverb: *longē.*

b) **Heavy or long by position: a syllable containing a vowel that is followed by two or more consonants (even in the following word) or by a double consonant (*x, z*) is heavy by position.** Note that the syllable is heavy or long even if the vowel is and remains short. For example, the second *a* in *nātūram* is short, but in *nātūramque* the syllable *-ram* is heavy or long because the *ă* is followed by two consonants, *m* and *qu*. Also, in *postquam* the *a* is short, but in *postquam manus* the syllable *-quam* is heavy or long because of the double consonant *mm*.

Exception 1. The *u* (as semi-consonant) and the weak *h* do not count as consonants for the rule "heavy or long by position." Therefore, the first syllable in *aqua* is short, as is the last syllable of *tristis* in *tristis hiems*.

Exception 2. If a short vowel is followed by a stop and a liquid, both belonging to the next syllable, then the syllable containing the short vowel is not heavy or long. (It is heavy if the vowel is long or if the stop goes with that syllable.)
pă-tris (short *ă*): first syllable is **not long** by position (*t* and *r* in the next syllable).
ab-la-tum (short *ă*): first syllable is **long** by position (*b* and *l* not together).
mā-tris (long *ā*): first syllable is **long** by nature.

8. **A syllable is short or light** in the following cases:
   a) A syllable with a **short vowel** that is not long/heavy by position is short or light. Therefore, both syllables are short/light in *du-ce;* all three are short/light in *re-ge-re*. But despite its short vowel *ĕ*, the syllable (word) *mens* is long by position.
   b) Final *-a* and final *-e* are short, as in *rosa* (nom.), *duce* (abl. sg. consonant declension), *vincere, scribe,* and *dulce,* except for the cases mentioned in § 7a.
   c) A vowel that in the same word is followed with another vowel or *h* is short: *rē-gi-us, au-di-ō, pro-hi-be-ō*. Exception. The following syllables are heavy/long: *is-tī-us, il-lī-us, di-ē-i, Ae-nē-ās* (from the Greek diphthong ει: Αἰνείας).
   d) A final syllable ending with one consonant is short/light: *ro-sam, vo-cat, in-ter, vo-cā-mus, men-sis, ca-pis*. Some final syllables with *-s* are heavy: *ro-sīs, ser-vīs* (dat./abl. pl.), *audīs* (in the ī-conjugation), *a-mās* (in the ā-conjugation), *ro-sās* (acc. pl.) (§ 7a).

Word stress or spoken accent

9. In words of three or more syllables, the stress falls on the second syllable from the end (the underlined penultimate) if the syllable is heavy (either by nature or by position): *cer-tā̱-men, pau-pē̱r-tās, re-gi-ō̱-nis, vo-lū̱p-tās.*

   If the penultimate is light/short, the stress falls on the third syllable from the end (the underscored antepenultimate): *re̱-gi-ō, co̱r-po-ris, re̱-ge-re.*

   In words of two syllables, the stress falls on the penultimate (= the first syllable).

   If a word is combined with a word without its own accent, such as *-que -ve, -ne, -met* (enclitics), then the two words are considered together as one phonological word, with the stress on the penultimate: *vi̱-rum,* but *vi-ru̱m-que; lū̱-mi-na,* but *lū-mi-na̱-que; e̱-go,* but *e-go̱-met.*

PART 2

Morphology

2

The Word

10. **The parts of speech** in Latin are almost the same as in English. Only the article is lacking. It should be clear from the context whether a noun should be accompanied in translation by an indefinite article, a definite article, a possessive adjective (§ 56), or nothing.

Words variable (inflected) by **declension** (§ 10a–c) or **conjugation** (§ 10d) are

a) **the noun** or **substantive**: the head of a noun phrase, like *chapter* in the phrase *this difficult chapter*. It has its own gender and is declined for number and case. It is the name of a person, animal, thing, or abstract concept.

b) **the adjective**: functions primarily as an attribute (modifier) in the noun phrase, as does *difficult* in the phrase *this difficult chapter*. It can also be used as a predicate adjective with a copula, as in *this chapter is difficult,* and as a predicative complement, as in *the students consider this chapter difficult.* It is declined for gender, number, and case. Participles and gerundives are adjectives derived from a verb.

• There are descriptive adjectives: they give the property (*difficult*) or the state (*lost, unfinished*) of the noun (chap. 4).

• There are determiners: numerals (often indeclinable) (chap. 4); possessive (*your*), demonstrative (*those*), interrogative (*which?*), and indefinite (*each*) adjectives (chap. 6).

c) **the pronoun**: refers to or stands "for" (*pro-*) a noun, such as *it (= the chapter)* in *it is difficult.* It is declined for gender (except the personal pronoun), number, and case. Pronouns are personal (*we*), possessive (*mine*), demonstrative (*this* in *this chapter is difficult*), interrogative (*who?*), indefinite (*something*), or relative (*who, that*) (chap. 6).

d) **the verb**: syntactically, a word that is the grammatical center of the predicate and agrees with the subject in person and number. Morphologically, it is conjugated for tense, mood, voice, aspect, person, and number. Semantically, a verb expresses an act, an occurrence, a position, or a state of being. Auxiliaries (*can, should, must*) and the copula (*to be*) generally lack some of these properties.

Invariable words are

e) **the adverb**: functions as the modifier of a verb (*never* in *they **never** consider*), an adjective (*very* in ***very** difficult*), an adverb (*almost* in *almost never*), or an entire sentence (*fortunately* in **fortunately** *he arrived*). Many adverbs are derived from adjectives by means of a suffix (*forti-ter* 'strong-**ly**'); others only exist as adverbs (*numquam* 'never'). Adverbs can indicate a place, direction, time, frequency, degree, manner, modality, negation, and so on. Closely connected to the adverbs are **the particles**, expressing an emphatic, emotional, or appreciative attitude: *utĭnam* (in Latin wishes) and Latin question particles.

f) **the preposition**: belongs to a small group of words (*in, to, under, with*, etc.) that can be combined with a (pro)noun or noun phrase, as in **after** *this chapter,* **in** *his sleep,* **during** *classes,* **without** *her.* The preposition and noun phrase form a prepositional phrase, which is mostly connected as an adverbial modifier to a verb. Postpositions function in the same way but occur after the (pro)noun, as in *vobiscum* 'with you' and *Urbem* **versus** 'City**wards**'.

g) **the conjunction**: joins two or more elements. Coordinating conjunctions (*and, or, but*) join two or more elements (words, phrases, or clauses) on the same level; subordinating conjunctions (*because, although*) join a subordinate clause to a governing clause.

h) **the interjection**: ejaculatory utterance (*alas, Heavens*), usually lacking grammatical connection (§ 380).

11. A **variable word** can consist of **several constituents (morphemes): root, derivational affix, thematic vowel**, and **ending**.

The **root** is the smallest possible meaningful unit (morpheme) in a word. In *victōrem,* the root *vic-* carries the meaning 'win, conquer'. A **compound word** like *signifer* 'standard-bearer' contains more than one root: the root *sign-* and the root *fer-*. The number of root morphemes that occur in Latin is very large, almost as large as the number of words in a dictionary.

An **affix** (derivational morpheme) **adds a meaning** to the root. The number of affixes that occur in Latin is limited (§ 12–16). The root and the affixes together form the **stem** of a word.

a) A **prefix** preceeds the root: *in-vic-tu-s* '**un**conquered'.

b) A **suffix** follows the root and can form the stem of another class of words (part of speech): *vic-tor* (noun) 'winner'. There can be several suffixes: *vic-tōr-ia* (noun) 'victory', *vic-tōr-i-ōsu-* (adjective) 'victorious'. Suffixes occur both as derivatives (§ 14–16) and as inflectional endings.

c) An **infix** occurs within the root: *vinc-e-re* 'to conquer'. (The *-n-* is an infix in some imperfective stems.)

A **stem** is followed by an **inflectional ending**: a **declensional ending** for nouns, adjectives, and pronouns; a **conjugational ending** for verbs. The final sound of the stem often merges with the ending, so that the separation between stem and ending is sometimes difficult to indicate (the stem *victōria* + the dat. pl. ending *-īs* > *victōriīs*). The stem and the ending together form the **word**.

Every **word** has a root but does not necessarily have derivational affixes. Every stem has an ending, but sometimes the ending is zero (ø). But a ø-affix or a ø-ending also has a meaning. In *victōr-ēs*, the ending *-ēs* indicates the nominative/accusative plural; in *victor*, the absence of an ending indicates the nominative singular. In *amā-ba-t*, the suffix *-ba* indicates the imperfect tense, and the ending *-t* indicates the third-person singular active. But in *ama-t*, the lack of a tense suffix indicates the present tense; and in *amā*, the lack of a suffix and of an ending indicates the present imperative second-person singular active. An extreme case of a root without suffix or ending is the imperative *I* 'Go!' This form is at the same time a root, a stem, a word, a sentence, and a speech.

A **thematic vowel** sometimes occurs between a stem and an ending (*reg-i-t, reg-u-nt, reg-e-re*) or between two roots (*sign-i-fer*).

12. The following **prefixes**, which also exist separately as prepositions, can be added to **verbs**, **adjectives**, and **nouns**. They can undergo changes when they are positioned before certain sounds. A changed morpheme is called an ***allomorph***. So, in the table that follows *ā-*, *abs-*, and *au-* are allomorphs or variants of the morpheme *ab-*. Also, the root vowel of the verb can undergo changes (*facere: perficere*).

Prefix	Meaning	Example
ab- (ā-, abs-, au-)	separation: away from	*āvertere* 'turn aside', *abdūcere* 'lead away', *auferre* 'carry off', *abscondere* 'hide'
ad- (ac-, af-, ag-, al-, ap-, as-, at-, a-)	direction: toward, near	*adīre* 'go to, visit', *afferre* 'bring to', *accurrere* 'rush to', *attingere* 'touch', *aspicere* 'look at'
ante-	before	*antepōnere* 'prefer', *anteīre* 'precede'
circum-	around	*circumvenīre* 'encircle'
contra-	against	*contrādīcere* 'contradict'
cum- (com-, con-, col-, co-)	1) together, with 2) completely	*compōnere* 'put together, compare' *commovēre* 'move thoroughly', *conficere* 'complete, finish off'
dē-	1) from above 2) away 3) completely	*dēcurrere* 'run down' *dēterrēre* 'deter, put off' *dēvincere* 'conquer completely'
ex- (ē-, ef-)	out (completely)	*extrahere* 'extract', *exhaurīre* 'draw from, exhaust', *ēligere* 'elect', *effugere* 'escape'
in- (il-, im-, ir-)	in, on	*ingredi* 'enter', *importāre* 'import', *incidere* 'fall on'
inter-	1) between, among 2) thoroughly	*intermittere* 'leave between, interrupt', *intercedere* 'intervene', *interficere* 'kill'

ob- (oc-, of-, op-, os-)	against, opposite	*obstāre* 'stand in the way', *occurrere* 'run to meet', *offendere* 'push against, offend', *ostendere* 'hold out, show'
per-	through, until the end, thoroughly	*percurrere* 'run through', *perficere* 'complete', *perterrēre* 'frighten terribly', *perdulcis* 'very sweet'
post-	after	*postpōnere* 'postpone, disregard'
prae-	1) before, ahead 2) very, intensively	*praemittere* 'send ahead', *praeficere* 'put at the head of'; *praeclārus* 'very brilliant'
praeter-	beside	*praetermittere* 'let pass'
pro- (prod-)	forth, forward, to the profit, on behalf of	*prōdūcere* 'bring forth, produce', *prō-scrībere* 'publicize (in writing)', *prō-desse* 'benefit', *prōconsul* 'proconsul'
sub- (su-, suc-, sup-, sus-)	under, from under up, secretly, a little	*subicere* 'put under, subject', *subīre* 'go up', *sustinēre* 'support', *subrīdēre* 'smile'
super-	over	*superesse* 'remain, be left over'
trans- (tra-)	across	*transīre* 'cross', *trādere* 'hand over'

13. The following **prefixes** are inseparable: they only occur in combination with verbs, adjectives, or nouns.

Prefix	Meaning	Example
amb- (am-)	around, about	*ambīre* 'go about', *amplecti* 'embrace'
dis- (di-, dif-, dir-)	apart	*distribuere* 'distribute', *dīmittere* 'send away, let go', *differre* 'postpone'
in- (im-)	un- (negation)	*iniustus* 'unjust', *impar* 'odd (not even)'
intro-	in (inward)	*intrōdūcere* 'bring in'
ne- (neg-)	negation	*nescīre* 'not know', *neglegere* 'not choose > neglect', *negōtium* 'no leisure > business'
re- (red-)	back, again	*redīre* 'return', *repetere* 'ask back, ask again, repeat'
se- (sed-)	apart, away	*sēcēdere* 'leave', *sēd-i-tio* 'separation, mutiny', *sēcūrus* 'without cares, secure'

14. The following **suffixes** add a meaning to the root of the verb.

Suffix	Meaning	Example
-it, -t, -tit	frequentative, iterative	*dictitāre* 'say repeatedly', *iactāre* 'throw frequently', *clamitāre* 'shout repeatedly'
-sc	inchoative: 'begin to'	*cognoscere* 'get acquainted, get to know', *lūcescere* 'become light'
apophony or ablaut: change in the root vowel (affix)	causative: 'cause to'	*cadere* 'fall': *caedere* 'make fall > fell, kill'; *meminisse* 'remember': *monēre* 'remind'

15. The following **suffixes change a verbal or nominal root into an adjective**.

Suffix	Meaning	Example
-ilis, -bilis	possibility	*crēdibilis* 'credible', *ūtilis* 'useful', *facilis* 'easy', *nōbilis* 'who can be known, famous'
-īlis	proper to	*puerīlis* 'childish'
-eus	made from	*aureus* 'golden', *purpureus* 'purple'
-ānus, -icus, -īnus, -ensis	originating from	*Rōmānus* 'Roman', *Athēniensis* 'Athenian', *Capitolīnus* 'from the Capitoline', *Africus* 'African'
-ōsus	full of	*perīculōsus* 'dangerous', *studiōsus* 'sedulous'
-ax	strongly inclined to	*audax* 'audacious, bold', *rapax* 'rapacious'

16. Many **nouns** are formed by adding a **suffix** to the root of a verb, an adjective, or another noun.

Suffix	Meaning	Example
-(t)or, -(s)or	agent (m.)	*victor* 'victor', *cursor* 'runner'
-trix	agent (f.)	*victrix* 'victress'
-(t)io, -(s)io, -(t)us, -(s)us	activity	*actio* 'act', *salūtātio* 'greeting', *exitus* 'exit', *rīsus* 'laughter'
-ia, -itia, -(e)tās, -(i)tās, -(i)tūdō, -tūs	abstract property	*iustitia* 'justice', *libertās* 'freedom', *pietās* 'piety, respect', *fortitūdō* 'strength, courage', *iuventūs* 'youth'
-mentum, -trum, -culum, -crum	instrument	*ornāmentum* 'ornament', *arātrum* 'plough', *vehiculum* 'vehicle', *sepulcrum* 'grave'
-ellus, -olus, -(c)ulus, -(el)la, -ola, -ula	diminutive (also with adj.)	nouns: *agellus* 'little field', *homunculus* 'little man', *fīliola* 'little daughter', *flammula* 'little flame' adjectives: *parvus* 'small' > *parvulus*, *miser* 'wretched' > *misellus*

3
The Noun

General concepts

17. **Nouns** or **substantives** fall into **five** classes or **declensions**. The declension to which a noun belongs is most easily seen from the form of the **genitive singular**. By convention, the genitive singular of every noun is listed in its dictionary entry.

> A noun of the **first** or **a-declension** has a genitive singular in *-ae*.
> A noun of the **second** or **o-declension** has a genitive singular in *-i*.
> A noun of the **third** or **consonant/i-declension** has a genitive singular in *-is*.
> A noun of the **fourth** or **u-declension** has a genitive singular in *-us*.
> A noun of the **fifth** or **e-declension** has a genitive singular in *-ei*.

18. A noun has **two numbers: singular** and **plural**.

Some nouns, known as pluralia tantum, only exist in the plural: *moenia, moenium* 'town walls'; *Athēnae, -ārum* 'Athens'; *arma, -ōrum* 'weapons'. Some nouns have a different meaning in the singular and the plural: *cōpia, -ae* 'supply', but *cōpiae, -ārum* 'troops'; *auxilium, -i* 'help', but *auxilia, -ōrum* 'auxiliary troops'; *aedēs, -is* 'temple', but *aedēs, -ium* 'house'.

The **dual** has disappeared, except in the two words *duo* 'two' and *ambō* 'both' (nom. and acc.: see § 45).

19. Nouns are **declined**. The stem of a noun is followed by an **inflectional ending**, which indicates **case and number**. Latin has **six cases: nominative, vocative, genitive, dative, accusative,** and **ablative**.

There were originally two other cases, the **locative** and the **instrumental**. They have, for the most part, merged with the ablative. But remnants of the locative singular ending in *-ī* are preserved in some forms and constructions (§ 25h, 28d, 30a, 133, 300, 305).

Cases indicate certain syntactic and semantic relations in the structure of the sentence and its parts. The syntactic functions and the semantic roles of the cases are explained in chapters 9 (with a summary in § 178) and 10 (§ 179–80, 184–88).

The cases have some general characteristics.

a) The **vocative** is like the nominative, except in the masculine o-declension singular: words of the type *servu-s* have a vocative singular *servĕ* with a weakened stem vowel and without a case ending.

b) The **nominative, vocative, and accusative neuter** are always the same. In the plural of these cases, the ending is -*a* in all declensions.

c) The **dative and ablative plural** are always alike in all genders in all declensions.

The stem is seen most clearly when the ending -*um* or -*rum* of the genitive plural is taken away. But in other cases, the stem and the endings have often merged, particularly when the stem ends in a vowel. Therefore, stem and ending cannot always be distinguished any longer. In the declension tables that follow in this book, the ending of a word is printed in bold type, although it may contain a part of the stem, as in *rosā* (stem *rosă* + length for the abl. sing.), *servīs* (stem *servo-* + -*īs* for the dat./abl. pl.), or *rex* (stem *reg-* + ending -*s* for the nom. sg.). In the tables, (shift of) word stress is sometimes indicated by an underlined syllable, because the stress may vary according to the number and the quantity of the syllables (§ 7–9).

20. Latin has **three grammatical genders: masculine, feminine, and neuter**. This is a simple distinction of form shown by a noun and by the adjective agreeing with it or by a pronoun agreeing or referring to it. The **grammatical gender (genus)** corresponds to the **natural gender or sex (male, female, and neither of those)** only to a limited extent.

Masculine is the gender of names and professions of all **males** and of names of **winds** and of many **rivers** and **months**, irrespective of their declension: *nauta* 'boatman', *Aquilō* 'the north wind', *Garumna* 'the Garonne', *Tiberis* 'the Tiber', *Aprīlis (mensis)* 'April'.

Feminine is the gender of the names and designations of **females** and of most **trees, countries, islands**, and **cities**: *anus* 'old woman', *arbor* 'tree', *quercus* 'oak', *Aegyptus* 'Egypt', *Dēlus* 'Delos', *Corinthus* 'Corinth'.

Neuter is the gender of **indeclinable nouns, infinitives**, and **phrases treated as indeclinable nouns**: *fās* '(divine) right', *errāre hūmānum est* 'to err is human', *triste valē* 'a sad farewell'.

21. If natural gender or sex does not play a role, the following rules apply for **grammatical gender**.

	Masculine	**Feminine**	**Neuter**
1st or a-declension		words in *-a*	
2nd or o-declension	words in *-us* and *-er*		words in *-um*
3rd or consonant/ i-declension	words in *-er* and *-or* also *fons, mons, pons, piscis, amnis, ignis, collis, mensis, ensis, lapis, orbis, finis, pānis, postis, sanguis torrens, oriens, dens, aquilō, ordō, sermō*	words in *-s, -o, -x* exceptions: see masculine and neuter columns	words in *-e, -al, -ar, -ma, -men, -ur* words in *-us* with the genitive in *-eris* or *-oris*
4th or u-declension	words in *-us*	*manus, domus, Idus, tribus*	words in *-u*
5th or e-declension	*diēs* (often), *merīdiēs*	words in *-es*	

First or a-declension

22. Nouns of the **first** or **a-declension** have a nominative singular in *-a* without case ending and a genitive singular ending in *-ī* (*rosa-ī*), which in spelling has changed to *-e* (*rosae*).

	Singular	**Plural**
Nominative	rọsa	rosae
Vocative	rosa	rosae
Genitive	rosae	rosārum
Dative	rosae	rọsīs
Accusative	rosam	rosās
Ablative	rosā	rọsīs

23. Remarks

    a) Originally the genitive singular ended in *-s*. This ending is still found in archaic expressions, such as *pater familias* 'head of the household'.

    b) Greek nouns of the first declension often retain their Greek endings in some cases: *Aenēās* (Greek nom.), *Aenēae* (Latin gen. and dat.), *Aenēan* (Greek acc.).

Second or o-declension

24. Masculine nouns of the **second** or **o-declension** have a nominative singular ending in *-s* (*servu-s*) or zero (*puer*) and a genitive singular ending in *-ī*. Neuter nouns have a nominative singular ending in *-m* and a genitive singular ending in *-ī*.

	Masculine		Masculine		Neuter	
	Singular	Plural	Singular	Plural	Singular	Plural
Nominative	servus	servī	puer	puerī	templum	templa
Vocative	serve	servī	puer	puerī	templum	templa
Genitive	servī	servōrum	puerī	puerōrum	templī	templōrum
Dative	servō	servīs	puerō	puerīs	templō	templīs
Accusative	servum	servōs	puerum	puerōs	templum	templa
Ablative	servō	servīs	puerō	puerīs	templō	templīs

25. Remarks

a) Nouns like *ager, agrī* 'field' are declined like *puer* but lose the vowel *e* in cases other than the nominative and vocative singular. *Vir, virī* 'man' is declined like *puer.*

b) The vocative singular of *fīlius* 'son' and of proper names ending in *-ius* ends in *-i: fīlī, Vergilī, Gāī.*

c) Nouns ending in *-ius* and *-ium* often have a contracted genitive singular ending in *-ī.*

d) The genitive plural originally ended in *-um.* This archaic genitive still occurs in poetry (*regīna deum* 'the queen of the gods', *virum terrea prōgeniēs* 'the earthly species of men'), in such archaic expressions as *praefectus fabrum* 'chief engineer', and in such genitives as *superum, sestertium, talentum, triumvirum,* and *līberum.*

e) *Deus* 'god' has a vocative singular *deus*, nominative plural *deī/diī/ dī* and dative/ablative plural *deīs/diīs/dīs.*

f) *Locus* (m.) has a neuter plural (*locă* 'places') and a masculine plural (*locī* 'passages in a book').

g) *Vulgus* 'populace' is neuter and has a nominative, vocative, and accusative singular *vulgus.* Also neuter are *vīrus* 'poison' and *pelagus* 'sea'. *Humus* and several Greek nouns, such as *methodus, paragraphus,* and *periodus,* are feminine.

h) The old locative (in *-ī*) survives in *humī* 'on the ground', *vesperī* 'in the evening', and *domī bellīque, domī militiaeque* 'at home and in war' = 'in peacetime and in wartime' (§ 19, 133, 305).

Third or consonant/i-declension

26. Nouns of the **third declension** end in *-is* in the genitive singular and *-um* in the genitive plural. The stem of this declension sometimes ends in a consonant, sometimes in the vowel *-i.* Two words having a stem in *-u* (*sūs* 'pig, sow', *grūs* 'crane') sometimes behave like consonant stems (see § 28f).

The ending of the nominative singular masculine and feminine is either *-s,* as in *lex* (< *leg-s*), *cīvitās* (< *cīvitāt-s*), and *sū-s,* or zero (ø), as in *victor-ø, regiō* (< *regiōn-ø*). The nominative singular neuter is always zero (ø): *corpus-ø, mare* (< *mari-ø*), *animal* (< *animāli-ø*).

The nouns of this declension fall into **four types**, but the majority of the nouns follow the paradigm (example) of *lex* and *corpus* (type I: see § 27).

	Masculine and feminine		Neuter	
	Singular	**Plural**	**Singular**	**Plural**
Nominative	lex	legēs	corpus	corpora
Vocative	lex	legēs	corpus	corpora
Genitive	legis	legum	corporis	corporum
Dative	legī	legibus	corporī	corporibus
Accusative	legem	legēs	corpus	corpora
Ablative	lege	legibus	corpore	corporibus

27. The nouns of this declension have different kinds of stems: **consonant stems** (including two u-stems) and **i-stems**. Types II, III, and IV present some deviations from type I (*lex, corpus*), the most frequent type. The types are presented in the table in order of decreasing frequency.

Type	Paradigm	Accusative singular masculine/ feminine	Ablative singular masculine/ feminine/neuter
I. **True consonant stems: imparisyllabic* nouns with one consonant** before *-is* in the genitive singular Also **u-stems**	*lex, legis* (f.) *cīvitās, civitātis* (f.) *leō, leōnis* (m.) *corpus, corporis* (n.) *sūs, suis* 'pig, sow'	-em	-e
II. **Old i-stems keeping the *i* only in the genitive plural** before the ending *-um* (*cīvi-um, urbi-um*) but declined as the consonant stems (type I) in other cases: **a) imparisyllabic* nouns with more than one consonant** before *-is* in the genitive singular** **b) parisyllabic* nouns** ** Ablative singular in *ī* (cf. type IV) and accusative plural in *-īs* (*cīvīs*) also occur.	*mons, montis* (m.) *urbs, urbis* (f.) *os, ossis* (n.) *cīvis, civis* (m.)	-em	-e
III. **Neuter i-stems ending in the** nominative singular with **-e, -al, -ar** keep the *i* in the genitive plural and have a long vowel *ī* in the ablative singular (as in the a-/o-/u-/e- declensions). Final short *ĭ > ĕ*.	*mare, maris* (n.) *animal, animālis* (n.)	—	-ī

IV. Some, mainly feminine i-stems with nominative and genitive singular in -is keep the i in the accusative and ablative singular and the genitive plural.	*Tiberis* (m.), *turris,* *sitis, vis, Neāpolis,* *puppis, secūris*	-m	-ī

* **Imparisyllabic** nouns have one more syllable in the genitive singular than in the nominative singular. **Parisyllabic** nouns have the same number of syllables in the nominative and the genitive singular.

** The nouns of the so-called family group belong to type I (without *i* in the gen. pl.): *pater, māter, frāter, iuvenis, senex, parens* (gen. pl. *parentum* or *parentium*), *canis, pānis.* Some other nouns may vary in the genitive plural: *civitat(i)um, mens(i)um, palūd(i)um,* etc.

28. Remarks

a) Some nouns are irregular, such as *Iuppiter, Iuppiter, Iovis, Iovī, Iovem, Iove.* The plural of *bos* 'cow, ox' is *bovēs, bovēs, boum, būbus/bōbus, bovēs, būbus/bōbus.*

b) Some nouns are defective. *Vīs* 'force' does not have a genitive or dative singular; it does have an accusative (*vim*) and an ablative (*vī*) and is regular in the plural (*vīrēs, vīrium,* etc.).

c) Nouns (particularly proper nouns) borrowed from Greek sometimes retain their Greek endings: accusative singular *aera, Marathōna, Amarylida, Socraten;* accusative plural *Cyclōpas.*

d) The locative singular survives in *rūrī* (from *rūs, rūris*) 'in the countryside' and *Karthāginī* 'at Carthage'.

e) *Corpus* has no ending in the nominative/vocative/accusative singular. In the other cases, the final -*s* of the stem (*corpos-*) has changed to *r* between two vowels. This phenomenon is called **rhotacism** and also occurs in English: *I was, we were.* The same phenomenon occurs in *flōs, flōris.* But in *honōs, honōris,* the nominative adapted to the rest of the declension **by analogy** and became *honor.*

f) The ending of the dative and ablative plural is -*bus* in the i-stems: *mari-bus/turri-bus.* But, taken from *mar-ibus/turr-ibus,* the ending is -*ibus* in the consonant stems. The two words with stems in -*u* can have *su-ibus, gru-ibus* or *sū-bus, grū-bus.*

Fourth or u-declension

29. The nouns of the **fourth** or **u-declension** have a stem in -*ŭ*. Masculine nouns have a nominative ending in -*s* and a genitive singular ending in -*s* with lengthening of the preceding *u*. Neuter nouns have a zero ending in the nominative and a genitive ending in -*s* with lengthening of the preceding *u*.

	Masculine		Neuter	
	Singular	**Plural**	**Singular**	**Plural**
Nominative	fructus	fructūs	cornu	cornua
Vocative	fructus	fructūs	cornu	cornua
Genitive	fructūs	fructuum	cornūs	cornuum
Dative	fructuī (fructū)	fructibus	cornū	cornibus
Accusative	fructum	fructūs	cornu	cornua
Ablative	fructū	fructibus	cornū	cornibus

30. Remarks

    a) The word *domus* (f.) has borrowed several forms from the second or o-declension: ablative singular *domō*, genitive plural *domōrum* or *domuum*, and accusative plural *domōs* or *domūs*. In addition, the old locative singular *domī* 'at home' still exists (§ 19, 25, 300, 305).

    b) Some nouns of this declension exist almost only in the ablative singular: *iussū* 'by order', *nātū* 'by birth', *permissū* 'with permission'.

Fifth or e-declension

31. The nouns of the **fifth** or **e-declension** have a stem in *-ē*. The nominative singular ends in *-s,* and the genitive singular ends in *-ī.*

	Singular	**Plural**
Nominative	rēs	rēs
Vocative	rēs	rēs
Genitive	reī	rērum
Dative	reī	rēbus
Accusative	rem	rēs
Ablative	rē	rēbus

4

The Adjective

Adjectives of the first group: a- and o-declensions

32. Adjectives of the first group are declined like nouns of the **a- and o-declensions**, that is, like *servus, puer,* and *ager* for the masculine, like *rosa* for the feminine, and like *templum* for the neuter.

	Singular			Plural		
	M.	**F.**	**N.**	**M.**	**F.**	**N.**
Nominative	longus	longa	longum	longī	longae	longa
Vocative	longe	longa	longum	longī	longae	longa
Genitive	longī	longae	longī	longōrum	longārum	longōrum
Dative	longō	longae	longō	longīs	longīs	longīs
Accusative	longum	longam	longum	longōs	longās	longa
Ablative	longō	longā	longō	longīs	longīs	longīs

	Miser			Niger		
	M.	**F.**	**N.**	**M.**	**F.**	**N.**
Nominative-Vocative	miser	misera	miserum	niger	nigra	nigrum
Genitive	miserī	miserae	miserī	nigrī	nigrae	nigrī
	etc.	etc.	etc.	etc.	etc.	etc.

33. Remark. Adjectives of the type *miser, misera, miserum* keep the *e* in their stem in all cases. Adjectives of the type *niger, nigra, nigrum* loose the *e* of the stem in all cases, except in the nominative and vocative masculine singular. Some adjectives, such as *dexter, dext(e)ra, dext(e)rum,* sometimes keep the *e.*

34. Pronominal adjectives. Some adjectives that, through their meaning, are close to indefinite pronouns follow the **a- and o-declensions** but have in all three genders a **genitive singular** in *-īus* and a **dative singular** in *-ī,* just like the pronouns. These so-called pronominal adjectives are

Nominative	Genitive singular	Dative singular
ūnus, -a, -um 'one'	*ūnīus*	*ūnī*
nūllus, -a, -um 'none'	*nūllīus*	*nūllī*
ūllus, -a, -um 'any'	*ūllīus*	*ūllī*
sōlus, -a, -um 'alone'	*sōlīus*	*sōlī*
neuter, neutra, neutrum 'neither'	*neutrīus*	*neutrī*
alius, -a, -ud 'other'	*(alterius)*	*aliī*
uter, utra, utrum 'which of the two?'	*utrīus* (but *utriusque*)	*utrī*
tōtus, -a, -um 'whole'	*tōtīus*	*tōtī*
alter, -a, -um 'other of two'	*alterius*	*alterī*

Adjectives of the second group: third or consonant/i-declension

35. **Adjectives of the second group** are declined like **nouns of the third declension**. But unlike the nouns, most adjectives (in all genders) belong to type III (i-stems: see § 27). Only a few adjectives belong to type I (§ 26, 37).

36. Most adjectives of the third declension are **i-stems** and belong to type III, with ablative singular in *-ī*. The genitive singular is always *-is,* and the accusative singular masculine and feminine is always *-em*. In the nominative singular, three groups can be distinguished.

   a) A very small number of adjectives have **three endings in the nominative singular**: *celer* (m.), *celeris* (f.), *celere* (n.) 'swift'; *ācer* (m.), *ācris* (f.), *ācre* (n.) 'sharp'; *equester* (m.), *equestris* (f.), *equestre* (n.) 'equestrian'; and a dozen others. The feminine form in *-is* is also the form of the genitive. Except for the three endings in the nominative singular, the declension of these adjectives is the same as the adjectives with two endings in the nominative singular (*dulcis, dulce:* see § 36b).

   b) Many adjectives have **two endings in the nominative singular**: *dulcis* (m./f.), *dulce* (n.) 'sweet'.

   c) Some adjectives have only **one ending in the nominative singular**: *ingens* (m./f./n.), *ingentis* 'huge'; *felix, felicis* 'happy' (with *-s* in even the neuter form). The imperfective active participle (IAP) belongs to this category.

	Singular		Plural	
	M./F.	**N.**	**M./F.**	**N.**
Nominative	dulcis	dulce	dulcēs	dulcia
Vocative	dulcis	dulce	dulcēs	dulcia
Genitive	dulcis	dulcis	dulcium	dulcium
Dative	dulcī	dulcī	dulcibus	dulcibus
Accusative	dulcem	dulce	dulcēs (-īs)	dulcia
Ablative	dulcī	dulcī	dulcibus	dulcibus

	Singular		Plural	
	M./F.	**N.**	**M./F.**	**N.**
Nominative	ingens	ingens	ingentes	ingentia
Vocative	ingens	ingens	ingentes	ingentia
Genitive	ingentis	ingentis	ingentium	ingentium
Dative	ingentī	ingentī	ingentibus	ingentibus
Accusative	ingentem	ingens	ingentēs (-īs)	ingentia
Ablative	ingentī	ingentī	ingentibus	ingentibus

37. **A small number of imparisyllabic (§ 27) adjectives** with **one consonant** before the ending *-is* of the genitive singular and with **one form in the nominative singular** are declined in the same way as the nouns of type I

(*lex, corpus*), with the ablative singular in *-e*. They have no *i* in the nominative/vocative/genitive/accusative plural. Some of those adjectives are *vetus, veteris* 'old'; *compos, compotis* 'possessing'; *dīves, dīvitis* 'rich'; *inops, inopis* 'poor'; *memor, memoris* (abl. sg. *-i*) 'mindful'; *particeps, participis* 'sharing'; *pauper, pauperis* 'poor'; and *superstes, superstitis* 'surviving'. See also the comparatives in § 41.

38. Remark. Adjectives that are declined according to the paradigm *ingens, ingentis* have an ablative singular in *-e* in the following instances:

    a) the imperfective active participle (IAP), if it is used as the predicate of an ablative absolute: *Augustō regnante* 'during the reign of Augustus';

    b) an adjective or IAP, if it is used as a noun: *ā sapiente* 'by a wise man' (but *ā sapientī virō* 'by a wise man').

Degrees of comparison

39. The adjective has three degrees of comparison.

    a) The **positive** is the form of the adjective as given in the dictionary.

    b) The **comparative**, indicating an increased quality or quantity, is formed from the positive by adding the suffix *-ior* (m./f.) or *-ius* (n.) to the last consonant of the stem.

    c) The **superlative** indicates the utmost degree, generally by means of the suffix *-(is)simus, -a, -um*. This superlative can be absolute (meaning 'very long') or relative to others (meaning 'the longest'). This formation is applicable to the vast majority of the adjectives.

Positive		Comparative	Superlative
longus 'long'	*long-(i)*	*long-ior, long-ius* 'longer' (gen. *long-iōr-is*)	*long-issim-us, -a, -um* 'longest / very long'
dulcis 'sweet'	*dulc-(is)*	*dulc-ior, dulc-ius*	*dulc-issim-us, -a, -um*
ingens 'huge'	*ingent-(is)*	*ingent-ior, ingent-ius*	*ingent-issim-us, -a, -um*

40. Irregular formations occur in some adjectives.

    a) **Adjectives ending in *-er*** (of both the first and second groups) have a **superlative ending in *-rimus, -a, -um*.**

        miser 'wretched'   *miserior/-ius*   *miser**rimus*** (<*miser-simus*)
        celer 'swift'   *celerior/-ius*   *celer**rimus***

    b) **Six (and only these six) adjectives in *-ilis*** have a **superlative with *-limus, -a, -um*.**

        facilis 'easy'   *facilior*   *facil**limus*** (<*facil-simus*)
        difficilis 'difficult'   *difficilior*   *difficil**limus***
        similis 'similar'   *similior*   *simil**limus***
        dissimilis 'unlike'   *dissimilior*   *dissimil**limus***
        gracilis 'slender'   *gracilior*   *gracil**limus***
        humilis 'humble'   *humilior*   *humil**limus***

c) **Completely irregular** degrees of comparison are formed on **different stems**.

bonus 'good'	*melior, melius* 'better'	*optimus* 'best, very good'
malus 'bad'	*pēior, pēius* 'worse'	*pessimus* 'worst, very bad'
magnus 'great'	*māior, māius* 'greater'	*maximus* 'greatest, very great'
parvus 'small'	*minor, minus* 'smaller'	*minimus* 'smallest, very small'
multus 'much'	neuter *plus* 'more'	*plūrimus* 'very much'
multi 'many'	*plūrēs, plūra*, genitive	*plūrimī* 'very many'
	plūrium 'more'	*plērīque, -aeque, -aque* 'most'

d) **Comparatives and superlatives** are sometimes formed on an **adverb or preposition of place** with the **same stem**.

(*prae/pro* 'before')	*prior* 'earlier'	*primus* 'first'
(*cis/citra* 'on this side')	*citerior* 'on this side'	—
(*ultrā* 'beyond')	*ulterior* 'farther'	*ūltimus* 'farthest, ultimate'
(*intrā* 'within')	*interior* 'inner'	*intimus* 'innermost'
(*extrā* 'outside')	*exterior* 'outer'	*extrēmus* 'outermost'
(*prope* 'near')	*propior* 'nearer'	*proximus* 'nearest'
(*dē* 'down')	*deterior* 'worse'	*deterrimus* 'worst'
(*post* 'after')	*posterior* 'later'	*postrēmus* 'last'
		postumus 'late-born'
(*suprā* 'above')	*superior* 'higher'	*suprēmus* 'supreme'
		summus 'highest'
(*infrā* 'below')	*inferior* 'lower'	*infimus* 'meanest'
		īmus 'lowest'

41. The declension of comparatives follows the paradigm of type I of the third declension: *lex* and *corpus* (§ 26) and *vetus, -eris* (§ 37). Hence, the ablative singular ends in **-e**, and there is no *i* in the nominative/vocative/genitive/accusative plural.

Superlatives are declined like adjectives of the first group (a- or o-declension: see § 32).

42. Remarks.

a) When two people or things are compared, Latin, like English, uses the comparative: *Quattuor relīquās (legiōnēs) in castra **maiora** reduxit*, "He brought the four legions back to the **bigger** camp." (Caes. *B.G.* 1.49.5)

b) For the construction of the second member of the comparison, or the lack thereof, see § 168, 318.

c) In some expressions, degrees of comparison are strengthened by adverbs.
longē *nobilissimus* 'by far the most known'
quam *maximus* 'the biggest possible'
eō *facilior* 'the easier'
multō *melior* 'much better'

Numerals

43. There are three kinds of numeral adjectives: **cardinal numerals** (not many of which are declined), **ordinal numerals**, and **distributive numerals**. There also exist some **multiplicative numerals**, such as *simplex, duplex, triplex*, and *quadruplex*. For numeral adverbs, see § 48d.

Roman figures	Cardinal numerals (one, two, etc.)	Ordinal numerals (first, second, etc.)	Distributive numerals (one . . . each)
I	ūnus, -a, -um	prīmus, -a,-um; prior	singulī, -ae, -a
II	duo, duae, duo	secundus, -a, -um; alter, -a, -um	bīnī, -ae, -a
III	trēs, tria	tertius, -a, -um	ternī, etc.
IIII / IV	quattuor	quartus, etc.	quaternī
V	quinque	quintus	quīnī
VI	sex	sextus	sēnī
VII	septem	septimus	septēnī
VIII	octō	octāvus	octōnī
VIIII / IX	novem	nōnus	novēnī
X	decem	decimus	dēnī
XI	ūndecim	ūndecimus, -a, -um	ūndēnī, -ae, -a
XII	duodecim	duodecimus	duodēnī
XIII	tredecim	tertius decimus	ternī dēnī
XIV	quattuordecim	quartus decimus	quaternī dēnī
XV	quīndecim	quintus decimus	quīnī dēnī
XVI	sēdecim	sextus decimus	sēnī dēnī
XVII	septendecim	septimus decimus	septēnī dēnī
XVIII	duodēvigintī	duodēvīcēsimus	duodēvīcēnī
XIX	ūndēvigintī	ūndēvīcēsimus	ūndēvīcēnī
XX	vīgintī	vīcēsimus	vīcēnī
XXI	vīgintī ūnus, -a, -um	vīcēsimus, -a, -um prīmus, -a, -um	vīcēnī, -ae, -a singulī, -ae, -a
XXX	trīgintā	trīcēsimus, -a, -um	trīcēnī, -ae, -a
XL	quadrāgintā	quadrāgēsimus, etc.	quadrāgēnī, etc.
L	quinquāgintā	quinquagēsimus	quinquāgēnī
LX	sexāgintā	sexagēsimus	sexāgēnī
LXX	septuāgintā	septuagēsimus	septuāgēnī
LXXX	octōgintā	octōgēsimus	octōgēnī
XC	nōnāgintā	nōnagēsimus	nōnāgēnī
C	centum	centēsimus	centēnī
CC	ducentī, -ae, -a	ducentēsimus, -a, -um	ducēnī, -ae, -a
CCC	trecentī, etc.	trecentēsimus, etc.	trecēnī, etc.
CCCC	quadringentī	quadringentēsimus	quadringēnī
D	quingentī	quingentēsimus	quīngēnī
DC	sescentī	sescentēsimus	sescēnī
DCC	septingentī	septingentēsimus	septingēnī
DCCC	octingentī	octingentēsimus	octingēnī
DCCCC	nongentī	nongentēsimus	nongēnī
M	mīlle	millēsimus	singula mīlia (noun)

44. Numerals from two thousand up are not adjectives but are formed by means of the plural declinable noun *mīlia, mīlium* 'thousands'. Such a numeral is construed with an attributive partitive genitive (§ 127).

> *Mille mīlites* 'a thousand soldiers' (indeclinable adjective)
> *Duo mīlia mīlitum* 'two thousand soldiers' (declinable noun)
> *Cum duōbus mīlibus mīlitum* 'with two thousand soldiers'
> *Mīlia passuum ducenta quadrāginta* '240,000 paces' = '240 miles'
>   = '360 kilometers' (*ducenta* agrees with *mīlia; quadrāgintā* is indeclinable)
> *Centum mīlia sestertium* '100,000 sesterces'; or *centēna mīlia sestertium;* or simply *sestertium* (taken as nom. sg. n. instead of gen. pl. n.), with omission of *centum mīlia.*
> *Vīciēs sestertium* [= *vīciēs centum mīlia sestertium*] 'two million sesterces'

45. Declension. Numerals with *ūnus* and *alter* are declined like the adjectives of the first group (a-/o-declension) in most cases but like the pronominal adjectives (§ 34) in the genitive and dative singular: *ūnus, ūnius, ūnī, ūnum, ūno; alter, alterius, alterī, alterum, altero.*

Unus is used in the plural with pluralia tantum (§ 18): *ūnae litterae* 'one epistle'. But the distributive numeral *bīnī* is used in *bīnae littěrae* 'two epistles' (as opposed to *duae litterae* 'two letters').

Duo 'two' (and *ambō* 'both') and *trēs* are declined as follows (the ending *-o* in *duo* and *ambō* is an archaic dual: see § 18):

Nominative	duo	duae	duo	trēs	tria
Genitive	duōrum	duārum	duōrum	trium	trium
Dative	duōbus	duābus	duōbus	tribus	tribus
Accusative	duōs/duo	duās	duō	trēs	tria
Ablative	duōbus	duābus	duōbus	tribus	tribus

5

The Adverb

46. **Adverbs modify a verb** (§ 293, 295), **an adjective, another adverb, or an entire sentence** (§ 381). See also § 366.

Adverbs are often derived from adjectives.

  a) To the last consonant of the stem of an adjective of the **first group** (**a- and o-declensions**), *the suffix -ē* is added.

  b) To the stem of an adjective of the **second group** (**consonant/i-declension**), **the suffix -(i)ter** is added. With stems in **-nt, tt > t**: *prudent-ter > prudenter*.

Adjective	Adverb
longus, -a, -um 'long'	*longē*
miser, -a, -um 'wretched'	*miserē*
pulcher, -chra, -chrum 'beautiful'	*pulchrē*
celer, -is, -e 'swift'	*celeriter*
dulcis, -e 'sweet'	*dulciter*
felix, genitive *felīcis* 'happy'	*felīciter*
prudens, stem *prudent-* 'aware'	*prudenter*

47. **Irregular adverbs** are

Adjective	Adverb
bonus, -a, -um 'good'	*bene* 'well'
facilis, -e 'easy'	*facile* 'easily' (= acc. sg. n.)

48. Some adverbs were productively formed in earlier times but are fixed in the classical period and mentioned as such in the dictionary. They can be derived from adjectives, nouns (often acc. or abl.), pronouns (§ 305), verbs, and so on.

  a) **Adverbs in -um** (= old acc. sg. n.): *multum* 'much', *paulum* 'a little', *sōlum* 'only', *tantum* 'only', *cēterum* 'for the rest', *nimium* 'too much', *prīmum* 'first', *plērumque* 'mostly', *vērum* 'but', and so on.

  b) **Adverbs in -o** (= old abl. sg. n.): *citō* 'quickly', *crebrō* 'frequently', *vērō* 'indeed', *manifestō* 'clearly', *modo* 'only', *primō* 'at first', *rārō* 'rarely', *subitō* 'suddenly', and so on.

  c) **Adverbs in -tim** or **-sim** (= old acc. sg. f.): *partim* 'partly', *nominātim* 'by name', *statim* 'at once', *paulātim* 'little by little', *passim* 'here and there', and so on.

d) **Numeral adverbs**, mostly in *-iēs* or *-iens*: *quotiens* 'how often', *semel* 'once', *bis* 'twice', *ter* 'trice', *quater* 'four times', *quinquie(n)s* 'five times', *sexie(n)s* 'six times', *decie(n)s* 'ten times', and so on.

e) **Adverbs with various formations**: *praetereā* 'besides', *adeō* 'so', *ibi* 'there', *imprīmīs* 'in the first place' (prep. + abl.), *adhūc* 'until now', *nōn* 'not', *noctū* 'by night' (abl.), *quemadmodum* 'how?', *scīlicet* 'of course, namely', and so on.

49. **Correlative adverbs** have a close relation with each other with regard to their meaning and often to their form. Each series contains an interrogative (with *qu-* or *u-*), an indefinite (with *ali-*), a demonstrative (often with *t-*), a relative (with *qu-* or *u-*), and an indefinite relative adverb (with *-cumque*, *-vīs* 'you want', *-libet* 'pleases'). See § 71.

Interrogative	Indefinite	Demon-strative	Relative	Indefinite relative
quandō 'when'	*aliquando* 'ever'	*tum, tunc* 'then'	*quandō* 'when'	*quandō(cum)que* 'whenever'
quotiens 'how often'	*aliquotiens* 'a few times'	*totiens* 'so often'	*quotiens* 'so often as'	*quotienscumque* 'however often'
quam (with adj.) 'how'	—	*tam* 'so'	*quam* '(so) as'	*quamquam, quamvīs* 'however, though'
quōmodo, ut (with verbs) 'how'	—	*ita, sic* 'so'	*ut* '(so) as'	*utcumque* 'in whatever way, howsoever'
quantum 'how much'	*aliquantum* 'somewhat'	*tantum* 'so much'	*quantum* '(so) as'	*quantumcumque* 'however much'
ubi 'where'	*alicubi* 'somewhere'	*ibi* (§ 305) 'there'	*ubi* 'where'	*ubicumque, ubivīs* 'wheresoever'
quō 'whither, where to'	*aliquō* '(to) somewhere'	*eō* (§ 305) 'thither'	*quō* 'whither'	*quōcumque, quōvīs* '(to) wherever'
unde 'whence, from where'	*alicunde* 'from somewhere'	*inde* (§ 305) 'thence'	*unde* 'whence'	*undecumque* 'from wherever'
quā 'along which road, by what means'	*aliquā* 'somehow'	*eā* (§ 305) 'this way'	*quā* 'which way'	*quācumque* 'whichever way, any way'

50. The **degrees of comparison of regularly formed adverbs** are parallel to the degrees of the adjective. Irregularities in the degrees of comparison of the adjective (§ 39–40) also exist in the adverbs.

a) The **comparative of the adverb** is the **accusative singular neuter** of the adjective.

b) The **superlative of the adverb** is formed regularly with the **suffix -ē**.

Adjective	Adverb Positive	Adverb Comparative	Adverb Superlative
longus	longē	longius	longissimē
pulcher	pulchrē	pulchrius	pulcherrimē
miser	miserē	miserius	miserrimē
celer	celeriter	celerius	celerrimē
dulcis	dulciter	dulcius	dulcissimē
felix	felīciter	felīcius	felīcissimē
prudens	prudenter	prudentius	prudentissimē
humilis	humiliter	humilius	humillimē
bonus	bene	mēlius	optimē
malus	malē	pēius	pessimē
magnus	magnō	magis	maximē
parvus	parvum	minus	minimē
multus	multum	plūs	plērumque 'mostly'
			plūrimum 'very much'
—	prope	propius	proximē
—	saepe	saepius	saepissimē

51. Remarks.

a) The constructions mentioned for adjectives (§ 42) also occur with adverbs.

b) The interrogative particles *-ne, num, nonne, utrum,* and *an* can be considered as interrogative adverbs. They indicate that the entire sentence is a question.

6

The Pronoun

Personal pronouns

52.

	Singular			Plural		
	1st person	**2nd person**	**3rd-person reflexive**	**1st person**	**2nd person**	**3rd-person reflexive**
Nom.	ego 'I'	tū 'you'	—	nōs 'we'	vōs 'you'	—
Gen.	meī	tuī	suī	nostrī nostrum	vestrī vestrum	suī
Dat.	mihi	tibi	sibi	nōbīs	vōbīs	sibi
Acc.	mē	tē	sē	nōs	vōs	sē
Abl.	mē	tē	sē	nōbīs	vōbīs	sē

53. Remarks about the forms

a) **The vocative** of the second person also exists: *tū* 'you', *vōs* 'you' (pl.).

b) **The genitives *nostrum* and *vestrum*** are used as partitive genitives: *Quis nostrum* 'Who among us?' Compare *Mementō nostrī* 'Remember us!' See also § 365, remark.

c) **The preposition *cum* 'with'** stands as a "postposition" (§ 117) after a personal pronoun in the ablative: *mēcum* 'with me', *nōbīscum* 'with us', and so on.

d) **Personal pronouns can be intensified with particles** (*-met, -te, -pte*) and with the demonstrative pronoun *ipse, -a, -um* 'self': *egōmet* 'I (myself)', *tūte* 'you yourself', *tibimet ipsī* 'to yourself'. *Sē* is sometimes doubled to *sēsē*.

54. Remarks about the meaning

a) The **personal pronoun** is used only independently as a pronoun. The other pronouns (treated later in this chapter) can occur both as determiners (attributes) and as pronouns.

b) The personal pronouns of the first and second person can be reflexive or not.

c) The personal pronoun of the third person (*suī*, etc.) is **reflexive**: it **refers to the subject of the clause in which it stands or to the subject**

of the governing clause (§ 190–91). For that reason, it lacks a nominative. It can also be used **reciprocally**: *inter sē* 'among themselves'.

> *Hī cum per sē minus valērent...* "Since these by themselves were less strong ..." (Caes. *B.G.* 6.12.2) (*Se* refers to the subject *hī*.)
> *Caesar omnem senātum ad sē convenīre iussit.* "Caesar ordered the whole senate to come to him." (Caes. *B.G.* 2.5.1) (*Sē* refers to the subject *Caesar* of the governing sentence. Note that *sē* is not necessarily translated by 'himself'.)
> *... omnēs Belgās obsidēs inter sē dare.* "... that all the Belgae were exchanging hostages." (Caes. *B.G.* 2.1.1)

d) For lack of a non-reflexive pronoun of the third person, Latin uses the demonstrative pronoun *is, ea, id* to refer to the just mentioned person. In the formula *At ille,* the demonstrative pronoun *ille, -a, -ud* indicates a turn in the text to the other (already known) actor or speaker.

e) If the personal pronouns are not stressed, they are not used in classical Latin, except in the comedies. If they indicate a contrast or a change of theme, they are used in classical Latin.

> *Vēnī, vīdī, vīcī.* "I came, I saw, I conquered." (Suetonius *Caes.* 37.3)
> *Sī valēs, benest.* "If you are doing well, that's fine." (Cic. *Fam.* 5.1.1)
> *Sī vōs valētis, bene est; ego quidem valeo.* "If you all are doing well, that's fine. I for my part am doing well." (Cic. *Fam.* 15.1.1)

Possessive pronouns

55. The **possessive pronouns/adjectives** are

- first-person singular: *meus, mea, meum* 'my, mine';
- second-person singular: *tuus, tua, tuum* 'your, thy, thine' (referring to one person);
- third-person singular and plural: *suus, sua, suum* 'his, her, its, their (own)';
- first-person plural: *noster, nostra, nostrum* 'our, ours';
- second-person plural: *vester, vestra, vestrum* 'your, yours' (referring to several persons)

The possessive adjectives are used attributively (*mare* **nostrum** 'our sea'); the possessive pronouns are used independently (*nostrī* 'our men'). They **are declined** like the adjectives of the **first group (a- and o-declensions)**—*longus, -a, -um* and *niger, nigra, nigrum*—with the exception that the vocative masculine singular of *meus* is *mī*.

56. Remarks about use and meaning

a) The possessive adjective is not used if it is sufficiently clear from the context who the possessor is. In English translation, the possessive adjective is always used (see the five examples in § 56c). In Latin, it is only expressed for reasons of clarity or emphasis. An English equivalent for this emphasis has to be found.

> *Cervus in liquōre vīdit effigiem* **suam**. *Rāmōsa mīrans laudat cornua.* "A deer saw **its own** image in the water. Full of admiration, it praised **its** spreading antlers." (Phaedrus 1.12 *Cervus ad fontem* 3–5). (The Latin possessive adjective does not refer to the gender and number of the possessor, as in English, but agrees with its head in the noun phrase, as in French and Spanish.)

b) **The possessive adjective of the third person is reflexive** (§ 54c): it refers to the subject of the clause or the subject of the governing clause (§ 190–91).

> *[Caesar] reperiēbat [Belgās] sōlōs esse quī Teutonōs Cimbrōsque intrā fīnēs* **suōs** *ingredī prohibuerint.* "Caesar learned that the Belgae were the only ones who had prevented the Teutons and the Cimbri from entering their territory." (Caes. *B.G.* 2.4.1–2) (*Suōs* refers not to the subject *Teutonōs Cimbrōsque* but to *quī*, the subject of the governing verb *prohibuerint.*)

c) Latin lacks a non-reflexive possessive adjective of the third person. **Therefore, it uses the possessive genitive (*ēius, eōrum, eārum*) of the demonstrative pronoun *is, ea, id*.** The English possessive adjectives *his, her, its,* and *their* can be reflexive or not.

> *Fīlius dēcessit. Huīc illa ita fūnus parāvit ut ignōrāret marītus. Quotiens cubiculum* **ēius** *intrāret, vīvere filium simulābat.* "**Their** son died. She organized **his** burial in such a way that **her** [sick] husband did not know it. Every time she entered **his** bedroom, she feigned that **their** son was still alive." (Pliny 3.16.3–4)

Demonstrative pronouns

57. There are three demonstrative pronouns/adjectives (used attributively or independently), **indicating a place with respect to the speaker**:

– *hic, haec, hoc* 'this' (here near me/us, the speaker or the first person);
– *iste, ista, istud* 'that' (there near you, the person[s] spoken to or second person);
– *ille, illa, illud* 'that (yonder)' (there near the third person, not near you or me).

If there are references to several persons or objects, *hic* refers to the one nearest in the text, the last mentioned; *ille* to the one furthest away, the first mentioned (§ 410).

Hic 'this' is usually anaphoric (referring back). Sometimes it is cataphoric (referring to what follows): *Coniūrandī hās esse causās.* "The causes of the conspiracy were the following." (Caes. *B.G.* 2.1.2) On anaphora as a figure of style, see § 407.

Iste often has a pejorative, uncomplimentary connotation, *ille* a positive connotation. These demonstratives can be combined with possessive/personal pronouns.

> *Furor iste tuus* ... "That madness of yours ..." (Cic. *Cat.* 1.1)
> *Ego ille quem nostī* ... "That famous me, whom you know ..." (Pliny 1.6.1)

58. The demonstrative pronouns/adjectives are **declined** like adjectives of the **a- and o-declensions**. Some characteristics, however, of the demonstrative and other pronouns are

- the somewhat irregular nominative singular (to be learned with the vocabulary);
- the typical pronominal genitive singular in *-ius* and dative singular in *-ī* (all genders);
- the ending *-d* in the nominative and accusative singular neuter in most pronouns;
- the unusual nominative and accusative plural neuter: *haec* and *quae*.

The declension of *ille, illa, illud* is the same as *iste, ista, istud*.

	Singular			Plural		
	M.	**F.**	**N.**	**M.**	**F.**	**N.**
Nom.	hic	haec	hoc	hī	hae	haec
Gen.	hūius	hūius	hūius	hōrum	hārum	hōrum
Dat.	huīc	huīc	huīc	hīs	hīs	hīs
Acc.	hunc	hanc	hoc	hōs	hās	haec
Abl.	hōc	hāc	hōc	hīs	hīs	hīs
Nom.	iste	ista	istud	istī	istae	ista
Gen.	istīus	istīus	istīus	istōrum	istārum	istōrum
Dat.	istī	istī	istī	istīs	istīs	istīs
Acc.	istum	istam	istud	istōs	istās	ista
Abl.	istō	istā	istō	istīs	istīs	istīs

Remarks. The *-c* at the end of several forms of *hic* is a remnant of the deictic (demonstrative) enclitic particle *-ce*. This particle can also be added to other forms and other pronouns: *hūiusce, hōsce;* also *istuc* (< *istudc*), *illaec* (< *illae+ce*). If the interrogative particle *-ne* is added to these forms, the *e* in *-ce* is weakened to *i*: *hicine, haecine, hocine, huncine,* etc.; in addition to *hicne,* etc.

59. **The declension of *is, ea, id*,** a demonstrative pronoun/adjective that can be used attributively or independently, has the characteristics mentioned in § 58.

	Singular			Plural		
	M.	**F.**	**N.**	**M.**	**F.**	**N.**
Nom.	is	ea	id	eī (iī)	eae	ea
Gen.	ēius	ēius	ēius	eōrum	eārum	eōrum
Dat.	eī	eī	eī	eīs (iīs)	eīs (iīs)	eīs (iīs)
Acc.	eum	eam	id	eōs	eās	ea
Abl.	eō	eā	eō	eīs (iīs)	eīs (iīs)	eīs (iīs)

60. Use and meaning of *is, ea, id*

   a) **The demonstrative *is, ea, id*** refers to someone or something mentioned earlier. The translation can vary from 'this/these' to 'that/those' to 'the said person/thing': *eārum rērum memoria* 'the remembrance of those (aforementioned) events', *eā dē causā* 'for this reason', *id bellum* 'the war in question'.

      If *is, ea, id* is used not as a determiner of a head but independently, it is translated as 'he, she, it', 'this one', 'that one'. It never refers to the subject of the clause or sentence.

      Is coniūrātiōnem fēcit. "He [= this man] laid a plot." (Caes. *B.G.* 1.2.1)
      ... *alter paulō amplius ab īs absit.* "... the other [officer] was a little further away from them." (Caes. *B.G.* 5.27.9)

   b) Because there is no non-reflexive possessive adjective, the possessive genitive of the demonstrative *is, ea, id* is used (§ 56c).

      *[Ambiānī] sē dēdidērunt. **Eōrum** fīnēs Nerviī attingēbant.* "The Ambiani surrendered. **Their** nearest neighbors were the Nervii." (Caes. *B.G.* 2.15.2–3) (*Eōrum* and *their* are non-reflexive: both refer not to the Nervii but to the Ambiani.)

   c) *Is, ea, id* often announces that a relative clause is to follow. The demonstrative pronoun, as antecedent of that relative clause, is often omitted if it has the same case as the relative pronoun. The same omission can occur in English.

      Is quī fugitīvum cēlāvit, fūr est. "He who has hidden a fugitive slave is a thief." (Ulpianus *Ad edictum aed. cur.* 1, *D.* 11.4.1)
      Quī mancipia vendunt, nātiōnem cūiusque in venditiōne prōnuntiāre dēbent. "Those who sell slaves have to declare publicly the nationality of each at the sale." Or "Whoever sells ... has to ..." (Ulpianus *Ad edictum aed. cur.* 1, *D.* 21.1.31)

61. *Idem, eadem, idem* 'the same' has the same declension as *is, ea, id* plus the suffix *-dem*, but with some changes in the nominative singular. An *m* before a dental is assimilated to *n*.

	Singular			Plural		
	M.	**F.**	**N.**	**M.**	**F.**	**N.**
Nom.	īdem	eadem	idem	eīdem (iīdem)	eaedem	eadem
Gen.	ēiusdem	ēiusdem	ēiusdem	eōrundem	eārundem	eōrundem
Dat.	eīdem	eīdem	eīdem	eīsdem (iīsdem)	eīsdem	eīsdem (iīsdem)
Acc.	eundem	eandem	idem	eōsdem	eāsdem	eadem
Abl.	eōdem	eādem	eōdem	eīsdem (iīsdem)	eīsdem	eīsdem (iīsdem)

62. *Ipse, ipsa, ipsum* 'self' is **declined** like *iste, ista, istud*, except in the nominative and accusative singular neuter (***ipsum***). It can be used attributively or independently.

Ipse is an intensive pronoun/adjective. It is often used, particularly in indirect speech, for clarity's sake. It then refers to the subject of the main clause (the speaker), whereas *se* and *suus* can refer to the subject of the dependent clause or the subject of the main clause.

Sed Caesar legi paruit ipse suae. "But Caesar himself obeyed the rule, his own rule." (Mart. *Liber spect.* 29.4)
[Caesar] vehementer eōs incūsāvit cūr dē suā virtūte aut dē ipsīus dīligentiā dēspērārent. "Caesar accused them violently, asking why they despaired of their own courage or his wise generalship?" (Caes. *B.G.* 1.40.1–4)

Relative pronouns

63. The **relative pronoun *qui, quae, quod*** 'who, that, which' has a somewhat irregular declension, but it does have the typical pronominal endings **-ius** and **-ī** in the genitive and dative singular (§ 58).

	Singular			Plural		
	M.	**F.**	**N.**	**M.**	**F.**	**N.**
Nom.	quī	quae	quod	quī	quae	quae
Gen.	cūius	cūius	cūius	quōrum	quārum	quōrum
Dat.	cuī	cuī	cuī	quibus	quibus	quibus
Acc.	quem	quam	quod	quibus	quibus	quibus
Abl.	quō	quā	quō	quōs	quās	quae

Remark. If the relative pronoun is combined with the preposition *cum*, then *cum* sometimes follows it: *cum quō/quā/quibus* or *quōcum, quācum, quibuscum* (§ 117).

64. Use. The relative pronoun introduces a dependent clause, the relative clause, which functions as an attributive clause modifying a noun or pronoun. **The relative pronoun has its own function and therefore its own case** in that dependent clause, but **in gender and number it agrees with its**

antecedent (= the word in the governing clause to which it relates)
(§ 367–69).

65. **Translation.** The relative pronoun can be translated 'who', 'whom',
'whose', 'which', or 'that'. Unlike Latin, English can delete the relative
pronoun if it is a direct object. Latin cases other than the nominative can
be rendered in English by the declined forms of *who* (for persons), but
which and *that* (for things) are not declinable.

vir, quī 'the man, who'	*castra, quae* 'the camp, that/which'
vir, cūius 'the man, whose'	*castra, quōrum* 'the camp, of which'
vir, cuī 'the man, to/for whom'	*castra, quibus* 'the camp, to/for which'
vir, quem 'the man, (whom)'	*castra, quae* 'the camp, (which)'
vir, cum quō 'the man, with whom'	*castra, in quibus* 'the camp, in which'

66. **The connecting relative pronoun** (*quī = et is*) introduces an independent
sentence. (In indirect speech, such a sentence is an infinitive clause, not a
relative finite clause: see § 273b.) This *quī* is best translated by a demonstrative or personal pronoun, possibly preceded by the conjunction *and*.
See § 374.

67. There are two **indefinite relative pronouns**, *quīcumque, quaecumque,
quodcumque* (attributive or independent) and *quisquis, quidquid* (only independent), both with the meaning 'whoever, whatever'. Except in the
nominative singular, they are both declined like *quī, quae, quod*. See also
§ 369.

> *Licēre illīs **quāscumque** in partēs velint sine metū proficiscī.* "They were
> allowed to leave without fear, in whichever direction they wanted."
> (Caes. *B.G.* 5.41.6)
> ***Quidquid** id est, timeō Danaōs et dōna ferentēs.* "Whatever it is, I fear
> the Greeks, even when [they are] bringing gifts." (Virg. *Aen.* 2.49)

68. **The correlative relative pronouns** are treated in § 71.

Interrogative pronouns

69. **The interrogative pronouns/adjectives are declined** like the relative pronoun *quī, quae, quod* (§ 63), except for the forms of the nominative listed
here.

> *quis, quid* 'who, what' (independent)
> *qui(s), quae, quod* 'which' (attributive). (*Qui* 'what kind of?') is ask-
> ing for a property.

> **Remark.** The genitive of the independent pronoun *cūius* is itself
> sometimes used as a declinable adjective: *cūia vox?* 'whose voice?',
> *cūium pecus?* 'whose flock?'

quisnam, quidnam 'who/what, pray' (independent)
quīnam, quaenam, quodnam 'which, pray' (attributive)

Uter, utra, utrum 'who/which of two' is declined like the adjectives of the first group (**a- and o-declensions**: *niger, nigra, nigrum*) but has in the genitive and dative singular the pronominal forms *utrīus* and *utrī*, respectively. The plural is only used with plural nouns.

The correlative interrogative pronouns are treated in § 71.

Indefinite pronouns

70. **The indefinite pronouns/adjectives** containing the letters *qu-* are declined like the relative pronoun *quī, quae, quod* (§ 63), except in the forms of the nominative listed here.

aliquis, aliquid 'somebody, someone or other, something'
     (independent)
aliquī, aliqua, aliquod 'any, some' (attributive)
   Remarks
   a. The nominative/accusative plural neuter is *aliqua*.
   b. *Aliquis* (etc.) is indefinite for both the speaker and the hearer.
   c. After such short conjunctions as *nē, ut, nisi, sī,* the shortened form *quī(s)* is used.

quīdam, quaedam, quiddam 'a certain one, a certain thing'
     (independent)
quīdam, quaedam, quoddam 'a certain' (attributive)
   Remarks
   a. *Quīdam* (etc.) is indefinite for the hearer but definite for the speaker. The speaker does not want to give more information.
   b. Before a dental, the *m* changes to *n: quendam, quōrundam,* and so on.

(unus)quisque, (ūnum)quidque 'every single one' (independent)
(unus)quisque, (ūna)quaeque, (ūnum)quodque 'every single'
     (attributive)

   Remark. Both parts of this word are declined: *ūnīuscūiusque, ūnamquamque,* and so on.

quīlibet, quaelibet, quidlibet (independent)/**quodlibet** (attributive) 'any one, anything you please'
quīvīs, quaevīs, quidvīs (independent)/**quodvīs** (attributive) 'any one, whatever you like'

Remark. The second part of these pronouns originally was a verb (*libet, vīs*). The first pronoun may be separated by tmesis (§ 461) into *quī* and *libet.*

quisquam, quicquam 'anyone at all' (in sentences with some negative or interrogative meaning)

uterque, utraque, utrumque 'each of two, either'
neuter, neutra, neutrum 'neither of two' (three syllables: *ne-u-ter*)

Remark. These and other compounds with *uter* are declined like the adjectives of the first group (a- and o-declensions), but with the typical pronominal forms of the genitive and dative singular for all three genders: *utrīusque, utrīque; neutrīus, neutrī* (§ 34).

nēmō 'nobody' (gen. sg. *nēminis/nūllīus,* dat. *nēminī/nūllī,* acc. *nēminem/nūllum,* abl. *nēmine/nūllō*).
nihil (nīl) 'nothing' (only nom. and acc. sg.; the other cases are supplied by *nūllīus reī, nūllī reī, nūllā rē*).

Correlative pronouns

71. Correlative pronouns/adjectives are closely related to each other (§ 49). Each series contains an **interrogative**, an **indefinite**, a **demonstrative**, a **relative**, and an **indefinite relative pronoun/adjective** (with an indefinite part, *-cumque, -vīs,* or *-libet*).

Interrogative	Indefinite	Demon-strative	Relative	Indefinite relative
quis, quid 'who, what?'	*aliquis, -quid* 'some one, something'	*is, ea, id* 'he/she/it, this/that'	*quī, quae, quod* 'who, which'	*quīcumcumque, quaecumque, quod-cumque* 'whoever'
quālis, quāle 'of what kind?'	–	*tālis, tāle* 'such'	*quālis, quāle* 'as'	*quālis-, quālecumque* 'of whatever kind'
quantus, -a, -um 'how great?'	*aliquantus, -a, -um* 'somewhat great'	*tantus, -a, -um* 'so great'	*quantus, -a, -um* 'as'	*quantus-, quanta-, quantumcumque* 'however great'
quot (indeclinable) 'how much?'	*aliquot* 'some, several'	*tot* 'so many'	*quot* 'as'	*quotcumque* 'however many'

*Cum **quantō** in perīculō imperātor versārētur cognōvissent* ... "As they knew in what great danger the general was ..." (Caes, *B.G.* 2.26.5)
Quot hominēs, tot sententiae. "So many people, so many opinions." Literally, "There are as many opinions as there are people." (Ter. *Ph.* 454)

7

The Verb

Concepts

Conjugations and stems

72. The regular verbs fall into **five conjugations** on the basis of the **final sound of the imperfective stem** (also called present stem). Most dictionaries list the verbs according to the form of the first-person singular of the present indicative, followed by the other information needed to know the three principal parts (§ 73). Other dictionaries classify them according to the form of the infinitive. The five conjugations are

First or **a-conjugation**: *amō, -āre, amāvī, amātum*	or *amāre, -ō, -ās, -āvi, amātum*
Second or **e-conjugation**: *habeō, -ēre, habuī, habitum*	or *habēre, -eō, -ēs, habuī, habitum*
Third or **u-/consonant conjugation**: *vincō, -ere, vīcī, victum*	or *vincere, -ō, -is, vīcī, victum*
Fourth or **ī-conjugation**: *audiō, -īre, audīvī, audītum*	or *audīre, -iō, -īs, audīvī, audītum*
Fifth or **ĭ-conjugation**: *capiō, -ere, cēpī, captum*	or *capere, -iō, -is, cēpī, captum*

73. **All verbal forms are built on one of the three stems** found in the dictionary entry. The stem is obtained by leaving out the ending **-o, -i, -um,** or **-(e)re.** Each verb thus has

- **an imperfective stem:** *amā-, habē-, vinc-, audī-, capi-;*
- **a perfective stem:** *amāv-, habu-, vic-, audīv-, cēp-;*
- **a supine stem:** *amāt-, habit-, vict-, audīt-, capt-.*

Remark. The imperfective stem of the **a-conjugation** (*amāre*) loses the final *-a* before the personal ending *-o* (*amaō > amō*). In verbs of the ĭ-conjugation, the **final short *-ĭ* of the stem changes to *-ĕ*** before an *r* or at the end of a word (*capĭre > capĕre*).

74. The **imperfective stem** may coincide with the **root** of the verb, as in *reg-* (§ 11), or it may consist of **a root and an affix,** as in *vinc-*. However, such an affix is not a regular marker of this stem.

The imperfective stem *vinc-* contains a root (*vic-*) and an imperfective infix (*-n-*). The imperfective stem of *dictāre* contains a root (*dīc-*) and a suffix (*-tā*). The imperfective stem of *cognoscere* contains a prefix (*cō-*), a root (*gnō-*), and an inchoative suffix (*-sc:* see § 14). Some of these affixes (*-n-, -sc*) only occur in the imperfective stem.

75. The **perfective stem** (active) can be formed in several ways, but the different formations do not express a different meaning any more than the past tense of an English weak verb (*work-ed*) expresses another meaning than the past tense of a strong verb (*swam*). The different formations are learned by memorizing the principal parts. For determining the right meaning or translation, see § 217–19.

The **regular perfective stem contains the marker -v.** This type of perfect chiefly occurs in the first and fourth conjugation: *amā-v-ī, audī-v-ī;* also *dēlē-v-i, cognō-v-ī.*

Closely related to the preceding marker is the marker -u, chiefly in the second conjugation: *habēre: habu-ī, monēre: monu-ī;* also *colere: colu-ī.*

Some **perfective stems end in the consonant of the root,** often **with change in the color or the length of the stem vowel:** *vincere: vīc-ī, iŭvāre: iūv-i, sedēre: sēd-ī, agere: ēg-ī, venīre: vēn-ī.*

Some **perfective stems end in -s** (a dental consonant is left out before an *s*): *manēre: māns-ī, regere: rex-i, mittere: mīs-ī, sentīre: sens-ī.*

Some **perfective stems are formed with a reduplication: a repetition of the first consonant (or *st* or *sp*) and the first stem vowel (or an *e*).** This reduplication also occurs in compounds of *dare, stāre, poscere,* and usually *currere,* but not in other compounds: *mordēre: mo-mordī, cadere: ce-cid-ī, (dē)currere: (dē)cucurr-ī, (circum)dare: (circum)de-d-ī, (circum)stāre: (circum)ste-t-ī, poscere: po-posc-ī, spondēre: spo-pond-ī, pellere: pe-pul-ī;* but *dē-pellere: dē-pul-ī.*

In two instances, **the perfective stem is completely different from the imperfective stem** (as in English *be: was*): *esse (sum): fu-ī, ferre: tul-ī.*

76. The **supine** (active) is formed mostly with **-tum,** sometimes with **-sum:** *amāre: amātum, habēre: habitum, vincere: victum, audīre: audītum, capere: captum, manēre: mansum.* The supine stem is found by omitting the ending **-um.** The supine stem is the base for the perfective passive participle (PPP), the future active participle (FAP), and the supine itself.

Tenses

77. The **three imperfective tenses** and the **three perfective tenses** for the most part correspond to the English tenses. (For the differences, see § 210–23.) In both instances, there is **a present, past, and future tense,** each with its own tense marker (tense suffix).

Imperfective tenses are constructed on the imperfective stem, which expresses incompleteness and simultaneousness (§ 210–11).

- **present** or **present imperfective tense**
- **imperfect** or **past imperfective tense**
- **future** or **future imperfective tense**

Perfective tenses are formed on the perfective stem in the active voice and with a PPP in the passive voice. This aspectual stem and the PPP express a completeness and anteriority (§ 210–11).

- **perfect** (§ 217–19)
- **pluperfect** or **past perfective tense**
- **future perfect** or **future perfective tense**

Moods

78. The **moods** (§ 224) are divided into two classes. In three moods, the **verb is finite**: it indicates which grammatical person is the subject. These moods are

- the **indicative mood**: six tenses (§ 83–84);
- the **subjunctive mood**: four tenses (§ 85);
- the **imperative mood**: two tenses (§ 86).

The verbs of **five non-finite moods** do not indicate a person but are nominal (substantive or adjective).

a) The **infinitive** is a verbal noun with properties of both verbs and nouns. As a noun, it is neuter. As a verb, it can be active or passive and imperfective, perfective, or future. Hence, there are six infinitive forms (§ 87). The infinitive can have an object or an adverbial modifier. It can have a subject in the infinitive clause.

b) The **supine** is a verbal noun with only two cases:
   - the supine in *-um* (acc.), an adverbial modifier of purpose (§ 355);
   - the supine in *-ū* (abl.), an adverbial modifier of restriction (§ 319).

c) The **gerund** is a verbal noun (a declined active infinitive) with only four case endings (gen., dat., acc., abl.). It is neuter and has no number. It has verbal properties: it can have an object or an adverbial modifier.

d) The **gerundive** is a passive verbal adjective with the meaning 'must', 'can (not)', or 'may (not)'. It is fully declined for case, number, and gender.

e) **The participle** is a verbal adjective. It is declined for case, number, and gender. It can be an attribute or part of the predicate. It also has verbal properties in a participial phrase. The verbal system lacks three participles: perfective active, imperfective passive, and future passive. There exist
   - the **imperfective active participle (IAP)**, expressing simultaneity;
   - the **perfective passive participle (PPP)**, expressing anteriority;
   - the **future active participle (FAP)**, expressing posteriority.

Voices

79. There exists an **active voice**, without any particular morphological characteristic, and a **passive voice**, often with the characteristic *r* in the personal endings.

The passive of some transitive verbs can express a **reflexive** (or related) meaning (§ 209).

Some verbs only exist in the **passive voice with an active meaning**. These are **deponent verbs**, which have "put down" (*dē-pōnere*) their passive meaning (§ 101–3, 209).

Person, number, and gender

80. The **personal forms of the verb** or **finite verbs** refer to an expressed or understood subject of the **first person** (the speaker), the **second person** (the addressee), or the **third person** (the person or thing talked about). Furthermore, they express a **number: singular** or **plural**. In the compound tenses (perfective passive tenses) and in the periphrastic conjugation (§ 100), the nominal part of the verb also agrees with the subject in **gender** and **number**.

Sometimes a **thematic vowel** (§ 11) is inserted between the stem and the personal ending. Usually it is a *ĭ*, which changes to *ĕ* before an *r* and at the end of the word, but *u* before *-nt*. There is no thematic vowel in some tenses of the regular conjugations and in some irregular verbs.

The **personal endings** (which also indicate number) are the same in all tenses and moods except for the active perfect indicative and the imperative. The endings are the same in all conjugation types.

Person and number	Active			Passive	
	Indicative/ subjunctive	**Perfect indicative**	**Imperative**	**Indicative/ subjunctive**	**Imperative**
1st singular	-m / -ō	-ī		-(o)r	
2nd singular	-s	-istī	-ø (fut. -tō)	-ris	-re (fut. -tor)
3rd singular	-t	-it	(fut. -tō)	-tur	(fut. -tor)
1st plural	-mus	-imus		-mur	
2nd plural	-tis	-istis	-te (fut. -tōte)	-minī	-minī
3rd plural	-nt	-ērunt	(fut. -ntō)	-ntur	(fut. -ntor)

81. **Syncopated forms** can occur in the active voice. These forms lose the sounds *vi* before *s* and *v(e)* before *r*: *amastī* (= *amāvistī*), *amasse* (= *amāvisse*), *audiērunt* (= *audīvērunt*), *audissem* (= *audīvissem*), *amārant* (= *amāverant*), *nōrint* (= *nōverint*), *cognōrant* (= *cognōverant*).

82. **Shortened forms** occur in the third-person plural of the active perfect indicative (*-ēre [= -ērunt]*) and in the second-person singular passive (*-re [= -ris]*): *amāvēre* (= *amāvērunt*), *amābāre* (= *amābāris*).

Characteristics of tenses and moods

83.

	Imperfective tenses of the active and passive indicative			
Tense	Stem + characteristic	Thematic vowel (§ 80)	Endings (§ 80)	Remarks
Present	imperfective stem	1st or a-conjugation: none 2nd or e-conjugation: none 3rd or consonant-conjugation: -i-, -u- 4th or ī-conjugation: -u- in 3rd-person plural 5th or ĭ-conjugation: -u- in 3rd-person plural	-o, -or -s, -ris etc.	Notice ama-ō > amō ĭ > ĕ before r
Imperfect	imperfective stem + -bā- in 1st or 2nd conjugation -ēbā- in 3rd, 4th, or 5th conjugation	none	-m, -r -s, -ris etc.	
Future	imperfective stem + -b- in 1st or 2nd conjugation -a- / -ē- in 3rd, 4th, or 5th conjugation	1st or 2nd conjugation: -o-, -i-, -u- 3rd, 4th, or 5th conjugation: none	1st or 2nd conjugation: -ō, -or, etc. 3rd, 4th, or 5th conjugation: -m, -r, etc.	-a- in 1st-person singular, -ē- elsewhere

84.

Perfective tenses of the indicative (all conjugations)		
	Active	**Passive**
Perfect	perfective stem + special endings (§ 80)	PPP + present indicative of auxiliary verb *sum, es, est, sumus, estis, sunt* (For PPP + *fui* [etc.], see § 221.)
Pluperfect	perfective stem + endings -eram, -erās, -erat, -erāmus, -erātis, -erant	PPP + imperfect indicative of auxiliary verb *eram, erās, erat, erāmus, erātis, erant* (For PPP + *fueram* [etc.], see § 221.)
Future perfect	perfective stem + endings -ero, -eris, -erit, -erimus, -eritis, -erint	PPP + future simple indicative of auxiliary verb *ero, eris, erit, erimus, eritis, erunt*

85.

Subjunctive		
Active and passive		
Present	1st or a-conjugation: imperfective stem + characteristic *-e* (which replaces the stem vowel *a*) 2nd, 3rd, 4th, or 5th conjugation: imperfective stem + *-a*	active endings: *-m, -s,* etc. passive endings: *-r, -ris,* etc. (§ 80)
Imperfect	imperfective stem + characteristic *-re* + endings (= imperfective active inf. + endings)	
	Active	**Passive**
Perfect	perfective stem + endings *-erim, -eris, -erit, -erimus, -eritis, -erint*	PPP + auxiliary verb *sim, sīs, sit, sīmus, sītis, sint*
Pluperfect	perfective stem + endings *-issem, -issēs, -isset,-issēmus, -issētis, -issent* (= perfective active inf. + endings)	PPP + auxiliary verb *essem, essēs, esset, essēmus, essētis, essent*

86.

Imperative: constructed on the imperfective stem			
	Active	**Passive***	**Thematic vowel**
Present	2nd-person singular: no ending 2nd-person plural: *-te*	2nd-person singular: *-re*** 2nd-person plural: *-minī*	1) thematic vowel *-i-* in the 2nd-person singular and plural of the 3rd or *u-/* consonant conjugation*** 2) *ĕ > ĭ* before *r*** and at the end of a word***
Future	2nd-person singular: *-tō* 3rd-person singular: *-tō* 2nd-person plural: *-tōte* 3rd-person plural: *-ntō*	2nd-person singular: *-tor* 3rd-person singular: *-tor* 3rd-person plural: *-ntor*	3) thematic vowel *-u-* in the 3rd-person plural of the 3rd, 4th, or 5th conjugations.

* A passive imperative is only meaningful in deponent verbs.
** For all practical purposes, the present passive imperative 2nd-person singular equals in all conjugations the imperfective active infinitive.
*** The active imperative 2nd-person singulars of *dīcere, dūcere,* and *facere* are *dīc, dūc,* and *fac* without final *-ĕ* (whether from thematic vowel *-ĭ* in *dīcere* and *dūcere* or from stem vowel *-ĭ* in *facere*).

87.

Infinitive			
	Active	**Passive**	**Remarks**
Imperfective	imperfective stem + *-re* (thematic vowel in the 3rd conjugation)	1st, 2nd, or 4th conjugation: imperfective stem + *-ri* 3rd or 5th conjugation: imperfective stem + *-ī*	3rd or 5th conjugation: *ĭ* > *ĕ* before *r* in the active Hence: (active) *reg-e-re, cape-re* (passive) *regī, capī*
Perfective	perfective stem + *-isse*	PPP + auxiliary *esse*	The PPP (perfective passive participle) and FAP (future active participle) in these infinitives are declined.
Future	FAP + *esse*	supine + auxiliary *īrī* (indeclinable)	

88.

Nominal forms of the verb		
Supine (noun)	supine in *-um* (= 3rd principal part) supine in *-ū*	accusative of purpose (§ 355) ablative of restriction (§ 319)
Gerund (noun)	imperfective stem (+ thematic vowel *-e-* in the 3rd, 4th, or 5th conjugation) + *-nd* + endings: genitive *-ī*, dative *-ō*, accusative *-um*, ablative *-ō*	The gerund is a declined imperfective active infinitive.
Gerundive (adjective)	imperfective stem (+ thematic vowel *-e-* in the 3rd, 4th, or 5th conjugation) + *-nd* + endings *-us, -a, -um*	The gerundive is passive in meaning and also has the meaning 'must, can (not), may (not)'. E.g., *amandus* 'to be loved, lovable'
Participle (adjective)	**IAP (imperfective active participle):** imperfective stem (+ thematic vowel *-e-* in 3rd, 4th, or 5th conjugation) + characteristic *-ns, -ntis* (§ 36)	IAP: simultaneity
	PPP (perfective passive participle): supine stem + *-us, -a, -um* (§ 32)	PPP: anteriority
	FAP (future active participle): supine stem + *-ūrus, -ūra, -ūrum* (§ 32)	FAP: posteriority

Five paradigms

89. In the paradigm tables that follow in this chapter, forms constructed on the imperfective stem are not screened, forms constructed on the perfective stem are screened dark grey, and forms constructed on the supine stem are screened light grey.

In the tables, forms like *amātus sum* and *amāti sumus* have to be read as *amātus, -a, -um sum* and *amāti, -ae, -a sumus*, respectively.

90. First or a-conjugation: AMARE   ACTIVE

	Indicative	Subjunctive	Imperative	Infinitive	Participle
Present	'I love' amō amās amat amāmus amātis amant	amem amēs amet amēmus amētis ament	amā 'love!' amāte	amāre 'to love'	amans, -ntis 'loving'
Imperfect	'I loved' amābam amābās amābat amābāmus amābātis amābant	amārem amāres amāret amārēmus amārētis amārent			
Future	'I will love' amābō amābis amabit amābimus amābitis amābunt	periphrastic conjugation (§ 100, 279)	amātō amātō amātōte amantō	amātūrus, -a, -um esse 'to be going to love'	amātūrus, -a, -um
Perfect	'I loved/have loved' amāvī amāvistī amāvit amāvimus amāvistis amāvērunt	amāverim amāveris amāverit amāverimus amāveritis amāverint		amāvisse 'to have loved'	
Pluperfect	'I had loved' amāveram amāveras amāverat amāverāmus amaverātis amāverant	amāvissem amāvissēs amāvisset amāvissēmus amāvissētis amāvissent			

	Gerund	Supine
	Genitive amandī Dative amandō Accusative (ad) amandum Ablative amandō	 Accusative amātum Ablative amātū

Future perfect	'I will have loved' amāverō amāveris amāverit amāverimus amāveritis amāverint

91. First or a-conjugation: AMARE   PASSIVE

	Indicative	Subjunctive	Imperative	Infinitive	Participle
Present	'I am loved' amor amāris amātur amāmur amāminī amāntur	amer amēris amētur amēmur amēminī amēntur	amāre amāminī	amārī 'be loved'	
Imperfect	'I was loved' amābar amābaris amābātur amābāmur amābāminī amābāntur	amārer amārēris amārētur amārēmur amārēminī amārentur			
Future	'I'll be loved' amābor amāberis amābitur amābimur amābiminī amābuntur		amātor amātor amantor	amātum īrī 'to be going to be loved'	
Perfect	'I was/have been loved' amātus sum amātus es amātus est amātī sumus amātī estis amātī sunt	amātus sim amātus sīs amātus sit amātī sīmus amātī sītis amātī sint		amātus, -a, -um esse 'to have been loved'	amātus, -a, -um 'loved'
Pluperfect	'I had been loved' amātus eram amātus erās amātus erat amātī erāmus amātī erātis amātī erānt	amātus essem amātus essēs amātus esset amātī essēmus amātī essētis amātī essent			
Future perfect	'I'll have been loved' amātus erō amātus eris amātus erit amātī erimus amātī eritis amātī erunt				**Gerundive** amandus, -a, -um 'to be loved'

92. Second or e-conjugation: HABERE   ACTIVE

	Indicative	Subjunctive	Imperative	Infinitive	Participle
Present	'I have' habeō habēs habet habēmus habētis habent	hābeam hābeās hābeat hābeāmus hābeātis hābeant	habē habēte	habēre 'to have'	habens, -ntis 'having'
Imperfect	'I had' habēbam habēbas habēbat habēbāmus habēbātis habēbant	habērem habērēs habēret habērēmus habērētis habērent			
Future	'I'll have' habēbō habēbis habēbit habēbimus habēbitis habēbunt	periphrastic conjugation (§ 100, 279)	habētō habētō habētōte habentō	habitūrus, -a, -um esse 'to be going to have'	habitūrus, -a, -um
Perfect	'I had/have had' habuī habuistī habuit habuimus habuistis habuērunt	habuerim habueris habuerit habuerimus habueritis habuerint		habuisse 'to have had'	
Pluperfect	'I had had' habueram habuerās habuerat habuerāmus habuerātis habuerant	habuissem habuissēs habuisset habuissēmus habuissētis habuissent			

Gerund	**Supine**
Genitive habendī	

Dative
          habendō
Accusative
(ad) habendum
Ablative
          habendō
	Accusative
	habitum
	Ablative
	habitū

Future perfect   'I will have had'
habuerō
habueris
habuerit
habuerimus
habueritis
habuerint

93. Second or e-conjugation: HABERE   PASSIVE

	Indicative	Subjunctive	Imperative	Infinitive	Participle
Present	'I am held' habeor habēris habētur habēmur habēminī habentur	habear habeāris habeātur habeāmur habeāminī habeantur	habēre habēminī	habērī 'to be held'	
Imperfect	'I was held' habēbar habēbāris habēbātur habēbāmur habēbāminī habēbantur	habērer habērēris habērētur habērēmur habērēmini habērentur			
Future	'I'll be held' habēbor habēberis habēbitur habēbimur habēbiminī habēbuntur		habētor habētor habentor	habitum īrī 'to be go- ing to be held'	
Perfect	'I was/have been held' habitus sum habitus es habitus est habitī sumus habitī estis habitī sunt	habitus sim habitus sīs habitus sit habitī sīmus habitī sītis habitī sint		habitus, -a, -um esse 'to have been held'	habitus, -a, -um 'held'
Pluperfect	'I had been held' habitus eram habitus erās habitus erat habitī erāmus habitī erātis habitī erant	habitus essem habitus essēs habitus esset habitī essēmus habitī essētis habitī essent			
Future perfect	'I will have been held' habitus ero habitus eris habitus erit habitī erimus habitī eritis habitī erunt				**Gerundive** habendus, -a, -um 'to be held'

94. Third or u-/consonant conjugation: VINCERE   ACTIVE

	Indicative	Subjunctive	Imperative	Infinitive	Participle
Present	'I win' vincō vincis vincit vincimus vincitis vincunt	vincam vincās vincat vincāmus vincātis vincant	vince vincite	vincere 'to win'	vincens, -ntis 'winning'
Imperfect	'I won' vincēbam vincēbas vincēbat vincēbāmus vincēbātis vincēbant	vincerem vincerēs vinceret vincerēmus vincerētis vincerent			
Future	'I'll win' vincam vincēs vincet vincēmus vincētis vincent	periphrastic conjugation (§ 100, 279)	vincitō vincitō vincitōte vincunto	victūrus, -a, -um esse 'to be going to win'	victūrus, -a, -um
Perfect	'I won/have won' vīcī vīcistī vīcit vīcimus vīcistis vīcērunt	vīcerim vīceris vīcerit vīcerimus vīceritis vīcerint		vīcisse 'to have won'	
Pluperfect	'I had won' vīceram vīcerās vīcerat vīcerāmus vīcerātis vīcerant	vīcissem vīcissēs vīcisset vīcissēmus vīcissētis vīcissent			
Future perfect	'I will have won' vīcero vīceris vīcerit vīcerimus vīceritis vīcerint				

Gerund	Supine
Genitive vincendī **Dative** vincendō **Accusative** (ad) vincendum **Ablative** vincendō	 **Accusative** victum **Ablative** victū

95. Third or u-/consonant conjugation: VINCERE PASSIVE

	Indicative	Subjunctive	Imperative	Infinitive	Participle
Present	'I am conquered' vincor vinceris vincitur vincimur vinciminī vincuntur	vincar vincāris vincātur vincāmur vincāminī vincantur	vincere vinciminī	vincī 'to be conquered'	
Imperfect	'I was conquered' vincēbar vincēbāris vincēbātur vincēbāmur vincēbāminī vincēbantur	vincerer vincerēris vincerētur vincerēmur vincerēminī vincerentur			
Future	'I'll be conquered' vincar vincēris vincētur vincēmur vincēminī vincentur		vincitor vincitor vincuntor	victum īrī 'to be going to be con- quered'	
Perfect	'I was/have been conquered' victus sum victus es victus est victī sumus victī estis victī sunt	victus sim victus sīs victus sīt victī sīmus victī sītis victī sint		victus, -a, -um esse 'to have been conquered'	victus, -a, -um 'con- quered'
Pluperfect	'I had been conquered' victus eram victus erās victus erat victī erāmus victī erātis victī erant	victus essem victus essēs victus esset victī essēmus victī essētis victī essent			
Future perfect	'I'll have been conquered' victus ero victus eris victus erit victī erimus victī eritis victī erunt				**Gerundive** vincendus, -a, -um 'to be con- quered'

96. Fourth or ī-conjugation: AUDIRE   ACTIVE

	Indicative	Subjunctive	Imperative	Infinitive	Participle
Present	'I hear' audio audīs audit audīmus audītis audiunt	audiam audiās audiat audiāmus audiātis audiant	audī audīte	audīre 'to hear'	audiens, -ntis 'hearing'
Imperfect	'I heard' audiēbam audiēbās audiēbat audiēbāmus audiēbātis audiēbant	audīrem audīrēs audīret audīrēmus audīrētis audīrent			
Future	'I'll hear' audiam audiēs audiet audiēmus audiētis audient	periphrastic conjugation (§100, 279)	audītō audītō audītōte audiunto	audītūrus, -a, -um esse 'to be going to hear'	audītūrus, -a, -um
Perfect	'I (have) heard' audīvī audīvistī audīvit audīvimus audīvistis audīvērunt	audīverim audīveris audīverit audīverimus audīveritis audīverint		audīvisse 'to have heard'	
Pluperfect	'I had heard' audīveram audīverās audīverat audīverāmus audīverātis audīverant	audīvissem audīvissēs audīvisset audīvissēmus audīvissētis audīvissent			

	Gerund	**Supine**
	Genitive audiendī	
	Dative audiendō	
	Accusative (ad) audiendum	**Accusative** audītum
	Ablative audiendō	**Ablative** audītū

Future perfect	'I will have heard' audīverō audīveris audīverit audīverimus audīveritis audīverint

97. Fourth or ī-conjugation: AUDIRE　　　PASSIVE

	Indicative	Subjunctive	Imperative	Infinitive	Participle
Present	'I am heard' audior audīris audītur audīmur audīminī audiuntur	audiar audiāris audiātur audiāmur audiāminī audiāntur	audīre audīminī	audīrī 'to be heard'	
Imperfect	'I was heard' audiēbar audiēbāris audiēbātur audiēbāmur audiēbāminī audiēbantur	audīrer audīrēris audīrētur audīrēmur audīrēmini audīrentur			
Future	'I will be heard' audiar audiēris audiētur audiēmur audiēminī audientur		audītor audītor audiuntor	audītum īrī 'to be going to be heard'	
Perfect	'I was/have been heard' auditus sum auditus es auditus est auditī sumus auditī estis auditī sunt	auditus sim auditus sīs auditus sīt auditī sīmus auditī sītis auditī sint		audītus, -a, -um esse 'to have been heard'	audītus, -a, -um 'heard'
Pluperfect	'I had been heard' auditus eram auditus eras auditus erat auditi eramus auditi eratis auditi erant	auditus essem auditus essēs auditus esset auditī essēmus auditī essētis auditī essent			
Future perfect	'I'll have been heard' auditus ero auditus eris auditus erit auditi erimus auditi eritis auditi erunt				**Gerundive** audiendus, -a, -um 'to be heard'

98. Fifth or ĭ-conjugation: CAPERE   ACTIVE

		Indicative	Subjunctive	Imperative	Infinitive	Participle
Present		'I take' capiō capis capit capimus capitis capiunt	capiam capiās capiat capiāmus capiātis capiant	cape capite	capere 'to take'	capiens, -ntis 'taking'
Imperfect		'I took' capiēbam capiēbās capiēbat capiēbāmus capiēbātis capiēbant	caperem caperēs caperet caperēmus caperētis caperent			
Future		'I will take' capiam capiēs capiet capiēmus capiētis capient	periphrastic conjugation (§ 100, 279)	capitō capitō capitōte capiuntō	captūrus, -a, -um esse 'to be going to take'	captūrus, -a, -um
Perfect		'I took/have taken' cēpī cēpistī cēpit cēpimus cēpistis cēpērunt	cēperim cēperis cēperit cēperimus cēperitis cēperint		cēpisse 'to have taken'	
Pluperfect		'I had taken' cēperam ' cēperās cēperat cēperāmus cēperātis cēperant	cēpissem cēpissēs cēpisset cēpissēmus cēpissētis cēpissent			

	Gerund	**Supine**
Genitive	capiendī	
Dative	capiendō	
Accusative	(ad) capiendum	captum (Accusative)
Ablative	capiendō	captū (Ablative)

Future perfect — 'I will have taken'
cēperō
cēperis
cēperit
cēperimus
cēperitis
cēperint

99. Fifth or ĭ-conjugation: CAPERE   PASSIVE

	Indicative	Subjunctive	Imperative	Infinitive	Participle
Present	'I am taken' capior caperis capitur capimur capiminī capiuntur	capiar capiāris capiātur capiāmur capiāminī capiantur	capere capiminī	capī 'to be taken'	
Imperfect	'I was taken' capiēbar capiēbāris capiēbātur capiēbāmur capiēbāminī capiēbantur	caperer caperēris caperētur caperēmur caperēmini caperentur			
Future	'I will be taken' capiar capiēris capiētur capiēmur capiēmini capiēntur		capitor capitor capiuntor	captum īrī 'to be going to be taken'	
Perfect	'I was/have been taken' captus sum captus es captus est captī sumus captī estis captī sunt	captus sim captus sīs captus sit captī sīmus captī sītis captī sint		captus, -a, -um esse 'to have been taken'	captus, -a, -um 'taken'
Pluperfect	'I had been taken' captus eram captus erās captus erat captī erāmus captī erātis captī erant	captus essem captus essēs captus esset captī essēmus captī essētis captī essent			
Future perfect	'I will have been taken' captus erō captus eris captus erit captī erimus captī eritis captī erunt				**Gerundive** capiendus, -a, -um 'to be taken'

Periphrastic conjugation

100. The **periphrastic conjugation** is formed with a **future active participle + the auxiliary verb** *esse* (in the present/imperfect indicative and subjunctive). The meaning, however, is not the same as that of the future. *Moriar* is a future and means 'I will die'. *Moritūrus sum* is a present and means 'I am (now) on the point of dying, I am (now) about to die'; *moritūrus eram* means 'I was about to die'; and so on (§ 216).

This periphrastic conjugation with the auxiliary in the subjunctive (*sim/essem*) is also used, for lack of a future subjunctive, to express **posteriority in an indirect question** (§ 277–79).

There is also a periphrastic conjugation with the **gerundive + auxiliary** *esse* to express an obligation or possibility in the passive: 'must be, may (not) be, can (not) be'. (The passive is impossible to render in English.) Thus, *Nunc est bibendum* may mean 'Now drinking has to be done', 'Now there has to be drinking', 'Now one must drink', or 'Now we must drink'. (Hor. *Carm.* 1.37.1)

The compound tenses of the passive perfective could also be called "periphrastic," as they are composed of a PPP and the auxiliary verb *esse*.

Deponent and semi-deponent verbs

101. **Deponent verbs have a passive form but an active meaning.** They have "put down" (*dē-pōnere*) their passive meaning. (These verbs are remnants of a stage in the language when there were, as in classical Greek, three voices. The middle voice of all verbs was active in meaning and passive as to its form.) Deponent verbs are conjugated like the passive of the regular verbs.

First or **a-conjugation**: *hortor, hortārī, hortātus sum* 'exhort'	like *amārī* (passive)
Second or **e-conjugation**: *vereor, verērī, veritus sum* 'fear'	like *habērī* (passive)
Third or **u-/consonant conjugation**: *sequor, sequī, secūtus sum* 'follow'	like *vincī* (passive)
Fourth or **long i-conjugation**: *potior, potīrī, potītus sum* 'get hold of'	like *audīrī* (passive)
Fifth or **short i-conjugation**: *patior, patī, passus sum* 'endure'	like *capī* (passive)

Deponent verbs also have some **active forms** with **active** meaning: gerund, supine, IAP, FAP, and future active infinitive.

The **gerundive** of these verbs does have a **passive meaning**.

The meaning of the PPP is sometimes active, sometimes passive: for example, *populātus,* the PPP of *populārī* 'destroy', can mean not only 'having destroyed' but also 'destroyed'.

102. Four **semi-deponent verbs** have **active forms and active meaning** in the imperfective tenses and **passive forms and active meaning** in the perfective tenses. Thus, they are only deponent in the perfective tenses.

> *audeō, audēre, ausus sum* 'dare'
> *gaudeō, gaudēre, gavīsus sum* 'rejoice'
> *soleō, solēre, solitus sum* 'be used to'
> *fīdō, fīdere, fīsus sum* 'trust' and its compounds *confīdere* 'trust' and
>   *diffīdere* 'distrust'

The tenses of the indicative, for example, are

imperfective: active: *audeō, audēbam, audēbō;*
perfective: deponent: *ausus sum, ausus eram, ausus erō.*

103. There is **one reverse semi-deponent verb**: *revertor, revertī* (passive inf.), *revertī* (active indic.) 'return'.

This verb is deponent in the imperfective tenses (imperfective inf. *revertī*, indic. *revertor, revertēbar, revertar,* etc.) and active in the perfective tenses (indic. *revertī, reverteram, reverterō,* perfective inf. *revertisse,* etc.).

Irregular verbs

Esse

104. The verb *esse* 'to be' is

– an independent verb: 'to exist, there is/are';
– a copula ('to be') combined with the nominal part of the predicate;
– an auxiliary verb in the perfective tenses of the passive.

This verb is irregular in the imperfective tenses. The root is *es-* or *s-*. It is regular in the perfective active tenses, with the root/stem *fu-*.

It has no passive, no gerund, no gerundive, and no IAP. It does have an FAP and infinitive. Its compounds do have an IAP: *abesse* 'be absent' has the IAP *absens, -ntis.*

In the present subjunctive, the archaic forms *siem, siēs, siet, etc.* and *fuam, fuās, fuat, etc.* exist in addition to the classical *sim, sīs, sit, etc.* In the imperfect subjunctive, *forem, forēs, foret, etc.* exist beside *essem, etc.* The declinable *futūrus esse* alternates with the indeclinable *fore.*

	Indicative	**Subjunctive**	**Imperative**	**Infinitive**	**Participle**
Present	sum 'I am' es est sumus estis sunt	sim (siem) sīs sit sīmus sītis sint	es este	esse 'to be'	only in compounds: absens, -ntis
Imperfect	eram 'I was' erās erat erāmus erātis erant	essem (forem) essēs esset essēmus essētis essent			
Future	erō 'I will be' eris erit erimus eritis erunt	periphrastic conjugation (§ 100, 279)	estō estō estōte suntō	futūrus, -a, -um esse (= fore) 'going to be'	futūrus, -a, -um
Perfect	fui 'I was/have been' fuistī etc.	fuerim fueris etc.		fuisse 'have been'	
Pluperfect	fueram 'I had been' fuerās etc.	fuissem fuissēs etc.			
Future Perfect	fuerō 'I will have been' fueris etc.				

Posse

105. The irregular verb *posse* 'can, be able' consists of the root *pot-* and the verb *esse*. In the imperfective tenses, the *t* is assimilated to *s* before the forms of *esse* beginning with an *s*: *pot-sum > possum*.

The perfective tenses are regularly formed on the perfective stem *potu-*: perfect *potuī, potuistī, etc.*; pluperfect *potueram, etc.*; future perfect *potuerō, etc.*; infinitive *potuisse, etc.*

	Indicative	Subjunctive	Infinitive	Participle
Present	possum 'I can' potes potest possumus potestis possunt	possim possīs possit possīmus possītis possint	posse 'be able / can'	potens, -ntis 'able / capable'
Imperfect	poteram 'I could' poterās poterat poterāmus poterātis poterant	possem possēs posset possēmus possētis possent		
Future	poterō 'I will be able' poteris poterit poterimus poteritis poterunt			

Ferre

106. *Ferō, ferre, tulī, latum* 'carry, bring' (with two different roots, *fer-* and *telə-/ tlā-*) is regular in the tenses built on the active perfective stem and in the active and passive forms built on the supine stem. In some forms (in bold type in the table that follows) of the imperfective tenses, there is no thematic vowel. The passive forms contain the same irregularity as the active ones (*feror, ferris, fertur, ferimur, feriminī, feruntur, etc.*).

ACTIVE	Indicative	Subjunctive	Imperative	Infinitive	Participle
Present	ferō **fers** **fert** ferimus **fertis** ferunt	feram ferās ferat ferāmus ferātis ferant	**fer** **ferte**	**ferre**	ferens, -ntis
Imperfect	ferēbam ferēbās etc.	**ferrem** **ferres** etc.			
Future	feram ferēs etc.	periphrastic conjugation (§ 100, 279)	2nd-person singular: **fertō** 2nd-person plural: **fertōte**	latūrus, -a, -um esse	latūrus, -a, -um

Velle, nolle, malle

107. These three verbs are **irregular in the imperfective tenses**, partly because of the lack of a **thematic vowel** (infinitive *vel-re* > *velle*). They have no passive. The perfective tenses are regularly built on the perfective stem. The principal parts are

volo, velle, voluī 'want';
nōlō, nōlle, nōluī 'not wish' (*nōlle* < *non velle*);
mālō, mālle, māluī 'would rather, prefer' (*mālle* < *magis velle*).

Nōlī(te) + infinitive is used to express a prohibition (§ 234). *Velle* and *nōlle* also have IAPs: *volens, -ntis* 'willing' and *nōlens, -ntis* 'not willing'.

	Indicative			Subjunctive			Imperative
Present	volō	nōlo	mālō	velim	nōlim	mālim	
	vīs	nōn vīs	māvis	velīs	nōlīs	mālīs	nōlī
	vult	nōn vult	māvult	velit	nōlit	mālit	
	volumus	nōlumus	mālumus	velīmus	nōlīmus	mālīmus	
	vultis	nōn vultis	māvultis	velītis	nōlītis	mālītis	nōlīte
	volunt	nōlunt	mālunt	velint	nōlint	mālint	
Imperfect	volēbam	nōlēbam	mālēbam	vellem	nollem	mallem	
	volēbās	nōlēbās	mālēbās	vellēs	nollēs	mallēs	
	etc.	etc.	etc.	etc.	etc.	etc.	
Future	volam	nōlam	mālam				
	volēs	nōlēs	mālēs				
	etc.	etc.	etc.				
Perfect etc.	voluī	nōluī	māluī	voluerim	nōluerim	māluerim	
	voluistī	nōluistī	māluistī	volueris	nōlueris	mālueris	
	etc.	etc.	etc.	etc.	etc.	etc.	

Fieri

108. The irregular verb *fīō, fierī, factus sum* is used

- with the meaning 'become';
- as an impersonal verb, with the meaning 'happen';
- as passive of the verb *facere*.

This verb is irregular in the imperfective tenses. The perfective tenses are regularly formed by means of the PPP (*factus*) + auxiliary *esse*.

	Indicative		Subjunctive		Infinitive	Participle
Present	fīō	fīmus	fīam	fīāmus		
	fīs	fītis	fīās	fīātis	fierī	
	fit	fīunt	fīat	fīant		
Imperfect	fīēbam		fīerem			
	fīēbās		fīerēs			
	etc.		etc.			
Future	fīam				factum īrī	
	fīēs					
	etc.					
Perfect etc.	factus sum		factus sim		factus, -a, -um esse	factus, -a, -um
	etc.		etc.			

Ire

109. The verb *eō, īre, iī (īvī), itum* mostly follows the fourth conjugation (*audīre*). Some exceptions (based on an older *eire*), printed in bold type in the table that follows, are

- there is an *e-* (instead of an *i-*) before an *a, o,* or *u*;
- the imperfect has no *e* in the tense suffix *-ba*;
- the future has the tense suffix *-b* as in the first and second conjugations;
- the supine has a short *i*;
- the perfective tenses are regularly formed on the perfective stem *i-*, but *iī > ī* before *s*.

	Indicative		Subjunctive		Imperative	Infinitive	Participle
Present	eō	īmus	**eam**	**eāmus**			
	īs	ītis	**eās**	**eātis**	2nd-person singular: i		
	it	**eunt**	**eat**	**eant**	2nd-person plural: ite	ire	iens, euntis 'going'
Imperfect	**ībam**		īrem				
	ības		īres				
	etc.		etc.				
Future	**ībo**		periphrastic conjugation (§ 100, 279)		2nd-person singular: ītō 2nd-person plural: ītōte	itūrus, -a, -um esse	itūrus, -a, -um
	ībis						
	etc.						
Perfect	iī (īvī)	iimus	ierim				**Supine**
	īstī	**īstis**	ieris				**Accusative:** itum
	iit	iĕrunt	ierit			**īsse** 'have gone'	
			etc.				**Ablative:** itu
Pluperfect	ieram		**īssem**				
	ierās		**īsses**				
	ierat		**īsset**			**Gerund**	**Gerundive**
	etc.		etc.				
Future Perfective	ierō					**Genitive** eundī **Dative** eundō **Accusative** (ad) **eundum** **Ablative** eundō	eundum
	ieris						
	ierit						
	etc.						

Defective verbs

110. Verbs are called **defective** when some of their forms are lacking. There are some verbs of which only a very few forms are used.

111. *Coepī, coepisse, coeptum* 'have begun, begin' has no imperfective stem and only exists in the perfective tenses, with **regular** forms constructed on the perfective stem and supine stem: *coepī, coepistī* (etc.); pluperfect *coeperam, etc.*

If this verb is combined with a passive infinitive, its passive form is used: *Lapidēs iacī **coeptī sunt**,* "They started to throw stones," (literally, "Stones were started to be thrown") (Caes. *B.G.* 2.6.2)

112. *Meminisse* 'remember' and *ōdī* 'hate' exist almost exclusively in the perfective tenses, with an imperfective meaning: *meminī, meministī, etc.; memineram, etc.; meminerō; meminerim, etc.; meminissēs, etc.; meminisse; ōdī, ōdistī, etc.*

113. The verb *āiō* 'say' only occurs in a very few forms: present *āiō, ais, ait, —, āiunt;* imperfect *āiēbam, āiēbās, āiēbat, etc.;* perfect *ait, etc.*

114. *Inquit* (present and perfect) 'he says/he said' chiefly occurs in this form in the middle of direct speech ('says he').

8

The Preposition

Definition

115. Prepositions are indeclinable words that govern a noun or pronoun in a certain case. Some prepositions can be construed with both the accusative (mainly direction, extent) and the ablative (separation, place, etc.). Most prepositions govern only one case. The nouns *causā* and *grātiā* (in the abl.) preceded by a noun in the genitive can also be considered prepositional expressions. Apart from this instance, no preposition governs a nominative, vocative, genitive, or dative. A preposition together with its (pro)noun or noun phrase forms a **prepositional phrase**.

116. Originally, prepositions were adverbs that defined a case more precisely. Some prepositions still occur in classical Latin as adverbs (*post, contrā, ante, suprā, circā,* etc.).

117. Prepositions normally precede the noun or pronoun they govern. But in a distant past, they were "postpositions." This explains why *cum* + ablative still occurs **after** a pronoun (*sēcum, vōbīscum, quibuscum, etc.:* see § 53c, 63). See also § 408 on **anastrophe** as an archaic poetic device.

118. Many prepositions have in the first place a **local** meaning, furthermore a **temporal** meaning, and sometimes a more **figurative** meaning.

Prepositions governing both the accusative and the ablative

119. *in*   a) **with accusative**—'into, unto, in, on, against' (direction; also used figuratively): *in urbem* 'into the city', *dīvidere in partēs trēs* 'divide into three parts', *impetus in nostrōs* 'an attack on our men', *in diēs* 'from day to day, daily', *in longitūdinem* 'lengthwise'.

       b) **with ablative**—'in, on' (place, time, circumstance): *in urbe* 'in the city', *in murō* 'on the wall', *in armīs* 'under arms', *in consulātū* 'during the consulate'.

   sub a) **with accusative**—'(to a place) under' (direction, time): *sub iugum mittere* 'bring under the yoke', *sub noctem* 'just before night', *sub occasum sōlis* 'at sunset'.

       b) **with ablative**—'(in a place) under, up to' (place, time): *sub rūpe* 'at the foot of the rock', *sub imperiō* 'under the domination'.

super   a) **with accusative**—'upon, over' (place, direction): *curret super ōra* '(traveling in a litter) he will pass above the faces (of the people)'.

   b) **with ablative** (mainly poetic)—'upon' (place): *fronde super viridī* 'on green leaves'.

Prepositions governing the accusative

120. *ad*   'near, to, toward' (direction, place, purpose): *ad urbem* 'to the city', *ad arma currere* 'take up arms', *ad caelum* 'toward heaven', *ad vesperum* 'by evening', *ūtilis ad nāvigandum* 'fit to sail', *ad ūnum ōmnēs* 'down to the last man'.

adversus   'against, toward, opposite to' (sometimes friendly, but usually hostile attitude): *adversus rem publicam* 'against the state'.

ante   'before' (place, time): *ante portās* 'before the gates', *ante lūcem* 'before dawn', *ante diem secundum Kalendās Māiās* 'the second day before the Kalends of May' = 'April 30'.

apud   'at, near' (place, mostly with persons): *apud Helvētiōs* 'among the Helvetii'.

circā, circum, circiter   'around' (place, time, approximation): *circum forum* 'around the forum', *circā sē habēre* 'have around himself', *circā eandem hōram* 'around the same hour'.

cis, citrā   'on this side of' (place): *cis Padum* 'on this side of the Po'.

contrā   'against' (place, direction, hostile attitude): *contrā populum Rōmānum coniūrāre* 'conspire against the Roman people'.

ergā   'toward' (friendly attitude): *fidēs ergā hominēs* 'faithfulness toward the people'.

extrā   'outside, without' (place; used figuratively): *extrā murōs* 'outside the walls', *omnēs extrā ducem* 'all except the leader'.

inter   'between, amidst' (place, time): *inter Sequanōs et Helvētiōs* 'between the Sequani and the Helvetii', *inter falcāriōs* 'among the scythemakers' = 'in the scythemakers' street', *inter sē* 'among themselves', *inter cēnam* 'during dinner'.

intrā   'inside, within' (place, time): *intrā mūrum* 'within the wall', *intrā annum* 'within a year'.

iuxtā   'next to, beside' (place): *iuxtā Viam Appiam* 'next to the Appian Way'.

ob   'because of, on account of, over against' (cause, place): *ob eam causam* 'for that reason', *quam ob rem* '(and) therefore', *ob oculōs versāri* 'be present before the eyes'.

per 'through' (the road followed, extent in time, means): *per prōvinciam* 'through the province', *per manūs* 'from hand to hand', *multōs per annōs* 'for many years', *per lēgātōs* 'through the envoys', *per dolum* 'by means of a trick', *per mē licet* 'I let you', *per omnēs deōs* 'Good Heavens!'

post 'behind, after' (place, time): *post mē* 'after me', *post proelium* 'after the battle'.

praeter 'beside' (used figuratively): *praeter ea* 'moreover', *omnēs praeter ūnum* 'all except one'.

prope 'near' (place): *prope castra* 'near the camp'.

propter 'near, on account of' (place, reason): *propter aliquem stāre* 'stand next to someone', *propter metum poenae* 'out of fear for punishment', *propter mē* 'as far as I am concerned'.

secundum 'along, next to, according to' (place, time; used figuratively): *secundum flūmen* 'along the river', *secundum comitia* 'immediately after the assembly', *secundum nātūram vīvere* 'live according to nature'.

suprā 'above' (place, time, rank): *suprā caput esse* 'hang above one's head', *suprā hanc memoriam* 'before our time', *suprā modum* 'exceedingly'.

trans 'across' (place, direction): *trans Rhēnum incolere* 'live on the other side of the Rhine', *trans Rhēnum dūcere* 'bring over the Rhine'.

versus, versum 'toward' (direction) (always occurs after the noun when used alone [see § 117]; in combination with *in* or *ad* before the noun, except for names of towns and small islands): *in Galliam versus* 'toward Gaul', *Rōmam versus* 'toward Rome'.

Prepositions governing the ablative

121. *a, ab* 'from, off' (separation in space or time), 'by' (agent modifier with passive verbs): *ab aliīs ad aliōs* 'from the ones to the others', *ab altō nīdō* 'from a high nest', *ā nōmine dicta* 'called after his name', *ab Urbe conditā* 'since the foundation of Rome', *ā parentibus mittuntur* 'they are sent by their parents'.

cum '(together) with' (accompaniment, manner; see also § 117): *cum hostibus* 'with the enemy', *cum gladiō* 'having a sword with him' (not 'by means of a sword'), *cum maximā cūrā* 'with the greatest care', *cum prīmā lūce* 'at dawn'.

dē 'down from, away from, immediately after, about' (separation, time; used figuratively): *dē mūrō dēicere* 'throw from the wall', *homo dē plēbe* 'a man from the plebs', *dē mediā nocte* 'immediately after midnight', *gravī dē causā* 'for a serious reason'; *dē rērum nātūrā* 'about the nature of things'.

ex, ē 'out, out of, from' (separation, time; used figuratively): *ē manibus* 'out of the hands', *ex oppidō* 'out of the town', *ex eō tempore* 'since that time', *ex lege* 'under the law', *statua ex aere facta* 'a statue made of bronze', *ūnus ex hīs* 'one of these' (§ 127, remark).

prae 'before, in front of, because of' (causal; in classical Latin, used only in negative sentences), 'in comparison with' (place, reason, comparison): *prae sē agere* 'drive in front of himself', *prae lacrimīs scrībere non possum* 'on account of my tears I could not write', *prae vīcīnīs* 'in comparison with my neighbors'.

prō 'before, for, instead of, in relation to' (place; used figuratively): *prō castrīs* 'before the camp', *prō pătriā morī* 'die for his fatherland', *prō consule* 'in the name of the consul', *prō amīcō habēre* 'consider a friend', *prō multitūdine hominum* 'in relation to their high population'.

sine 'without' (separation): *sine morā* 'without delay', *sine uxōre* 'without spouse'.

PART 3

Semantics and Syntax
of the Cases

9

Semantics and Syntax of the Cases

Introduction

122. This chapter examines the meaning or semantic role of the morphological category of case (morphosemantics). The major syntactic functions expressed by each case are also indicated here. Although case gives a strong indication about function, it is not systematically used for one function. Particularly, constructions used in adverbial modifiers in the sentence may also be used for other functions (§ 177, 366, 380–81). The functions are treated systematically in this book's chapters on the sentence and the text (chaps. 10–17). Such fundamental concepts as function, role, form, and level are explained in chapter 10.

Nominative

123. The nominative is the case of the **subject** of the sentence, if the predicate of the sentence is a finite verb or a historical infinitive. Because of the rules of agreement, it is also the case of the **nominal part of the predicate—predicate noun, the predicate adjective, or the participle of a compound tense** (§ 193–202).

> *Daedalus intereā clausus erat pelagō.* "In the meantime Daedalus was closed in by the sea." (Ovid *Met.* 8.183–85)

The nominative is also the case of the **noun** and **adjective** (**nomen substantivum** and **nomen adiectivum**) given in the dictionary entry and used in the **title** of a work, as in Cicero's title *Laelius vel dē amīcitiā* (Laelius, or On Friendship).

Vocative

124. The vocative, with or without the interjection *o*, has **an appeal function**; that is, it does not refer to a person but calls his/her attention to the sentence(s) or text that is or will be spoken/written. It is also used in **exclamations.** The noun in the vocative indicates a function not in the sentence but in the text (letter, speech, etc.) as a whole (§ 379).

> *"Pȳrame"*, *clāmāvit*, *"quis tē mihi casus adēmit? Pȳrame, respondē."* "'Pyramus', she cried, 'what event took you away from me? Pyramus, answer.'" (Ovid *Met.* 4.142–43)

Genitive

Genitive as constituent of the noun phrase

125. The vast majority of nouns in the genitive are **attributes of another noun**. Therefore, they themselves are not a sentence constituent but a part of a constituent (or noun phrase). **They modify the head** of the noun phrase (§ 358, 365).

The semantic relation between a noun in the genitive and its head noun is not always the same. The nature of their relation is to a large extent determined by the meaning of both words in their context. In English translation, the preposition *of* is often used, but other prepositions, possessive adjectives, and compound words occur as well.

126. The **possessive genitive** indicates that the noun in the genitive is the **possessor** of the head noun it determines. Even if the noun in the genitive is not a living being, it can be classified under this category.

*Id fierī posse, sī Haeduī suās cōpiās in fīnēs **Bellovacōrum** intrōduxerint et **eōrum** agrōs populārī coeperint.* "This could happen if the Haedui brought their troops into the territory **of** the Bellovaci and started to destroy **their** fields." (Caes. *B.G.* 2.5.3)

*Etiam necessitātēs **valētūdinis** frūgālitāte restringit.* "Even what is needed **for** his health he cuts down for reasons of economy." (Pliny 5.19.9)

127. The **partitive genitive**, or **genitive of the whole**, indicates the whole to which a part belongs. The head noun denotes a part, a certain quantity; it may also be a pronoun, an ordinal numeral, a superlative, an adverb, or a neuter singular adjective or pronoun (nom. or acc. only). English translation often employs the preposition *of,* sometimes such prepositions as *among,* and sometimes no preposition.

*. . . ut [Sequanī] partem **finitimī agrī** possidērent.* ". . . so that the Sequani possessed a part **of** the neighboring territory." (Caes. *B.G.* 6.12.4)

*[Fīnēs] mīlia **passuum** ducenta quadrāgintā patēbant.* "The territory extended for 240,000 paces [= 240 miles = 360 kilometers]." (Caes. *B.G.* 1.2.5) (see § 44).

*Nihil **novī** sub sōle.* "Nothing new under the sun." (Ecclesiastes 1:9)

***Hōrum omnium** fortissimī sunt Belgae.* "The most courageous **of** [or among] all these are the Belgae." (Caes. *B.G.* 1.1.3)

*Satis **ēloquentiae**, **sapientiae** parum.* "Enough eloquence, little wisdom." (Sall. *Cat.* 5.4)

*Ubinam **gentium** sumus?* "Where **in** the world are we?" (Cic. *Cat.* 1.9)

Remark. Instead of the partitive genitive, the prepositions *ex* and *dē* + **ablative** or *inter* + **accusative** may be used: *paucī dē nostrīs* 'a few of our men', *ūnus ē multīs* 'one of the many', *Croesus inter regēs opulentissimus* 'Croesus, wealthiest of kings'.

128. The **subjective genitive** represents what would be the subject of an action or feeling of a verb corresponding to or contained in the head noun on which the genitive depends.

> *Nōs transeuntis rīsus excitat turbae.* "The laughter **of** the passing crowd disturbs us." (Mart. *Ep.* 12.57.26) (The crowd laughs: *turba ridet.* The noun *rīsus* contains the verb *rīdēre,* of which *turba* is the subject.)
> *Sancienda [sunt] consulum imperia.* "The orders **of** the consuls have to be sanctioned." (Livy 8.7.19) (The noun phrase contains the idea: *consulēs* [subject] *imperant.*)

129. The **objective genitive** indicates what would be the object of a verb corresponding to or contained in the head noun of the noun phrase. Often a preposition other than *of* is used in English translation.

> *Silvae magna cōgitātiōnis incitamenta [sunt].* "The forest is a great stimulus **for** thinking." (Pliny 1.6.2) (The forests stimulate the thinking: *thinking* is the object of *incitāre.*)
> *Agitābātur animus conscientiā scelerum.* "His mind was roused by the awareness **of** his crimes." (Sall. *Cat.* 5.7) (He knows or is aware of his crimes.)

> **Remark.** Out of context, a genitive could be either a subjective or an objective genitive. The context should indicate which interpretation is correct.
> *Metus hostium,* for example, can mean 'the fear **of** the enemy (for us)', in which case *hostium* is a subjective genitive, because "they" fear "us." But this noun phrase can also mean that someone fears the enemy, in which case *hostium* is an objective genitive.
> *Imperium populī Rōmānī* will in most cases mean 'the domination of the Roman people' (subjective gen.); but *imperium Britanniae* can in a certain context (Caes. *B.G.* 2.4.7) mean 'the domination over Britain' (objective gen.).

130. The **genitive of quality**, or **descriptive genitive**, expresses size, age, rank, or physical or mental property. The noun in the genitive always has an adjective or numeral with it. (See also § 135, 177.)

> *Caesar mūrum in altitūdinem pedum sēdecim perduxit.* "Caesar constructed a wall sixteen feet high." (Caes. *B.G.* 1.8.1)
> *[Nerviōs] esse hominēs ferōs magnaeque virtūtis.* "The Nervii were wild people **of** great courage." (Caes. *B.G.* 2.15.5)

131. The **explanatory genitive**, or **genitive of specification**, explains or specifies a generic word. Latin poets use this explanatory genitive also for geographical proper names, whereas prose authors in such a case would prefer **an apposition in the same case** (*Urbs Rōma, flūmen Rhēnus*). This construction in the genitive is sometimes translated in English by the preposition *of,* sometimes by an apposition.

> *Triste est nōmen ipsum carendi.* "The word *carēre* [to lack] itself is something sad." (Cic. *Tusc.* 1.87)
> *... quō minus hospitiī et amīcitiae iūs officiumque praestāret.* "... to fulfill his holy duty **of** hospitality and friendship." (Cic. *Fam.* 14.4.2)
> *Quis genus Aeneadum, quis Troiae nesciat urbem?* "Who would not know the family **of** the descendants of Aeneas, who would not know the city **of** Troy?" (Virg. *Aen.* 1.565)

Genitive as constituent of the sentence

132. The noun or noun phrase in the genitive can be a **genitive object** (**indirect object**, an obligatory sentence constituent) of **a verb, an adjective, or a participle**. In English translation, either a direct object or a prepositional object will be needed.

> *... ut mihi aut rēī publicae aut meī meōrumque oblīviscendum sit.* "... so that I must either forget the State or myself and my family." (Livy 8.7.16)
> *... hominēs cupidī bellandī ...* "... people longing for warfare ..." (Caes. *B.G.* 1.2.4)
> *Corpus patiens inediae, algōris, vigiliae.* "His body could endure hunger, cold, and wakefulness." (Sall. *Cat.* 5.3)

The **verbs** governing the genitive are not very numerous: *meminisse* 'remember', *oblīviscī* 'forget'; *potīrī (rērum)* 'seize (power)'; *miserēri* 'pity'; judicial verbs, as in *accūsāre aliquem alicūius rēī* 'accuse someone of something', *damnāre aliquem alicūius rēī* 'condemn someone for something', *damnare aliquem capitis* 'condemn someone to death'; impersonal verbs, as in *mē paenitet* 'it repents me, I repent' (§ 247, 263), *interest, rēfert* 'it is to the interest of' (§ 245).

Adjectives governing the genitive are *avidus* 'greedy for', *cupidus* 'eager for, longing for', *edax* 'devouring', *expers* 'not experienced in', *ignārus* 'unaware of', *inops* 'poor', *insuētus* 'not used to', *memor* 'mindful of', *immemor* 'forgetful of', *perītus* 'skillful in', *particeps* 'participating in', *plēnus* 'full of', *reus* 'guilty of'.

Participles expressing a permanent property govern the genitive: *patiens* 'enduring', *appetens* 'eager for', *amans* 'fond of'. If these participles express a transient attitude, they are construed with an object in the accusative: *amans* 'loving, one who loves', *patiens* '(one who is) bearing'.

133. With proper names of towns and small islands of the a- and o-declensions singular, the genitive is used for **adverbial modifiers of place**. The locative, an old case that ended in *-ī* (as in the archaic locative *domī*), resembled the genitive singular of those two declensions. Therefore, the locative *Rōma-ī* became, after some time, *Rōmae*. The adverbial modifier of place in the genitive does not occur in the plural or in other declensions, where the locative has merged with the ablative. See § 298–300, 305.

> *Sī es **Rōmae**, iam mē adsequī non potes.* "If you are in Rome, you cannot catch up with me anymore." (Cic. *Att.* 2.5)
>
> *Non fuerat mihi dubium quīn tē **Tarentī** aut **Brundisiū** visūrus essem.* "I had not had any doubt that I would see you in Tarentum or Brundisium." (Cic. *Att.* 3.6)

134. *Causā* and ***grātiā*** in the ablative can be preceded by an attributive noun in the genitive. The whole phrase is then an **adverbial modifier of reason or purpose**. (*Causā* and *grātiā* actually are nouns in the ablative but are weakened and considered as "postpositions.")

> *Divicīācus **auxiliī petendī** causā Rōmam ad senātum profectus [est].* "Diviciacus left for Rome in order to ask for support from the senate." (Caes. *B.G.* 6.12.5) (See § 357.)

135. The **possessive** genitive (§ 126), the **descriptive** genitive (§ 130), and the genitive of **price or value** (as an adverbial modifier: see § 317) can occur as the **nominal part of the predicate**.

> *... Galliam potius esse **Ariovistī** quam **populī Rōmānī**.* "... that Gaul belongs to Ariovistus rather than to the Roman people." (Caes. *B.G.* 1.45.1)
>
> *... nec Graecum esse nec Rōmānum nec **ūllīus gentis nōtae**.* "... he was not Greek, nor Roman, nor of any known nation." (Seneca *Apoc.* 5.2)
>
> *Nōlī spectāre **quantī** homo sit.* "Don't consider how much the fellow is worth." (Cic. *Ad Quintum fratrem* 1.2.14)

Dative

136. A noun (usually an animate or abstract noun) in the dative has the **semantic role of a person involved (more rarely a thing), a recipient, a beneficiary, an advantage, a similarity, a proximity, a friendly inclination, or the opposite of these.**

This sentence constituent in the dative can have several syntactic functions: it can be an obligatory constituent in the kernel, or it can be an adverbial modifier. Whatever its function, the dative is usually translated by English *to* or *for*. But modern Western languages have a tendency to make a person the subject of the sentence. Therefore a dative object is often translated as the subject of the sentence with a different verbal construction, as can be seen in the examples in § 138b, d, and e.

137. An **indirect object in the dative** occurs with **verbs that express a transmission of words or things to a recipient, such as** *dare, dīcere,* and *ostendere.* Such an indirect dative object is the third obligatory constituent, with the predicate, in the kernel, in addition to the subject and the direct object. In English translation, the preposition *to* is used if the indirect object follows the direct object. If, in English, the indirect object precedes the direct object, the preposition is omitted. Unlike in English (e.g., "All Italics were given citizenship"), the indirect object cannot be the subject of a passive sentence.

> *[Gracchus] dabat cīvitātem* **omnibus Italicīs.** "Gracchus gave citizenship to all Italics." (Velleius Paterculus *Hist. Rom.* 2.6.2)
> *Cūr non mittō meōs* **tibi,** *Pontiliāne, libellōs? Nē* **mihi** *tū mittās, Pontiliāne, tuōs.* "Why do I not send you, Pontilianus, my little books? In order that you not send your little books to me, Pontilianus." (Mart. *Ep.* 7.3)

138. A **dative object** occurs in the kernel as the **second or third obligatory constituent with a number of verbs and adjectives.** In English translation, either a direct object or a prepositional object is used. Unlike the accusative object with the role of patient, a dative object cannot be the (patient-)subject in a passive sentence. Its semantic role is one of those mentioned in § 136.

A **dative object** occurs with

a) **verbs** that are not immediately recognizable as such but that are listed in the dictionary with the information *cum datīvō* or *alicuī* or with an example in the dative. Some frequent verbs with the dative are

propinquāre 'approach'	*plācēre* 'please'	*crēdere* 'trust, believe'
favēre 'favor'	*licet* 'it is allowed'	*fīdere* 'trust'
nocēre 'harm'	*libet* 'it pleases'	*parcere* 'spare'
studēre 'be devoted to'	*(per)suādēre* 'persuade'	*nūbere* 'marry'
pārēre 'obey'	*vidērī* 'seem'	*servīre* 'serve'

> *[Nōnnūllī Gallī]* **novīs imperiīs** *studēbant.* "Some Gauls were inclined toward a change of government." (Caes. *B.G.* 2.1.3)

b) **adjectives** that express one of the semantic roles mentioned in § 136: *amīcus* 'friendly with', *cārus* 'dear to', *grātus* 'pleasing to, grateful to', *(dis)similis* '(un)like, (dis)similar', *ūtilis* 'useful to'.

> **Huīc** *bella intestīna, caedēs, rapīnae, discordia cīvilis grāta fuēre.* "This man was fond of civil wars, murder, raids, and civil discord." Literally, "To him wars ... were pleasing." (Sall. *Cat.* 5.1)
> *Nunc dēmum intellegō ūtilia* **mihi** *quam fuerint quae despexeram.* "Now I finally understand how useful for me were the things I had despised." (Phaedrus 1.12 *Cervus ad fontem* 13–14)

c) **many verbs compounded with the prefixes** *ad-, ante-, cum-, in-, inter-, ob-, post-, prae-, sub-, and super-.*

> *Hīs Pedium et Cottam praefēcit.* "At their head he put Pedius and Cotta." (Caes. *B.G.* 2.11.3)

d) **all compounds of** *esse* **(except** *abesse* **+ ablative).**

> *Neque illī tamen ad cavendum dolus aut astūtiae deerant.* "However, he was not in want of tricky ruses for staying on guard." (Sall. *Cat.* 26.2)

e) **existential** *esse* **+ person in the dative.** The dative signals the person to whom something belongs, and it is therefore called **dative of the possessor.** This dative is most conveniently translated in English as the subject of a verb (e.g., *to possess, to have*).

> *Nec cōgitandī nec quiescendī in urbe locus est **pauperī**.* "A poor person has no place to think or to rest in the City." (Mart. *Ep.* 12.57.3–4)

139. The noun in the dative can be an **adverbial modifier** (a non-kernel constituent). The most frequent instance is the **adverbial modifier of advantage or disadvantage** (*dativus commodi et incommodi*).

> *Non **vītae** sed **scholae** discimus!* "We learn not for life but for school!" (Seneca *Luc.* 106.12)
> *Nec **illī**, terra, grāvis fueris: non fuit illa **tibi**.* "Earth, don't be heavy for her: she has not been for you." (Mart. *Ep.* 5.34.9–10)
> *Atuatucī omnibus cōpiīs auxiliō **Nerviīs** [vēnērunt].* "The Atuatuci came with all their troops to the rescue of the Nervii." (Caes. *B.G.* 2.29.1)

140. The **adverbial modifier of purpose** occurs with such verbs as *mittere, venīre,* and *relinquere* (with *esse,* see § 143). It indicates the purpose of an action and often co-occurs with an adverbial modifier of advantage or disadvantage (§ 139).

> *Atuatucī omnibus cōpiīs **auxiliō** Nerviīs [vēnērunt].* "The Atuatuci came with all their troops to the Nervii's rescue." (Caes. *B.G.* 2.29.1)
> *Hunc sibi **domiciliō** locum dēligunt.* "They choose this place for [or "as"] their domicile." (Caes. *B.G.* 2.29.3)

141. The **adverbial modifier of the person involved** (§ 136) occurs with a **gerundive** (verbal adjective). The gerundive indicates that there is an obligation "for someone". To avoid confusion with other datives, the gerundive is sometimes construed with *a(b)* + ablative (§ 166).

> ***Caesarī** omnia ūnō tempore erant agenda.* "Caesar had to do everything at the same time." Literally, "For Caesar all things had to be done at the same time." (Caes. *B.G.* 2.20.1)

142. The **adverbial modifier of point of view** (*dativus iudicantis*) indicates for whom the action or situation holds good. It is less emotional than the "dativus ethicus" (§ 144).

> *Quintia formōsa est **multīs**, **mihi** candida, longa, recta est.* "Quintia is beautiful in the eyes of many; to me she is white, slender, and straight." (Catullus 86.1–2)
> *Caesar Gomphos vēnit, quod est oppidum prīmum Thessaliae **venientibus ab Epīrō**.* "Caesar arrived at Gomphi. This is the first town of Thessalia to those coming [i.e., "as you come"] from Epirus." (Caes. *B. Civ.* 3.80.1)

143. The **dative of purpose** is part of the **predicate** if it occurs with the copula *esse.* Only a few nouns occur in this semantic role, such as *auxiliō* 'help', *honōrī* 'honor', *impedīmentō* 'hindrance', *salūtī* 'health, safety', and *ūsuī* 'advantage'. This nominal part of the predicate thus takes the dative, but it is often translated in English with a regular predicate noun or adjective or another construction.

> *Caesar pollicitus est sibi eam rem **cūrae** futūram [esse].* "Caesar promised that he would take care of that problem [or "would have that problem at heart"]." (Caes. *B.G.* 2.33.1)
> *Milltēs sibi ipsōs ad pugnam esse **impedīmentō** vīdit.* "He saw that the soldiers stood in each other's way for the battle." (Caes. *B.G.* 2.25.1)
> *Amīcitiam populī Rōmānī sibi **ornāmentō et praesidiō**, **non dētrīmentō** esse oportēre.* "The friendship of the Roman people should be a distinction and a protection for him, not a disadvantage." (Caes. *B.G.* 1.44.5)

144. The **dativus ethicus** is only used in pronominal forms indicating a **person who takes special interest in the action or situation expressed by the sentence**. This emotional **adverbial modifier** is not a modifier of the predicate but an attitudinal modifier to the sentence as a whole (§ 380). It belongs to the colloquial style and often occurs with *em, ecce* 'look'. The translation is rather difficult and should express some emotion.

> *Ecce **tibi** Ausoniae tellus.* "Look, there lies your Italic soil." (Virg. *Aen.* 3.477)
> *Quid **mihi** Celsus agit?* "What [or "how"] is my Celsus doing?" (Hor. *Epist.* 1.3.15)

145. The **exclamation in the dative** with the interjection *vae* 'woe!' is not a sentence constituent but functions as part of the text as a whole (§ 380).

> *Vae **victīs**.* "Woe to the conquered!" (Livy 5.48.9)

Accusative

146. The **semantic role** of the accusative in general is that of the **direction or goal** to which the action of the verb is directed. This holds not only for the adverbial modifiers but also for the direct object, whereby the action of the verb passes (Latin *transīre*) from the subject to (in the direction of) the direct object. This is the case with active **transitive verbs.** A transitive verb is one that can be transposed to the passive voice, such that the direct object of the active verb becomes the subject of the passive verb.

147. The **direct object of a transitive verb** is in the accusative. The action passes from the subject as agent to the object as the **patient (or goal or undergoer) of the action.** The direct object of an active verb can be the subject as patient of the corresponding passive verb. In the English translation of a sentence containing a transitive verb, there will be either a direct object or a prepositional object.

> *Cūr mē verberas?* "Why do you beat me?" (Plautus *Aul.* 42)
> *Parthōs amīcitiam populī Rōmānī petere coēgī.* "I forced the Parths to ask for the friendship of the Roman people." (August. *Res gestae* 29)
> *Per Macedoniam Cyzicum petebāmus.* "We are traveling through Macedonia to Cyzicus." (Cic. *Fam.* 14.4.3) (See § 215 on the epistolary imperfect.)

148. **Intransitive verbs** normally do not have a direct object. Sometimes they have a **cognate direct object (or inner object), when the meaning and sometimes also the root or stem of the direct object is already contained in the verb.** Such a cognate direct object usually includes an attribute limiting the idea contained in the verb. The most common form of this object is a neuter pronoun or adjective. The same phenomenon occurs in English. Such verbs as *vīvere* 'live', *morī* 'die', and *īre* 'go' normally do not have a direct object, but the following constructions are possible:

> *Longam incomitāta vidētur īre viam.* "She seemed to go a lóng way alone." (Virg. *Aen.* 4.467–68) (The accent on *long* renders the Latin hyperbaton § 432.)
> *Mīrum atque inscītum somniāvī somnium.* "A strange and uncanny dream did I dream." (Plautus *Ru.* 597)
> *Id eīs persuāsit.* "He convinced them of this idea." (Caes. *B.G.* 1.2.3)
> *Quid rīdētis?* "What [laughter] [or "why"] are you laughing?" (Plautus *Aul.* 718)

149. **Verbs of motion** normally are intransitive. They cannot have a direct object. But **they are transitive when compounded with the prefixes *circum-*, *praeter-*, and *trans-*.** Verbs of motion compounded with the prefixes *ad-*, *in-*, *ob-*, *per-*, and *sub-* are transitive mainly when used in a figurative sense.

*Germānōs consuescere **Rhēnum** transīre vidēbat.* "He saw that the Germani became used to crossing the Rhine." (Caes. *B.G.* 1.33.3)
*[**Unum Horātium**] trēs Cūriātiī circumsteterant.* "The three Curiatii had surrounded one Horatius." (Livy 1.25.6)
*[Mūcius] **senātum** adiit.* "Mucius approached the senate." (Livy 2.12.4)

150. Some transitive verbs compounded with the prefixes **trans-** or **circum-** can have **two objects: one direct object (patient object) of the verb and one object depending on the prefix (prefix object)**. In the passive voice, only the direct object depending on the verb can be the subject (as patient).

> *Caesar **funditōres sagittāriōsque pontem** trādūcit.* "Caesar led his slingers and archers across the bridge." (Caes. *B.G.* 2.10.1)
> *Belgās **Rhēnum** antīquitus trāductōs . . .* "Belgae who long ago were brought across the Rhine . . ." (Caes. *B.G.* 2.4.1)

151. Some other verbs are construed with **two objects in the accusative: one object of the person and one of the thing**. This construction usually occurs with *docēre* 'teach', *cēlāre* 'conceal', *rogāre* 'ask' (in the stereotyped expression *aliquem sententiam rogāre* 'ask someone for his opinion'), and *interrogāre* 'interrogate, ask'. In the alternative construction, these verbs have one object (the person) in the accusative and a prepositional object (the thing) with *dē* + ablative. Only the object of the person can be the subject of a passive sentence. Such verbs as *flāgitāre, petere, postulāre* 'demand', and *poscere* 'claim' can have either two accusatives or, more often, the alternative construction: one object (the thing) in the accusative and a prepositional object (the person) with *a(b)* or *e(x)* + ablative.

> *Tē tua fata docēbō.* "I'll tell you your destiny." (Virg. *Aen.* 6.759)
> *Caesar, rogātus **sententiam** ā consule, hūiuscemodī verba locūtus est.* "Caesar, asked by the consul for his opinion, spoke in the following manner." (Sall. *Cat.* 50.5) (The active sentence would read, *Consul **Caesarem sententiam** rogāvit.*)
> *Interim cotīdiē Caesar **Haeduōs frūmentum** flāgitāre.* "In the meantime, Caesar daily required grain from the Haedui." (Caes. *B.G.* 1.16.1)

152. The **adverbial modifier of direction (place to which)** is generally construed with the prepositions *ad, in,* and *sub* + accusative and with prepositions that, often more figuratively, indicate a direction, such as *ergā, contrā,* and *adversus* + accusative.

> *Hoc volunt persuadēre animās ab aliīs post mortem transīre **ad aliōs**.* "They want to persuade them that souls after death pass on from one to another." (Caes. *B.G.* 6.14.5)
> *Ignōtās animum dīmittit **in artēs**.* "He sets his mind upon únknówn crafts." (Ovid *Met.* 8.188) (The accents on *unknown* render the Latin hyperbaton § 432.)
> *[Caesar] certior fīēbat omnēs Belgās **contrā populum Rōmānum***

coniūrāre. "Caesar was informed that all Belgae were conspiring against the Roman people." (Caes. *B.G.* 2.1.1)

153. The **adverbial modifier of direction with names of towns and small islands** is put in the accusative without a preposition. The accusative and the meaning of the noun sufficiently indicate a direction. This is also the case with the words *domum* 'home(ward)' and *rūs* 'to the countryside' and often in poetry.

> *[Catilina] Manlium Faesulās mittit.* "Catilina sends Manlius to Faesulae." (Sall. *Cat.* 27.1)

154. The **adverbial modifier of duration (extent in time)** is in the accusative or is constructed with *per* + accusative.

> *Undēvīgintī annōs nātus exercitum parāvi.* "At the age of nineteen I levied an army." (August. *Res gestae* 1.1)
> *Lūdī per decem diēs factī sunt.* "Games were held for ten days." (Cic. *Cat.* 3.20)

155. The **adverbial modifier of distance (extent in space)** indicates the distance, the way covered, the height, the depth, the length, or the width.

> *Oppidum Rēmōrum nōmine Bibrax aberat mīlia passuum octō.* "A town of the Remi, called Bibrax, was at a distance of eight miles." (Caes. *B.G.* 2.6.1)

156. The **adverbial modifier of "the road by which"** is constructed with the preposition *per* + accusative (but see also § 175, 304–5). With persons, this construction indicates the agency through which something happens.

> *[Nīlus] per tōtam discurrit Aegyptum.* "The Nile runs through the whole of Egypt." (Seneca *Quaest. nat.* 4A.2.8)
> *Curius properē per Fulviam Cicerōnī dolum ēnuntiat.* "Curius quickly disclosed the trap to Cicero via Fulvia." (Sall. *Cat.* 28.2)

157. The **adverbial modifier of degree** (the so-called adverbial accusative) **indicates to which degree** something is true. It is used chiefly in adverbs and fixed expressions: *cēterum* 'for the rest, besides', *nihil* 'in no respect', *summum* 'at the most', *magnam partem* 'largely', and so on.

> *[Suēbī] non multum frūmentō, sed maximam partem lacte atque pecore vīvunt multumque sunt in vēnātiōnibus.* "The Suebi live to a small extent on grain, but for the most part on milk and cattle, and are very occupied in hunting." (Caes. *B.G.* 4.1.8)

158. The **adverbial modifier of respect** (also called Greek acc.) **indicates in what respect an action occurs.** In early Latin, **neuter accusative pronouns** are freely used as an accusative of respect. Later, under the influence

of Greek literature, especially *genus, mentem,* and **body parts** are mentioned.

> *Mīrābar quid maesta deōs, Amaryllī, vocārēs.* "I was wondering why [i.e., in what respect] you were sadly calling on the gods." (Virg. *Buc.* 1.36)
>
> *Hannibal femur trāgulā graviter ictus cecidit.* "Hannibal was seriously hit in the thigh by a javelin and fell." (Livy 21.7.10)

159. The accusative can also occur in **adverbial modifiers** with semantic roles depending on the meaning of a preposition: *ob* 'because of' (**reason**), *inter* 'between' (**place**), *post* 'after' (**time**), and so on.

160. The **accusative of exclamation** expresses a feeling, possibly accompanied by an interjection (*heu, ō, em, prō*) or an interrogative particle (*-ne*). It is not a part of the sentence (§ 380).

> *Heu mē miserē miserum!* "Alas, poor miserable me!" (Plautus *Aul.* 721)
>
> *O fortūnātōs agricolās!* "O blessed farmers!" (Virg., *Geo.* 2.458–59)
>
> *Huncine hominem, hancine impudentiam, iūdicēs, hanc audāciam!* "What a fellow, what impudence, judges, what a nerve!" (Cic. *Verr.* 2.5.62)

161. The accusative is also a characteristic of the subject and the predicate in the infinitive clause (§ 266–71).

Ablative

162. The **semantic roles** of nouns in the ablative diverge considerably because, historically speaking, three different cases have merged into the ablative. The ablative, properly speaking (*ab-latum* < *ab-ferre*), expresses a **separation**; the instrumental, a **means**; and the locative, a **place**. The exact semantic role of a noun in the ablative is identified within the sphere of one of those ancient cases, the meaning of the preposition (if any), the meaning of the word in the ablative, and the meaning of the verb it modifies (§ 187–88).

The **function** of a word in the ablative, in a few instances, is **object** (§ 163). In very numerous instances, including the ablative absolute (§ 349–54), it is an **adverbial modifier** (§ 164–76). There is also an instance of an ablative being **part of the predicate** (§ 177).

163. The ablative can be an **indirect object (obligatory sentence constituent) of some verbs and adjectives** (§ 250). Six deponent verbs (some with their compounds) express a means; some other verbs, a separation (or abundance); and a few others, a price or value. The adjectives generally indicate a separation or abundance. These verbs and adjectives require an ablative object or a prepositional object (*a(b)* + abl.).

(ab)ūti '(ab)use'	*vescī* 'feed oneself'	*dēsistere* 'desist'
fruī 'enjoy'	*vacāre* 'be free of'	*stāre* 'cost'
fungī 'acquit oneself'	*abundāre* 'abound in'	*(in)dignus* '(un)worthy'
(in)nītī 'lean on'	*carēre* 'miss'	*onustus* 'burdened'
potīrī 'possess oneself of'	*egēre* 'need'	*opus est* 'there is need of'

Germānī . . . eōdem victū et cultū corporis ūtuntur. "The Germani use the same food and the same attire." (Caes. *B.G.* 6.24.4)

Hōs pastor baculō stīvāve innixus arātor vīdit. "A shepherd leaning on his staff and a farmer leaning on his plow handle saw them." (Ovid *Met.* 8.217–19)

Rēmigiō carens non ūllas percipit aurās. "For want of oars he did not catch any wind." (Ovid *Met.* 8.228)

Helvētiī hōc cōnātū dēstitērunt. "The Helvetii abandoned this attempt." (Caes. *B.G.* 1.8.4)

Quō etiam māiōre sunt istī ōdiō suppliciōque dignī. "Those men deserve even greater hatred and punishment." (Cic. *Cat.* 3.22)

Remarks

a) Several of these verbs take an accusative object in comedy (in Plautus and, less frequently, Terence) and in later Latin.

b) *Potīrī* occurs also with a genitive object in the expression *potīrī rērum* 'seize power'.

164. The ablative is mostly used for **adverbial modifiers (non-kernel constituents)**. A very common semantic role is **separation (the place whence)**, whereas the term ***origin*** may be more appropriate with certain nouns or verbs. These modifiers are generally constructed with such prepositions as *a(b), dē, e(x),* and *sine* + ablative. Prepositions are omitted with names of towns and small islands and also quite frequently in poetry.

Eō ex fīnitimīs populīs turba omnis avida novārum rērum perfūgit. "There a whole crowd of people from neighboring tribes, eager for a new life, took refuge." (Livy 1.8.6)

Respice quotiens rīmōsa et curta fenestrīs vāsa cadant. "Look how often leaky and broken vessels fall from the windows." (Iuv. *Sat.* 3.268–71)

Ut mē omnēs tuō sanguine ortum vērē ferrent, haec spolia portō. "In order that all people may tell that I am truly born of your blood, I bring you this booty." (Livy 8.7.13)

Brindisiō profectī sumus. "We left Brundisium." (Cic. *Fam.* 14.4.3)

165. The **adverbial modifier of distance** is in the ablative without a preposition.

[Horātius] videt [hostēs] magnīs intervallīs sequentēs. "Horatius saw his enemies follow at great intervals." (Livy 1.25.8)

[Ariovistus] mīlibus passuum sex ā Caesaris castrīs cōnsēdit. "Ariovistus took up a position at six miles from Caesar's camp." (Caes. *B.G.* 1.48.1)

166. The **adverbial modifier of agent** is constructed with *a(b)* + ablative for animate beings (persons, animals, and personified abstract concepts) who perform the action of a passive verb. See also § 141, 206, 313.

> *Volturcius ā legatīs dēsertus est.* "Volturcius was abandoned by the envoys." (Sall. *Cat.* 45.4)

167. The **adverbial modifier of cause or reason** is in the ablative, usually without a preposition. A cause is a factual element that explains an event, while a reason is an argument given for an action or state. For other constructions, see § 134, 159, 312.

> *Plūrimus hīc aeger moritur vigilandō.* "Here many a sick man dies from lack of sleep." (Iuv. *Sat.* 3.232)
>
> *Clangōre eōrum ālārumque crepitū excitus [est] Manlius.* "Manlius was awakened by their clangor and the rattle of their wings." (Livy 5.47.4)

168. The **adverbial modifier of comparison (inequality with a comparative)** can be in the ablative without a preposition. The ablative expresses the "point from which" the comparison is viewed. For the more recent construction with *quam*, see § 318.

> *Lūce sunt clāriōra nōbīs tua consilia omnia!* "Clearer than the sunlight are all your plans for us!" (Cic. *Cat.* 1.6)

169. The **adverbial modifier of place** is constructed with a **preposition** (*in* 'in, on', *sub* 'under', *prō* 'before, on the front of') + **ablative**. There is **no preposition** with names of **towns and small islands**. The preposition is generally missing in phrases with *tōtus* 'entire' and with *locus* + attribute. The preposition *in* is also used less often in poetry. See also § 133, 159, 298–301, 305, 325.

> *Hōrum alterum in terrā linquit, alterum sub terrā locat.* "One of them she left on earth; the other she placed under the earth." (*C.I.L.* 6.15346)
>
> *Quā ex rē fierī uti magnum sibi auctōritātem in rē mīlitārī sūmerent.* "For that reason it happened that they acquired a great authority in military affairs." (Caes. *B.G.* 2.4.3)
>
> *Erat Athēnīs spatiōsa domus, sed infāmis.* "Once upon a time, there was in Athens a spacious but infamous house." (Pliny 7.27.5)
>
> *Undique tōtīs usque adeō turbātur agrīs.* "Everywhere there is constantly such disorder in all the fields." (Virg. *Buc.* 1.11–12)

170. The **adverbial modifier of time** is usually constructed with *in* + ablative. The preposition is not used if the noun itself indicates a time or is modified by an attribute. See also § 306–9. For dates, see § 308.

> *Quid in bellō [possunt]?* "What are they capable of in times of war?" (Caes. *B.G.* 2.4.1)

*In finēs Vocontiōrum **diē septimō** pervēnit.* "He reached the territory of the Vocontii on the seventh day." (Caes. *B.G.* 1.10.5)

***Sōlis occasū** suās cōpiās Ariovistus in castra rēdūxit.* "At sunset Ariovistus brought his troops back to his camp." (Caes. *B.G.* 1.50.3)

***Secundō Pūnicō Bellō** exhaustum [erat] aerārium.* "In the Second Punic War, the treasury was empty." (Valerius Max. 5.6.8)

*[Clōdius] respondit **trīduō** illum aut summum **quadrīduō** esse peritūrum.* "Clodius answered that he [Milo] would die in three or, at the most, four days." (Cic. *Mil.* 26)

171. The **adverbial modifier of limitation or restriction** indicates that the idea expressed by the verb or the adjective is limited to one domain. Also, the **supine in -*u*** is used in this sense with such adjectives as *facilis, incrēdibilis,* and *turpis.*

> *Helvētiī reliquōs Gallōs **virtūte** praecēdunt.* "The Helvetii surpass the other Gauls in bravery." (Caes. *B.G.* 1.1.4)
>
> *Incrēdibile **memorātū** est.* "It is incredible to mention." (Sall. *Cat.* 6.2)
>
> *Māiōrēs **nātū*** 'the elders' (i.e., 'greater in respect to birth')

172. The **adverbial modifier of means** (ablative without preposition) indicates the instrument with which something is done. Also, a group of persons can be considered as a (military) means. See also § 156, 173.

> *Tum [Daedalus pennās] **līnō** mediās et **cērīs** alligat īmās.* "Then Daedalus bound the feathers together in the middle with flaxen thread and at the bottom with wax." (Ovid *Met.* 8.193)
>
> *[Catilīna] opportūna loca **armātīs hominibus** obsidēre.* "Catiline occupied strategic places with armed men." (Sall. *Cat.* 27.2)

173. The **adverbial modifier of accompaniment** is constructed with ***cum*** + ablative. ***Cum*** means 'together with', never 'by means of'.

> *Dēsinant obsidēre **cum gladiīs** cūriam.* "Let them stop besieging the senate building armed with swords." (Cic. *Cat.* 1.32) (There is no action by means of swords.)
>
> *Constituēre eā nocte paulō post **cum armātīs hominibus** introīre ad Cicerōnem.* "They decided to get access to Cicero a little later that night, accompanied by armed men." (Sall. *Cat.* 28.1)

174. The **adverbial modifier of manner** can be constructed without a preposition or with ***cum*** + ablative. The noun may or may not be modified by an attribute.

> *Incrēdibilī **celeritāte** ad flūmen dēcucurrērunt.* "They ran down to the river at incredible speed." (Caes. *B.G.* 2.19.7)
>
> *Ventī ruunt et terrās **turbine** perflant.* "The winds dash down and blow in a whirl over the earth." (Virg. *Aen.* 1.82–83)

*Allobrogēs **magnā cum cūrā et dīligentiā** suōs finēs tuentur.* "The Allobroges protect their territory with great care and close attention." (Caes. *B.G.* 7.65.3)

175. The **adverbial modifier of "the road by which"** is expressed in the ablative without a preposition if the noun plus attribute indicates a road, a gate, a port, a bridge, a sea, and so on. In other cases, *per* + accusative is used (§ 156, 304–5).

> *Mediō ut līmite currās moneō.* "I advise you to follow the middle route." (Ovid *Met.* 8.203–4)
> *Aurēliā Viā profectus est.* "He left by the Aurelian Way." (Cic. *Cat.* 2.6)

176. The **adverbial modifier of price or value** is put in the ablative without a preposition. See also § 317 (price in abl. and gen.), 163 and 250 (price as object with *stāre*), and 135 (price as nominal part of the predicate).

> *Emi virginem **trigintā minīs.*** "I bought a young woman for thirty minae." (Plautus *Curc.* 343–44)

177. The **descriptive ablative** is either an **attribute** of a noun or a **part of the predicate** with a copula (§ 204; see also § 130, 135). A literal translation is almost never possible.

> *C. Valerium Procillum, **summā virtūte et hūmānitāte** adulescentem . . .* "C. Valerius Procillus, an extremely courageous and cultivated young man, . . ." (Caes. *B.G.* 1.47.4)
> *Catilīna fuit **magnā vī** et animī et corporis.* "Catilina was very strong with respect to mind and body." Or "Catilina had a very strong mind and body." (Sall. *Cat.* 5.1)
> *[Claudia] **sermōne** erat **lepidō.*** "Claudia had a charming way of talking." (*C.I.L.* 6.15346)

Synopsis of the use of the cases

178. **Remark.** The functions marked with an asterisk (*) in the table that follows are not sentence constituents but parts of the text as a whole. Those marked with two asterisks (**) are attributes.

Case	Function	Role
Nominative	1) subject	agent, non-agent, patient
	2) part of the predicate (predicative noun/adjective)	
Vocative	address,* exclamation*	
Genitive	1) attribute**	possessive, partitive, subjective, objective, descriptive, explanatory
	2) indirect object of verbs, adjectives, and participles	
	3) adverbial modifier	place (towns and small islands of the a- or o-declension sg.); price; reason/purpose with *causā/grātiā*
	4) part of the predicate	possessive, descriptive with *esse*
Dative	1) indirect object	recipient with verbs of giving and saying
	2) indirect object of verbs and adjectives	(dis)advantage, similarity, proximity; prefix object; dative of possessor
	3) adverbial modifier	(dis)advantage, purpose, person involved, point of view
	4) part of the predicate	purpose with *esse*
	5) exclamation*	disadvantage, *dativus ethicus*
Accusative	1) direct object	patient or role depending on the meaning of the prefix
	2) adverbial modifier	direction, duration (time), distance (space), degree, respect, road (with *per*), other (depending on the preposition)
	3) exclamation*	
	4) See infinitive clause.	
Ablative	1) indirect object of verbs and adjectives	means, separation
	2) adverbial modifier	separation/origin, distance, agent, cause/reason, comparison, place, time, means, limitation/restriction, accompaniment, manner, road by which, price
	3) attribute** or part of the predicate	descriptive

PART 4

Syntax and Semantics
of the Sentence and Its Parts

10
The Sentence

Sentence structure

179. Language consists, in the first place, not of words but of meaningful units separated by pauses in the spoken language and usually by periods in the written language. Such a unit conveys a meaning (*sententia*) and therefore is called a sentence (*sententia*). (For the sentence in its wider context and in the speech act, see § 375.) A sentence normally consists not of one word but of groups of words (phrases) and clauses that are combined into a pattern, with each phrase or clause fulfilling a **syntactic function**. The study of this coherent structure is called **syntax**.

These phrases or sentence constituents display not only a syntactic coherence (subject of, attribute of, agreement with, etc.) but also a meaningful content (agent, patient, place, purpose, reason, etc.). This is called the **semantic role**.

Role is connected to function but is not synonymous with it. For example, a noun in the nominative referring to an animate being may have the function of subject and the role of agent. In a passive sentence, however, that noun in the ablative may still have the role of agent, but its function will be an adverbial modifier. The semantic role also depends on the meaning of the word, with its semantic features. A word like *annus* 'year', with its semantic feature of time, will in the ablative be an adverbial modifier of time rather than an adverbial modifier of manner. The functions and roles are listed in § 178 and 184–88.

180. In the syntactic structure of the sentence, some parts or constituents are **obligatory: they form the kernel** of the sentence. Without the appropriate kernel, the sentence is not well formed. In addition to the kernel, there may be **non-obligatory constituents.**

The kernel is a minimal clause. How many and which constituents it must contain depends on the meaning of the predicate. The predicate is the basis of a kernel, and its predicate frame or valence determines the structure of the kernel. Some predicates require no other obligatory sentence constituent (also called **argument**) in their frame (quite rare); some require one, some two, and still others three. So there are zero-, one-, two-, and three-place predicates. The kernel thus can consist of a predicate and zero, one, two, or three other obligatory constituents.

Kernel	
Structure	**Example**
Predicate **without** any other obligatory constituent	*Pluit.* 'It is raining.'
Predicate with **one** other obligatory constituent: subject	*Conticuēre omnēs.* 'Silent were they all.' (Virg. *Aen.* 2.1)
Predicate with **two** other obligatory constituents: subject and direct object	*[Daedalus] dēvōvit suās artēs.* 'Daedalus cursed his crafts.' (Ovid *Met.* 8.234)
Predicate with **two** other obligatory constituents: subject and indirect object in the genitive, dative, or ablative	*Minimē Germānī agricultūrae student.* 'The Germans take very little to farming.' (Caes. *B.G.* 6.29.2)
Predicate with **three** other obligatory constituents: subject, direct object, and indirect object (recipient)	*[Daedalus] dedit oscula nātō.* 'Daedalus gave kisses to his son.' (Ovid *Met.* 8.211)
Predicate with **three** other obligatory constituents: subject, direct object, and indirect object	*Gallī mihi bellum intulērunt.* 'The Gauls made war on me.' (after Caes. *B.G.* 1.44.3)
Predicate with **three** other obligatory constituents: subject, direct object, and predicative complement	*Populus mē consulem creāvit.* 'The nation elected me consul.' (August. *Res gestae* 1)

181. If one constituent was lacking in one of the sentences in the table in § 180, the kernel, and hence the sentence, would be grammatically incorrect, and the sentence would not make sense. A constituent may be understood, if it has been mentioned in an earlier sentence. For example, in the original text of the sentences drawn from the poet Ovid, the subject *Daedalus* is understood in both sentences. But the structure of these sentences does contain a subject. We understand the subject from the context and from the fact that the ending of the predicate (*-t*) refers to a subject in the third-person singular (agreement).

All the sentences in the table in § 180 consist only of a **kernel: a minimal clause**. But they could contain additional, **non-obligatory constituents**—adverbial modifiers that modify the action, position, event, or state expressed by the predicate.

The predicative complement in the last sentence in the table is obligatory with such verbs as *creāre* 'elect' (§ 288), but with other verbs, the constituent '(as) consul' may occur as a non-obligatory predicative apposition (see examples in § 290a).

Sentence analysis

182. When we read a sentence, we go about it in a linear manner. We start with the first word or phrase; we make hypotheses about its meaning, function, and role. We then go to the next word or phrase and so on, until we have read the whole sentence. This is a reading method.

However, when we analyze a sentence, we look systematically for its grammatical structure. For this purpose, we should start with the basis on which the kernel and the whole sentence is built, that is, the **predicate** (verbal or nominal, § 192–93). Then we look step by step for the first additional obligatory constituent, the second, and so on. The rest of the sentence (outside the kernel) will consist of non-obligatory constituents (adverbial phrases or adverbial clauses, predicative appositions).

An example sentence analysis follows:

Belgae pătrum nostrōrum memoriā, omnī Galliā vexātā, Teutonōs Cimbrōsque intrā suōs fīnēs ingredī prohibuērunt. (Caes. *B.G.* 2.4.1, adapted)

1) The first step is to look for the basis on which the kernel and the whole sentence is construed. This sentence contains three verb forms: *vexātā*, a perfective passive participle (PPP); *ingredī*, an infinitive; and *prohibuērunt*, a finite verb. This last form, being a finite verb not introduced by a subordinating conjunction, is the basis of the kernel and of the sentence as a whole.

2) By itself, *prohibuērunt*, "hindered" or "kept away," is not a sentence. The second step is to look for a subject (possibly understood). The ending -*nt* refers to a plural subject. Looking for a nominative plural, we find *Belgae*. Thus we read, "The Belgae kept away."

3) *Belgae prohibuērunt*, "The Belgae kept away," is not a well-formed sentence in Latin (or in English). A second obligatory constituent is still needed in the predicate frame of *prohibēre*. We look for a (direct) object and find a noun cluster in the accusative: *Teutonōs Cimbrōsque*. This could make the kernel complete: "The Belgae kept the Teutons and the Cimbri away." But now we do not have an explanation for the infinitive *ingredī*. Therefore, we revise our analysis and interpret the whole infinitive clause, *Teutonōs Cimbrosque intra suos fines ingredi*, as the object of the predicate, *prohibuerunt:* "The Belgae prevented the Teutons and the Cimbri from entering their territory." This is a correct kernel. The rest of the sentence will contain non-obligatory constituents. (This is not to imply that these constituents are not important in the communication.)

4) With this kernel (consisting of one verb and two obligatory constituents), all kinds of adverbial phrases and clauses may occur. We may find explanations as to where, when, why, with whom, how, and so on.

   4a) The first non-obligatory noun phrase (noun + attributive gen.) is an adverbial modifier of time: *pătrum nostrōrum memoriā*, "in the time of our fathers."

   4b) The remaining three words, *omnī Galliā vexātā*, stand in the ablative, and one of them is a participle. We think of a participial clause or ablative absolute. These words form an adverbial clause without conjunction, but from the context, we infer that its semantic role is time or circumstance.

   4c) The prepositional group *intrā fīnēs suōs* is also an adverbial modifier, but it does not function on the level of the sentence (§ 190–91) and therefore is not a sentence constituent. It functions on the level of the dependent clause (the infinitive clause). Its position between *Cimbrōsque* and *ingredī* already brought us to this conclusion in the third step of this analysis. This dependent clause will not be analyzed here.

The complete sentence analysis is thus

	Belgae	*pătrum nostrōrum memoriā,*	*omnī Galliā vexātā,*
Function:	subject	adverbial modifier	adverbial clause
Role:	agent	time	time/circumstance
Form:	noun	noun phrase	ablative absolute

	Teutonōs Cimbrōsque intrā suōs fīnēs ingredī	*prohibuērunt.*
Function:	object	predicate
Role:	patient	—
Form:	infinitive clause	finite verb

The translation is "In the time of our fathers, when all of Gaul had been scourged, the Belgae prevented the Teutons and the Cimbri from entering their territory."

183. The following example has the same number of words but has more subordinate clauses and more levels in the grammatical hierarchy (§ 190–91). Here, the sentence level will be analyzed first, then the inner structure of some of the sentence constituents.

> *Curius, ubi intellegit quantum perīculum consulī impendeat, properē per Fulviam Cicerōnī dolum quī parābātur enuntiat.* (Sall. *Cat.* 28.2)

1) When looking for the predicate of the sentence, we encounter a great number of finite verb forms. The first one, *intellegit,* is introduced by the subordinating conjunction *ubi* and is therefore the predicate of a dependent clause. The finite verb *impendeat* depends on the interrogative pronoun *quantum* and is the predicate of an indirect question. *Parābātur* is introduced by *quī* and occurs in a relative clause. The only finite verb that does not depend on a subordinating word is *ēnuntiat.* This is the predicate of the kernel and of the sentence as a whole.

2) *Enuntiat* by itself is not a well-formed kernel. There must be a singular subject. The only nominative singular (besides the ones in the dependent clauses) is *Curius.*

3) *Curius ēnuntiat,* "Curius reported," is not a correct kernel in Latin (or in English). The predicate frame of *enuntiare* requires an object as well. *Fulviam* preceded by *per* cannot be a direct object. The only remaining candidate is *dolum,* together with its relative clause *quī parābātur.* This noun phrase is the direct object.

4) The predicate frame of a verb of saying (*verbum dicendi*) also requires an indirect object as recipient. The dative *consulī* occurs in the dependent clause and cannot fulfill this function and role in the main

clause. Therefore, the indirect object in the kernel is the dative *Cicerōnī*. We now have the kernel, with a predicate and its three arguments.

5) We now look for the non-obligatory constituents (words, phrases, or clauses).

5a) There is an adverbial clause of time, *ubi intellegit quantum perīculum consulī impendeat,* itself containing a dependent clause of the second degree (§ 190–91).

5b) There is an adverb, *properē* 'hastily', an adverbial modifier of manner.

5c) Lastly, there is the prepositional phrase *per Fulviam,* an adverbial modifier of means or "road by which."

The translation is "When Curius understood what a great danger threatened the consul, he hastily reported the trap that was being prepared, via Fulvia, to Cicero."

The sentence construction is

	Curius,	*ubi intellegit quantum perīculum consulī impendeat,*	*properē*
Function:	subject	adverbial clause	hastily
Role:	agent	time	manner
Form:	noun	clause	adverb

	per Fulviam	*Cicerōnī*	*dolum quī parābātur*	*ēnuntiat.*
Function:	adverbial modifier	indirect object	direct object	predicate
Role:	means	recipient	patient	—
Form:	prepositional phrase	noun	noun phrase	finite verb

Passing on to the analysis of the dependent clause of time introduced by *ubi,* we ask ourselves the same questions about the constituents of this clause.

1) *Impendeat* depends on *quantum* and is the predicate of an indirect question within the time clause. Therefore, the predicate of the time clause is *intellegit.*

2) The first obligatory constituent within the predicate frame of *intellegit* must be a singular subject. This subject is understood (ø), and the context tells us that it must be *Curius,* subject and theme (§ 383–84, 387d) of the main clause and the dependent clause.

3) The predicate of this kernel, *intellegit,* also requires a direct object (noun, noun phrase, or object clause). Here, the object clause is an indirect question in the subjunctive.

The construction of the adverbial clause of the first degree (§ 190–91) is thus

	(ubi)	*ø*	*intellegit*	*quantum perīculum consulī impendeat*
Function:		subject	predicate	object
Role:		agent	—	patient
Form:		ø	finite verb	dependent clause (indirect question)

The construction of the dependent clause of the second degree is analyzed in the same manner. The predicate frame of *impendeat* requires a subject and an object (a prefix object with a verb compounded with *im-:* see § 138c).

	quantum perīculum	*consulī*	*impendeat*
Function:	subject	object	predicate
Role:	agent	disadvantage	—
Form:	noun phrase	noun	finite verb

Function

184. The number of **syntactic functions** is very small. On the level of the active sentence, the following functions occur.

- **predicate** (obligatory basis: see § 180)
- **subject** (first obligatory constituent with the predicate)
- **object** (second obligatory constituent with the predicate)
  - either a direct object in the accusative (possible subject of a passive verb: see § 146–47)
  - or an indirect object in the genitive, dative, or ablative
  - or a prepositional object
- **indirect/prepositional object** (third obligatory constituent with the predicate)
- predicativum: **predicative complement** (third obligatory constituent)
- predicativum: **predicative apposition** (non-obligatory constituent)
- **adverbial modifier** (noun, phrase, or clause; non-obligatory constituent)

A sentence thus can have the following structures:

Sentence						
Kernel: Predicate + zero, one, two, or three arguments						**Non-obligatory constituents**
	1	**2**	**3**	Predicativum		
predi-cate	subject	direct object: accusative	indirect object: genitive, dative, ablative	**3** predi-cative comple-ment	predica-tive ap-postion	adverbial modifier
		indirect object: dative, genitive, ablative	prepositional object			
		prepositional object				

185. On a lower level, within the noun phrase (§ 358–73), the following functions occur.

- **head** or nucleus of the phrase (the noun or the pronoun)
- **attribute** or the attributive clause
- **apposition**

186. On a higher level (§ 378–81), the following functions occur.

- **address**
- **exclamation**
- **sentence adverbial modifier**

Semantic role

187. The **semantic roles** constituents can play in the sentence with regard to the predicate are quite numerous. The role of a constituent can be found on the basis of the following elements:

- the case of that constituent
- the meaning of the preposition (if any)
- the meaning of the word(s) of which the role is sought
- the meaning of the verb that is modified by that constituent

188. There is no one-to-one relation between the syntactic function and the semantic role of a sentence constituent. Furthermore, some roles occur both in the kernel and in the adverbial modifier. Finally, some occur only as phrases, others only as clauses, and some as both.

Roles of constituents in the kernel include agent, non-agent, patient (or undergoer), recipient, similarity, advantage, disadvantage, description, and so on.

Roles of adverbial clauses include time, cause/reason, comparison, concession, condition, purpose, and result.

Roles of adverbial modifiers include time, place, comparison, separation/origin, direction, road by which, duration, measure, respect, distance, agent, cause/reason, means, accompaniment, manner, price/value, restriction/limitation, degree, (dis)advantage, purpose, point of view, and so on.

Roles of attributive genitives in the phrase include possessive, partitive, subjective, objective, descriptive, and explanatory.

Form

189. Every constituent, whatever its level, has a certain form. This can vary from an **understood constituent** to a **word** or bigger construction, such as a **phrase**, a **clause**, a **sentence**, or a whole **text**. The following example contains only three constituents but with different forms: there is a noun phrase, a verb, and a complete (albeit short) speech.

	Pater infēlix	*dixit:*	*"Icare, ubi es? Quā tē regiōne requīram?"*
Function:	subject	predicate	object
Role:	agent	—	patient
Form:	noun phrase	verb	speech

The translation is

"The unlucky father said: 'Icarus, where are you? Where should I search for you?'" (Ovid *Met.* 8.231–32)

When a constituent consists of only one word, the form is the name of the part of speech: noun, adjective, pronoun, verb (more specifically, finite verb, infinitive, participle, supine, gerund, or gerundive), or adverb.

When a constituent consists of more than one word, the form is a phrase, a cluster, a clause, a sentence, or a text.

a) **Phrase**: noun phrase, pronoun phrase, adjective phrase, verb phrase (or infinitive phrase, participial phrase, copula + predicate n./adj.), prepositional phrase, adverbial phrase.

b) **Cluster**: noun cluster, noun phrase cluster, pronoun cluster, and so on. A cluster is a group of two or more equivalent elements (words, phrases, etc.)

c) **Clause**: finite clause with conjunction, relative clause, infinitive clause, ablative absolute, and so on.

d) **Sentence** (§179).

e) **Text**: speech, letter, poem, defense plea, report, direct order, quotation, etc.

Remark. It is sometimes hard to draw the dividing line between a phrase and a (concise) clause, as can be seen in several examples in § 353, 355–57.

Level

190. Sentence constituents, irrespective of their length or complexity, by definition function on the level of the sentence. Thus, the following sentence, already analyzed in detail in § 183, counts fifteen words and includes some dependent clauses but contains only seven sentence constituents: subject, three adverbial modifiers, indirect object, direct object, and predicate.

> *Curius,* | *ubi intellegit quantum perīculum consulī impendeat,* | *properē* | *per Fulviam* | *Cicerōnī* | *dolum quī parābātur* | *ēnuntiat.* "When Curius understood what a great danger threatened the consul, he hastily reported the trap that was being prepared, via Fulvia, to Cicero." (Sall. *Cat.* 28.2)

Sentence:

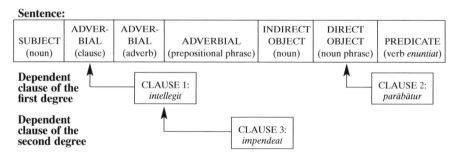

Some of the seven sentence constituents contain a clause on a **lower level**: these are **dependent clauses of the first degree**. The time adverbial consists of a dependent clause introduced by the conjunction *ubi*. This clause is **dependent** on its **governing** predicate, *ēnuntiat*, which at the same time is the main verb of the sentence. The direct object of the sentence, a noun phrase, **does not consist of but contains** a dependent clause of the first degree: the relative clause *quī parābātur*, which functions as an attributive clause to the head noun *dolum*. This relative clause is also governed by *ēnuntiat*.

As is shown in the preceding scheme, clause 1, the dependent adverbial clause, contains a dependent clause: *quantum consulī impendeat* (clause 3). This clause (an indirect question as direct object) is a dependent clause of the **second degree**, governed by *intellegit*.

Such **dependent clauses** depend on a governing verb, but two or more of them could be **conjoined by coordinating conjunctions** (*sed, et, -que, -ve, aut*). They are all made to depend on their governing verb by their common **clause marker** (subordinating conjunction, relative pronoun, interrogative pronoun, interrogative adverb, interrogative particle). In the case of infinitive clauses, ablative absolutes, and supine clauses, there is no subordinating word.

191. **The connection between a dependent clause and its governing clause** is important for the correct understanding of the **sequence of tenses** (§ 270, 277–83). This relative time relation holds between a dependent clause and its governing clause, never between dependent clauses.

The verb of clause 1 (historical present, instead of perfect) in the scheme in § 190 has a certain **time relation** (here **anteriority**) to the governing verb *ēnuntiat* (historical present, instead of perfect). The verb of clause 2 expresses a **simultaneity** with the governing verb, *ēnuntiat*. The verb *impendeat* of clause 3 is **simultaneous** with its governing verb, *intellegit* of clause 1. Clause 2 has no time relationship whatsoever with clause 1 or 3, or vice versa. The sentence thus has a **hierarchical organization**, in which every clause only has a relative time relation with its governing verb.

The level of the dependent clauses (showing subordinating words and verbs only) can also be presented by means of a left-right scheme.

Main clause	Dependent clause of the first degree	Dependent clause of the second degree
ēnuntiat		

↑——————— *ubi intellegit*

————————————————————— *quantum perīculum . . . impendeat*

————— *quī parābātur*

In § 401–2, two long sentences with many dependent clauses of the first, second, and third degree are presented by means of such a left-right scheme.

11
The Predicate

Definition and terminology

192. The **predicate** is the **basis of a kernel** (§ 180–81) **and of the sentence.** All other kernel and sentence constituents are related semantically and syntactically to this basis. **The predicate determines** how many and which constituents (subject, object, etc.) **necessarily** have to occur in the kernel in order to arrive at a well-formed sentence. In addition, the predicate may be modified by **non-obligatory sentence constituents (words, phrases, or clauses).**

The term *verb* indicates a part of speech like the term *noun*; *predicate* indicates a function (like *subject*). Therefore, it is correct to say that a sentence contains a subject and a predicate, whereas to refer to "a subject and a verb" is inconsistent. Furthermore, an ablative absolute, such as *Cicerōne consule,* although a correct clause, does not contain a subject and a verb, but it does contain a subject and a predicate.

193. The predicate can be a verb—a finite verb, a historical infinitive, an infinitive in an infinitive clause, a participle in the ablative absolute, a supine in a supine clause. In compound tenses with a PPP (perfective passive participle), an FAP (future active participle), or a gerundive, the auxiliary *esse* is sometimes omitted, more often in the infinitive than in the finite forms.

The predicate can consist of a nominal part (noun or adjective) and the copula *esse.* Such a predicate is thus called a **nominal predicate.** The copula is the carrier of the verbal categories of tense, mood, person, and number. Otherwise, it has no meaning and only serves to link the nominal part to the subject. The copula can also be omitted.

194. The predicate can have many forms (constructions). The following sentences or clauses all have the same structure with the functions subject and predicate. The subject is always a noun (form). But various forms fill the predicate slot.

Functions: subject + predicate	Form of the predicate
Corvus cantat. 'The raven sings.'	finite verb (active)
Corvō cantante ... 'While the raven is singing ...'	participle
... *corvum cantāre* '... that the raven sings.'	infinitive
Corvus decipitur. 'The raven is taken in.'	finite verb (passive)
Corvus deceptus est. 'The raven has been taken in.'	PPP + auxiliary
Corvus stultus est. 'The raven is stupid.'	adjective + copula
Corvus avis est. 'The raven is a bird.'	noun + copula

Agreement with the subject

195. The **predicate agrees with the subject in person, number, gender, and case**, if these categories are expressed by the predicate.

196. Agreement in person and number. If the speaker says something about himself/herself, the predicate takes the first-person singular: it agrees with an expressed or understood *ego* 'I'. The first-person plural refers to the speaker and some other person(s). If the speaker says something to the addressee(s) (*tū, vōs*), the predicate is in the second person (singular or plural). If the speaker talks about something or someone other than himself/herself or the addressee, the predicate is in the third person (singular or plural).

The Latin word *persōna* means 'stage mask' and indicates which role the subject plays in the speech act (§ 375): the first person, or speaker; the second person, or addressee; or the third "person," the person/thing referred to by the speaker.

> *Nōs satis facere reī pūblicae **vidēmur**, sī istīus furōrem ac tēla **vītāmus**.* "We seem to do enough for the state if we avoid the madness and the arms of that fellow." (Cic. *Cat.* 1.2)
> *Quid ais tū? Quid est? Quid rīdētis?* "What do you say? What is it? Why are you laughing?" (Plautus *Aul.* 717–18)

197. Agreement in gender and case. If the predicate contains declinable elements (predicate adjective, participle, gerundive), they agree with the subject in number, gender, and case. They are thus nominative in a clause with a finite verb or in a main clause, accusative in the infinitive clause, and ablative in the ablative absolute. The predicate noun has its own gender but agrees with the subject in case and often in number.

> ***Perditissimus** ego **sum** omnium in terrā.* "I am the most wretched of all on earth." (Plautus *Aul.* 723)
> *[Caesar] reperiēbat plērōsque Belgās **esse ortōs** ā Germānīs.* "Caesar found out that most Belgae descended from the Germani." (Caes. *B.G.* 2.4.1)
> *Tribūnō **recūsante, additus** [est] ab insolente Gallō ponderī gladius, **audītaque** intoleranda Rōmānīs vox "Vae victīs."* "As the tribune refused, a sword was added to the weight by the insolent Gaul, and one heard the words, intolerable for the Romans, 'Woe to the conquered!'" (Livy 5.48.9)

198. In the case of an **agreement *ad sensum*,** the predicate agrees with the subject in its natural gender and number, rather than in its grammatical gender and number.

> *[Orgetorix] cīvitātī* [sg.] *persuāsit ut dē fīnibus suīs **exīrent**.* "Orgetorix convinced his tribe to emigrate from their territory." (Caes. *B.G.* 1.2.1)

Magna pars [f. sg.] ***vulnerātī** aut **occīsī** [sunt].* "A large part were wounded or killed." (Sall. *Iug.* 58.2)

199. The predicate sometimes agrees with an **apposition** of the subject or with a **predicative apposition or complement** if this is nearer than the subject. Also, the copula may agree in number with the **predicate noun** rather than with the subject.

> *Poetae* [pl.] *suum quisque* [sg.] *opus ā vulgō consīderārī **vult**.* "Each poet wants his work to be admired by the public." (Cic. *Off.* 1.147)
> *Non omnis error* [m.] *stultitia* [f.] ***dīcenda est**.* "Not every error has to be called silliness." (Cic. *Div.* 2.90)
> *Amantium īrae* [pl.] *amōris integrātiō* [sg.] ***est**.* "Lovers' quarrels are love's renewal." (Ter. *And.* 555)

200. When there are **several subjects**, the predicate may agree with the nearest subject, particularly when each subject can be considered individually within the context of the sentence.

> *Neque enim domus . . . vel templa . . . aut quid morae **interiacēbat**.* "Indeed, there lay no houses, or temples, or any retarding obstacle in between." (Tac. *Ann.* 15.38.3)

201. When **persons or genders of various combined subjects are different**, the following agreements may occur.

    a) **The first person is preferred to the second, the second to the third.**
    b) **With animate subjects, the masculine gender is preferred to the feminine and the neuter.**
    c) **Inanimate subjects with different genders (and also various abstract feminine subjects) may have a neuter plural predicate.**

> *Sī tū et Tullia **valētis**, ego et suāvissimus Cicerō **valēmus**.* "If you and Tullia are doing well—dearest Cicero and I are doing well." (Cic. *Fam.* 14.5.1)
> *Pater mihi et māter **mortuī** [sunt].* "My father and my mother have died." (Ter. *Eun.* 517–18) (*Mihi* is a dativus ethicus [§ 144, 380] and is hard to translate.)
> *Mūrus et porta dē caelō **tacta erant**.* "The wall and the gate had been struck by lightning." (Livy 32.29.1)
> *Nī virtus fidēsque vostra satis **spectāta mihi forent**, . . .* "If your courage and fidelity had not been sufficiently clear to me, . . ." (Sall. *Cat.* 20.2)

202. When the subject is a **demonstrative or relative pronoun, reverse agreement occurs**. The subject pronoun agrees with the predicate noun. This is not the case in English translation.

Ista quidem vīs est! "But that is violence!" (Suetonius *Caes.* 82.1)

[Caesar] certior fīēbat omnēs Belgās, quam [not *quōs*] *tertiam esse Galliae partem dīxerāmus, coniūrāre.* "Caesar was informed that all Belgae, who—as we had said—constituted the third part of Gaul, were conspiring." (Caes. *B.G.* 2.1.1) (See § 373.)

See also the second example in § 142, where *quod* is not masculine plural.

203. Sometimes the predicate of an infinitive clause depending on an impersonal verb agrees with an understood subject. Sometimes it agrees with a person in the dative, if the impersonal verb is construed with the dative.

> *Nam expedit bonās esse vōbīs.* "Because it is in your interest to be honest." (Ter. *Heaut.* 388)
>
> *Per hanc cūram quiētō tibi licet esse.* "Through my concern you may be at rest." (Plautus *Epid.* 338)

204. In all the instances in § 197–203, the predicate is in the same case as the subject. But other constructions do occur.

a) The predicate can consist of a copula with a possessive genitive (§ 126, 135), a descriptive genitive (§ 130, 135), a genitive of price (§ 317), a dative of purpose (§ 143), or a descriptive ablative (§ 177).

> *Est virī fortis nē suppliciīs quidem movērī.* "It is proper to a courageous man not to become upset, not even by punishment." (Cic. *Mil.* 82)
>
> *Mīlitēs sibi ipsōs ad pugnam esse impedīmentō vīdit.* "He saw that the soldiers hindered each other in the battle." (Caes. *B.G.* 2.25.1)
>
> *Britannī capillō sunt prōmissō.* "The Britanni wear their hair long." (Caes. *B.G.* 5.14.3)

b) The predicate can consist of a copula with a prepositional phrase.

> *Illud [est] contrā omnia iūra Siculōrum.* "This is against all the rights of the Sicilians." (Cic. *Verr.* 2.3.38)
>
> *Ipse cum tēlō esse.* "He himself was armed." (Sall. *Cat.* 27.2)

c) The predicate can contain an adverb.

> *Res ita est.* "That is the situation." (Plautus *Bacch.* 721)
>
> *Neque inceptum ullum frustrā erat.* "Not a single enterprise was in vain." (Sall. *Iug.* 7.6)

Active and passive voices

205. **In the active voice, the subject is the first obligatory constituent with the predicate.** The semantic role of the subject may vary according to the meaning of the predicate. The subject very often is the agent (in control) of an action or a position. But there are also non-agent subjects of events or states. Whatever its semantic role, the subject of an active verb takes the nominative in a main clause or in a clause with a finite verb. It takes the accusative in the infinitive clause and the ablative in the ablative absolute.

> *Manlius spīculum inter aurēs equī **fixit**.* "Manlius drove the spear between the ears of the horse." (Livy 8.7.10) (subject as agent of an action)
>
> *Suessiōnēs fīnēs latissimōs ferācissimōsque agrōs **possidēre**.* "The Suessiones held an extensive territory and most fertile fields." (Caes. *B.G.* 2.4.6) (subject as agent in a position)
>
> ***Tabuerant** cērae.* "The wax had melted." (Ovid *Met.* 8.227) (non-agent subject of an event)
>
> *Apud Helvētiōs **longē nōbilissimus fuit et dītissimus** Orgetorix.* "Among the Helvetii Orgetorix was by far the best known and richest." (Caes. *B.G.* 1.2.1) (non-agent subject of a state)

206. **The passive voice has a subject as patient.** (It corresponds to the object as patient of the active voice.) This subject undergoes the action of the verb. A verb in the passive voice does not have a direct object except when it is a deponent verb (§ 209) or when it is a verb like *docēre* or *rogāre* (§ 151). The animate subject as agent of the active verb can occur in the passive sentence as an adverbial modifier of agent. It is not obligatory.

In the context of the speech act (§ 375), the agent modifier is often omitted, for various reasons.

a) The agent is unknown.

> *Petrosidius aquilifer ipse prō castrīs fortissimē pugnans **occīditur**.* "The chief standard-bearer Petrosidius himself is killed while fighting fiercely in front of the camp." (Caes. *B.G.* 5.37.5)

b) The agent is obvious and its mention superfluous.

> *Igitur comitīs habitīs, consulēs **dēclārantur** M. Tullius et C. Antōnius.* "When the elections were held, M. Tullius and C. Antonius were declared consuls." (Sall. *Cat.* 24.1)

c) The agent is omitted by the speaker/author for reasons of modesty (when he/she is talking/writing about himself/herself) or tact.

> *. . . in urbe **parāta esse** quae iusserit.* "[Lentulus writes to Catiline] that in Rome all the preparations had been made [by Lentulus] that he [Catiline] had ordered." (Sall. *Cat.* 44.6)

d) The omission of the agent with a passive verb draws the attention to the action of the verb itself, whereas an active verb (even with an understood subject) necessarily points to the agent subject.

> *Vīgintī minās dabin [= dabisne]? — **Dabuntur**.* "'The twenty minae, are you going to give them?' — They will be given." (Plautus *Pseud.* 1077–78)

*Quid **agitur**, Calidōre? — **Amātur** atque **egētur** acriter.* "What's up, Calidorus? — In love and no money—extremely so." (Plautus *Pseud.* 273) [In this dialogue the speakers' problem, as such, shows here to full advantage, whereas use of *agis, amō,* and *egeō* would draw the attention to the second and first person.)

207. **The passive voice is often used in narratives to signal a shift from one sequence of events to another sequence with different actors.** The passive verbs thus have to be explained not on the sentence level but in the context of the whole passage (§ 375a). (The reasons mentioned in § 206 for the use of the passive and/or the omission of the agent complement in a speech act may also apply in a narrative.) The following passage (Cic. *Cat.* 3.5–8), here broken into five sequences, is drastically shortened but contains all main verbs: the active (and deponent) main verbs are underlined; the passive main verbs are printed in bold type.

> *Praetōrēs ad mē vocāvī; rem exposuī; quid fierī placēret ostendī. Illī autem negōtium suscēpērunt et occultē ad pontem Mulvium pervēnērunt atque ibī bipertītō fuērunt. Eōdem autem et ipsī multōs fortēs virōs ēduxerant et ego complūrēs dēlectōs adulescentēs mīseram.*
> "I summoned the praetors to me; I explained the matter; I showed them what I wanted to happen. And they took the task up, arrived in secret at the Mulvian Bridge, and took post there in two groups. Moreover, they themselves had taken many strong men with them, and I had also sent several selected young men."
> *Cum pontem Allobrogēs ingredī inciperent, **fit** in eōs impetus. **Dūcuntur** et ab illīs gladiī et ā nostrīs. Rēs praetōribus **erat nōta** sōlīs, **ignōrābātur** ā cēterīs. Tum pugna **sēdātur**. Litterae **trāduntur**. Ipsī ad mē **dēdūcuntur**.*
> "As the Allobroges began to walk on the bridge, an attack on them occurred. Swords were drawn both by them and by our men. (The matter was only known to the praetors and not known by their men.) Then the fight was stopped. The letters were handed over. The Allobroges were brought to me."
> *Gabīnium statim ad mē vocāvī.*
> "I immediately sent for Gabinius."
> *Deinde **accersītus est** Statilius, post eum Cethēgus; tardissimē autem Lentulus vēnit*
> "Later, Statilius was summoned, and after him Cethegus; very late, Lentulus also arrived."
> *Negāvī . . . Arbitrābar . . . Senātum coēgī. Mīsī . . .*
> "I refused . . . It was my opinion . . . I convoked the senate. I sent . . ."

The first sequence deals with the activities of Cicero and the praetors.

The second sequence uses passive main verbs for the shift to the skirmish on the bridge.

In the third sequence, Cicero acts again (active verb).

The fourth sequence contains a shift (*accersītus est*) to the other three conspirators (all three in the nominative—which makes the last one the subject of the active verb *vēnit*).

The fifth sequence shows Cicero again in action (with the active verbs *negavi*, etc.). The ensuing interrogation of the conspirators is told chiefly in the active voice (the actors are Cicero and the conspirators), but with passive sentences for short shifts to activities (readings) by others: *erat scriptum* "there was written," *recitatae sunt tabellae* "the letter was read," *leguntur litterae* "the letter was read" (Cic. *Cat.* 3.8–12).

Throughout the passage, pluperfect and imperfect verbs (*ēduxerant, mīseram, erat nōta, ignōrābātur, arbitrābar*) signal background information (§ 213, 220), rather than the event line of the narrative, which is in the historical perfect (§ 218) or historical present (§ 212).

208. An **impersonal passive** of intransitive verbs and, to a lesser degree, of transitive verbs can also occur without an agent modifier. An impersonal passive exists only in the third-person singular and has no subject. In an **impersonal construction of the gerundive**, the passive meaning is contained in the gerundive. A literal translation of such an impersonal passive is not possible in English. One has to resort to other (active) constructions, possibly with indefinites, such as *one, we, people, they*.

> *Acriter utrimque usque ad vesperum **pugnātum est***. "There was a fierce battle on both sides until evening." Or "They fought fiercely on both sides until evening." (Caes. *B.G.* 1.50.2)
> *Undique tōtīs usque adeō **turbātur** agrīs*. "Everywhere there is constantly such disorder in all the fields." (Virg. *Buc.* 1.11–12)
> *Nunc est bibendum*. "Now we [or 'one'] should drink." (Hor. *Carm.* 1.37.1)

209. The passive voice is also used with **a reflexive or reciprocal meaning**. Historically speaking, the passive corresponds to the Greek middle voice, which, for all practical purposes, may be interpreted as a reflexive. This **reflexive use is also found in the Latin passive**. Such a verb is not passive in meaning, because **the subject is the agent of the action**.

If a verb has only passive endings and no active ones, it is called a **deponent verb**. Such a verb can hardly be distinguished from an active verb, because its subject is an agent, and the meaning often is not reflexive or reciprocal. For example, there is no difference in meaning between the active and the passive forms of the semi-deponent verbs (§ 102–3): *audeō* 'I dare,' *ausus sum* 'I dared'. Deponent verbs can be transitive or intransitive.

Several deponent verbs and also regular active verbs, when used in the passive voice, can have a reflexive, reciprocal, or similar shade of meaning.

a) reflexive

deponent: *revertor* 'turn oneself back, return'

non-deponent: *lavārī* 'wash oneself', *ornārī* 'dress oneself', *cingī* 'gird oneself', *exercērī* 'drill oneself, practice, exercise' (often replaced by *sē exercēre*)

b) reciprocal

deponent: *luctārī* 'wrestle', *amplectī* 'embrace'

non-deponent: *cōpūlārī dextrās* 'shake hands', *coniungī* 'join (each other)'

c) intransitive action of non-deponent verbs

volvere '(make) roll', passive intransitive *volvī* 'roll'; *vehere* 'carry, convey', *vehī* 'ride, sail, drive, travel'; *frangere* '(cause to) break', *frangī* 'break'; *minuere* 'make smaller', *minuī* 'diminish'. In both Latin and English, some verbs in the active voice are transitive and intransitive: *avertere* 'turn away,' *ruere* 'rush, dash down, turn up'.

> *[Ventī] vastōs **volvunt** ad litora fluctūs.* "The winds rolled huge waves to the shores." (Virg. *Aen.* 1.86)
>
> *Excutitur prōnusque magister **volvitur** in caput.* "The helmsman is thrown overboard and rolls head foremost [into the sea]." (Virg. *Aen.* 1.115–16)
>
> ***Franguntur** rēmī: tum prōra **āvertit.*** "The oars break: then the prow turns aside." (Virg. *Aen.* 1.104)

Tenses

210. Tense and aspect. As in English, there are three tenses in Latin: present, past, and future. Tenses indicate when an action or event is situated in time. But in the conjugation system (§ 77, 90–99), there appear to be six tenses (three times two). Therefore, another grammatical category must come into play here. This category, called **aspect, indicates how someone looks at (*ad-spicere*) the action or how someone presents it.** As will be clear from the description of the tenses that follows, tenses cannot be understood completely without the notion of aspect.

Latin does not make a distinction between the simple, the progressive, and the emphatic forms of a verb: *audit* can mean 'he listens', 'he is listening', or 'he does listen'.

211. The distinction between **imperfective** and **perfective** "tenses" is really a distinction of aspect, which is at the basis of the whole conjugation system.

All tenses formed on the **imperfective stem** (also called the **present stem**) indicate that an action or event is, was, or will be **incomplete** at the moment of speaking. This also implies that these tenses, when occurring in a dependent clause, are **simultaneous** with the governing verb.

All tenses formed on the **perfective stem** (active) or by means of the **PPP** (passive) indicate **completeness**. This means that the action or event is, was, or will be over and done at the moment of speaking. This also implies that in a dependent clause, these tenses are **anterior** to the governing verb.

212. The **present tense** presents the action or event as **present** and **not completed**. This means that it takes place at the moment of the speech act. Even when the action is past or future, the speaker/writer can experience and present the action as present.

> *Nisi mē frustrantur oculī, māter tibi coniunx et līberī adsunt.* "If my eyes do not deceive me, your mother, spouse, and children are here." (Livy 2.40.4)
>
> *Saepe tibi dīcō inesse vim Rēgulō.* "I told you often there is pith in Regulus." (Pliny 4.7.1) (This present has been going on for some time already.)
>
> *Tuēminī castra. Ego reliquās portās circumeō.* "Protect the camp. I'll go around the other gates." (Caes. *B.Civ.* 3.94.5) (This present may still last some time.)

The present is also used for **general truths**, which are not confined to the present but are timeless.

> *Verba volant, scripta mānent.* "Words fly, writings remain." (saying)

The **historical present** is often used for facts from the past that the speaker/writer wants to present as happening at the time of speaking/writing, as if he/she were present. **In this way, the addressee/ reader becomes a contemporary of those facts, which increases the vivacity of a text.** (A historical infinitive is also sometimes used for this purpose: see § 225.) In the translation, such a shift from the historic perfect to the historic present may be maintained by shifting from the past to the present tense. Whoever is not happy with such shifts in the next (shortened) text may translate the whole text in the past.

> *Caesar duās legiōnēs conscripsit et . . . mīsit. Ipse . . . ad exercitum venit. Dat negōtium Senonibus . . . Hī . . . nuntiāvērunt . . . Tum . . . existimāvit . . . Castra movet et . . . ad fīnēs Belgārum pervenit.* "Caesar raised two legions and sent . . . He himself goes to his army. He gives an order to the Senones . . . These announced . . . Then he thought . . . He breaks camp and arrives at the territory of the Belgae." (Caes. *B.G.* 2.2.2–6)

For the **durative, iterative, or habitual aspect** and the **conative aspect**, see § 213–14.

213. The **imperfect** presents the action or event in the **past** and as **not completed**. The imperfect is the tense par excellence for the **description of circumstances** (i.e., what is happening "in the meantime") and for **giving**

background information needed for the story, whereas the perfect gives the backbone, or event line, of the story (§ 218).

The description of situations may in certain contexts imply that such a situation lasted, repeated itself, or was a habit. This is the **durative, iterative, or habitual aspect** of the verb (which also occurs with the present tense). This aspect can also be expressed or strengthened by the frequentative suffix *-t* (§ 14). In English translation, one can sometimes use adverbs expressing such an aspect (*permanently, often, frequently, usually*), or one can use the progressive form.

> *Icarus ūnā **stābat** et **captābat** plūmās, flāvam pollice cēram **mollībat** lūsūque suō mīrābile pătris **impediēbat** opus.* "In the meantime Icarus was standing with him and often tried [iterative and conative (§ 214) aspect, expressed by the suffix *-t*] to catch the feathers, softened the golden wax with his thumb, and hindered through his play the wonderful work of his father." (Ovid *Met.* 8.195–200) (The four imperfect tenses give the background information for the narrative's event line [told in the historical perfect or historical present], the activities of Daedalus.)
>
> *At pater infēlix "Icare," dixit. "Icare," dixit, "ubī es? Quā tē regiōne requīram?" "Icare," **dīcēbat.*** "But the unhappy father said, 'Icarus.' 'Icarus,' he said, 'where are you? Where should I look for you?' 'Icarus,' he said the whole time." (Ovid *Met.* 8.231–33) (*Dixit* expresses the backbone event, *dicebat* the additional background activity.)
>
> *Erat Athēnīs domus spatiōsa sed infāmis. Strepitus vinculōrum **reddēbātur**. Mox **appārēbat** īdōlum. Catēnās **gerēbat quatiēbatque**. Inhabitantibus noctēs **vigilābantur. Proscrībēbātur.** Venit Athēnās philosophus Athēnodōrus. Legit titulum.* "Once upon a time, there was in Athens a spacious but infamous house. The sound of chains was heard. Soon the ghost appeared. He wore chains and shook them. The inhabitants passed the nights without sleep. The house was put up for sale. Then arrived the philosopher Athenodorus. He read the notice." (Pliny 7.27.5–7, considerably shortened) (The first seven imperfect verbs give background information about the situation. Then two verbs [*venit* and *legit*] in the historical present [= perfect] give the beginning of the event line, or backbone, of the narrative.)

214. The imperfect and the present can have a **conative aspect**. This means that someone is trying to do something but is not necessarily succeeding. This aspect includes an **imperfectum de conatu** and a **praesens de conatu**.

> *Pestilentem domum **vendō**.* "I am selling my unhealthy house." (Cic. *Off.* 3.55) (In context, *domum vendō* means [both in Latin and in English] "I am trying to sell my house" or "I am offering my house for sale.")
>
> ***Captābat** plūmās.* "He constantly tried to catch the feathers." (Ovid *Met.* 8.198)

215. In a letter, a Latin writer sometimes uses the **epistolary imperfect**. The writer sees his/her activity in the context of the speech act (§ 375) and takes the point of view of the reader, using the tense that counts for the reader when receiving the letter. This is not done in English.

> *Haec ego **scrībēbam** hōrā noctis nōnā.* "I am writing this at the ninth hour of the night." (Cic. *Att.* 4.3.5)

216. The **simple future** locates the action or event in the future. In this respect, Latin is more precise than English.

> *Namque **erit** ille mihi simper deus.* 'Indeed, for me he will always be a god.' (Virg. *Buc.* 1.7)
> *Certumst, **ībō** ad medicum.* "I have made up my mind: I'm going [literally, "I will go"] to the doctor." (Plautus *Merc.* 472)

Latin also has a **periphrastic future**, consisting of a **future active participle** + *esse*. This construction indicates an immediate future and is best translated 'I am about to, I intend to'. This periphrastic tense is used less in the indicative and more in the subjunctive, to express posteriority in the future infinitive (§ 271) and in indirect questions (for lack of a future subjunctive: see § 278–79).

> *Nec, ut sim miserrima, diū **futūra sum**.* "And, although I am very unhappy, I have no intent to be so for a long time." (Livy 2.40.8)

217. The **perfect** is a tense where two different aspectual stems have merged, as can be seen from the two different meanings, from the various formations of this tense, and from a comparison with classical Greek. The different formations (§ 75) no longer have any relevance for the meaning: all forms express a past action or event. But for a good understanding of this tense in context and for an adequate translation, the two aspects have to be distinguished. The **historical perfect** expresses an action or event at a certain point in the past. The **resultative perfect** (also called **present perfect**) expresses a completed action with a result that is still present.

218. The **historical perfect** expresses an action or event that is **over and done** and that took place at a certain moment in the **past**. This moment is considered as a point in time. This perfect has a **punctual aspect**. This tense is used for the **successive actions or events of a narrative in the past.** It provides the **backbone of the narrative**, the **thread of discourse**, whereas the imperfect describes situations that exist during the narrative. In other words, if, in a narrative, all the verbs in the imperfect tense are omitted and the verbs in the perfect are kept, there is still the backbone of the narrative; if only the verbs in the imperfect are kept, there is no narrative, only some descriptions. Thus, the choice between the perfect and the imperfect depends not on the sentence but on the text as a whole (§ 375a). In English, the simple past is used for the translation of both

Latin tenses. In the examples that follow, the imperfect verbs are under-lined; the perfect verbs are printed in bold type. Some additional adverbs are sometimes added in the translation to render the Latin imperfect tense. (For more examples, see § 213.)

> *Plānitiēs <u>erat</u> magna et in eā tumulus terrēnus satis grandis. Hic locus aequō ferē spatiō ab castrīs Ariovistī et Caesaris <u>aberat</u>. Eō, ut erat dictum, ad conloquium* **vēnērunt**. *Legiōnem Caesar quam equīs vexerat passibus dūcentīs ab eō tumulō* **constituit**. *Item equitēs Ariovistī parī intervallō* **constituērunt**. *Ariovistus ex equīs ut conloquerentur . . .* **postulāvit**. *Ubī eō* **ventum est**, *Caesar . . . beneficiīs* **commemorāvit** *. . . Quam rem paucīs contigisse . . . <u>docēbat</u> . . . <u>Docēbat</u> etiam . . .* **Postulāvit** *deinde eadem . . . Ariovistus ad postulāta Caesaris pauca* **respondit**. "There <u>was</u> [background information] a great plain and in it a rather high earthen hill. This place <u>was</u> [id.] at about the same distance from Ariovistus's camp and Caesar's. There they **met** [part of the backbone], as was arranged, for the negotiation. Caesar **stationed** [id.] the legion he had brought with him at two hundred steps from that hill. Ariovistus's horsemen also **halted** [id.] at the same distance. Ariovistus **demanded** [id.] that they negotiate on horseback. When they arrived there, Caesar **reminded** [id.] him of his favors. [In doing so] he <u>explained</u> [no new step, but additional information about *commemorāvit*] that this honor had not been bestowed on many. He also <u>explained</u> [id.] that . . . He then **formulated** [backbone: next action after *commemorāvit*] the same demands. Ariovistus **answered** [id.] little to Caesar's demands." (Caes. *B.G.* 1.43–44.1)

For examples of historical perfects and background imperfects and pluperfects, see § 207.

219. The **resultative perfect** expresses an action or event that started in the past and is now over and done but the result of which is still present. It thus has a **resultative aspect** and is translated by the present perfect. Several verbs can even be translated in the present tense, if this present tense is the result of an action (*perīre* 'die', perf. 'have died' = 'be dead'; *cognoscere* 'get to know', perf. 'have got to know' = 'know'; *consuescere* 'get accustomed', perf. 'be accustomed'; and other verbs with the inchoative suffix *-sc* [see § 14]).

> *Tellus ā nomine* **dicta** *[est] sepultī.* "The land is named after [and today still has the name of] the boy who is buried there." (Ovid *Met.* 8.235)
> *Gallia* **est divisa** *in partēs trēs.* "Gaul [until today] is divided into three parts." (Caes. *B.G.* 1.1.1)
> **Perī**. "I am a dead man." (Plautus *Aul.* 713)
> **Nōvī** *omnēs.* "I know you all." (Plautus *Aul.* 718)

The **gnomic perfect** is a resultative perfect used in maxims. The experience and sententious wisdom from the past is expressed in the perfect, whereas English may use the present tense for these general truths.

Otium et rēgēs prius et beātās perdidit urbēs. "Idleness has ruined both kings and prosperous cities before." (Catullus 51.15–16)
Nīl sine magnō vīta labōre dedit mortālibus. "Life does not give anything [literally, "Life has not given anything"] without great effort to humans." (Hor. *Sat.* 1.9.59–60)

220. In the active voice, the **pluperfect (past perfective)** is formed on the perfective stem. In the passive voice, it is formed by means of a PPP + an auxiliary verb. The pluperfect names an action that is **completed** and **anterior** to another action in the past. The pluperfect can occur in independent sentences: see *ēduxerant* and *mīseram* in the example passage in § 207 and *scripseram* (anterior to *est profectus*) in the first example that follows in the present section. It often occurs in dependent clauses: see *volueram* (anterior to *est profectus*) in the first example that follows. The second example that follows is different: the pluperfect stands in the governing clause and is anterior to the (present) verb of the dependent clause.

> *Scripseram ad tē epistulam. Sed is cuī dare volueram non est profectus.* "I had written a letter to you. But the man to whom I [had] wanted to give it, did not set out." (Cic. *Att.* 9.7.1)
> *Quod vispillō facit [Diaulus], fēcerat et medicus.* "What Diaulus does as an undertaker, he also had done as a doctor." (Mart. *Ep.* 1.47.2)

221. Remark. In the passive perfect and pluperfect, the auxiliaries *sum* (etc.) and *eram* (etc.) are generally used, but *fuī* (etc.) and *fueram* (etc.) also occur. However, there is a difference in meaning. Both auxiliaries express a completed action or event, but the tenses with *fuī* (etc.) and *fueram* (etc.) indicate that the result has been present for some time but not any longer.

> *Unum manēbat illud sōlācium, quod ēreptum est.* "There remained that one consolation, that has been taken away [and is still taken away]." (Cic. *Fam.* 4.6.2)
> *Quae sī hōc tempore non diem suum obīsset, paucīs post annīs tamen eī moriendum fuit, quoniam homo nāta fuerat.* "If she had not died in this moment, she should have died anyway a few years later, since she was born as a human being [but does not live anymore]." (Servius Sulpicius in Cic. *Fam.* 4.5.4)

222. The **future perfect (future perfective)** expresses (mostly in a subordinate clause) an **anteriority** to another future verb (mostly in the governing clause). Latin is very careful in expressing both completion and anteriority, whereas this tense is often translated by an English present or perfect tense.

> *Sī ad nōs vēneris, consilium tōtīus reī capiēmus.* "When you join us [literally, "will have joined us"], we will take a decision about the whole issue." (Cic. *Att.* 3.2)

*Effice, quidquid corpore **contigero**, fulvum vertātur in aurum.* "Make sure that whatever I touch [literally, "will have touched"] with my body changes into yellow gold." (Ovid *Met.* 11.102–3)

223. Synopsis of the meaning of the tenses in the indicative

Tense	Meaning	Translation	Example
Present	a) not completed in the present time	a) present	'he makes'
	b) sometimes durative, iterative, habitual, or conative aspect	b) present or present progressive	'he makes/is making'
	c) historical present	c) present or past	'he made/makes'
Imperfect	a) background information, description (in the past)	a) past	'he made'
	b) sometimes durative, iterative, habitual, or conative aspect	b) past or past progressive	'he made/was making'
	c) epistolary imperfect	c) present	'he makes'
Future	future	future	'he will make'
Perfect	**historical perfect**: backbone of the narrative in the past	past	'he made'
	resultative perfect: present result of a completed action or event	present perfect	'he has made'
Pluperfect	completed and anterior to another past verb	past perfect	'he had made'
Future perfect	completed and anterior to another future verb	present or perfect or future perfect	'he makes/has made/will have made'

Moods and sentence types

Modality

224. The **moods** of the verb are used to render certain **sentence types** and certain **modalities. Modality is the relation between the idea expressed and reality.** In a declarative sentence, the speaker/writer communicates something that he/she presents as **real, possible**, or **contrary to fact (counterfactual).** The same modalities can occur in a question (an interrogative sentence).

Sentences with a **volitive** character (expressing the will of the speaker/writer) each have their own relation to reality: **command, prohibition, wish, exhortation, concession**.

The **negation** in a declarative and interrogative sentence (in all modalities) is the modal adverb ***nōn***. In a volitive sentence, the speaker/writer rejects the idea of a certain action or event by means of the adverb ***nē***.

Modality is often expressed by modal adverbs: *certē* 'surely', *fortasse* 'probably', *vix* 'hardly', and so on. Modal auxiliary verbs can also be used for this purpose: *debēre* 'must', *oportet* 'it is needed', *posse* 'can'. Finally, there are periphrastic means for expressing modality, such as the verbs *spērāre* 'hope' and *timēre* 'fear' and intonation. All these means are used more frequently in English than in Latin, which employs mainly the moods of the verb.

Each sentence type has its own moods and, sometimes, tenses, as will be clear from the following paragraphs and the table in § 238. However, the **infinitive can also be used for some sentence types**. In such instances, the context makes clear which sentence type and modality are meant. The infinitive names the action, event, or state of affairs but is in itself unmarked as to various categories (not only sentence type and modality, but also person, number, gender, and tense).

Declarative sentence

225. In a **declarative sentence**, the speaker/writer very often presents something as **real**. Such a modality is expressed by the **indicative mood** (any tense). From time to time, in a lively narrative, there occurs a shift from the **historical perfect** or **historical present** to the **historical infinitive**. If such a shift is difficult in English, a translator should resort to a regular (past or present) finite verb.

> *[Catilīna] Manlium Faesulās, Septimium in agrum Pīcēnum, Iulium in Apuliam dīmīsit. Intereā Rōmae multa simul mōlīrī: consulibus insidiās tendere, parāre incendia,* . . . "Catiline sent Manlius to Faesulae, Septimius to the Picenian territory, Iulius to Apulia. In the meantime he undertook many activities: laying traps for the consuls, preparing fires, . . ." (Sall. *Cat.* 27.1–2)

Verbs expressing a possibility or obligation often occur in the indicative because the possibility or obligation is or was real, even if the action has not been realized. In English, frequent use is made of conditionals or modal auxiliaries.

> *Hīc tamen hanc mēcum poterās requiescere noctem.* "Yet you could have rested here this night with me." (Virg. *Buc.* 1.79)
> *Ad mortem tē, Catilīna, dūcī iam pridem oportēbat.* "You should already have been put to death long ago, Catiline." (Cic. *Cat.* 1.2)

226. A **declarative sentence** can express a **possibility** (a supposition that may not be fulfilled) in the **subjunctive mood**. For a possibility in **the present**, a verb in **either the present or the perfect** is used, without any difference in meaning. For a possibility in **the past**, a verb in **the imperfect subjunctive** is used. (Possibility in the past generally equals a contrary-to-fact modality in the present.)

*Hesperidās dōnasse **putēs**.* "You might think that the Hesperides had given them." (Ovid *Met.* 11.114)

*Satius itaque est compārārī ea quae ad coercendōs ignēs auxiliō esse **possint**.* "Therefore, it would be preferable to provide what could be useful for confining fires." (Pliny 10.34.2)

*Fūsile per rictūs aurum fluitāre **vidērēs**.* "You could have seen the molten gold flow through his open mouth." (Ovid *Met.* 11.126)

227. A **declarative** sentence expresses an idea that is **contrary to fact in the present time** with a verb in the **imperfect subjunctive**; it expresses an idea that was **contrary to fact in the past** with a verb in the **pluperfect subjunctive**. Such sentences are often accompanied by a conditional clause (§ 335–39). In English, frequent use is made of auxiliaries (*were, would, had been, would have, etc.*). An infinitive may also be used, although it in itself does not express any idea that may be contrary to fact.

*Ego nisi **peperissem**, Rōmam non **oppugnārētur**; nisi fīlium **habērem**, lībera in līberā pătriā **mortua essem**!* "If I had not given birth, Rome would not be besieged; if I did not have a son, I would have died as a free woman in my free native land." (Livy 2.40.8)

*Quod nī fēcisset, **perdere** litem.* "If he had not done that — case lost [= "he would lose the case"]." (Hor. *Sat.* 1.9.37)

Interrogative sentence

228. In a **direct question (interrogative sentence)**, usually the **indicative** is used, because usually someone asks for a **reality**, but the **possibility** and the **counterfactual** also occur. These modalities utilize the same moods and tenses used in declarative sentences (§ 225–27, 238).

A **yes-no question** is sometimes recognized by its **intonation only** but is generally introduced by the enclitic **interrogative particle –ne**, attached to the first word (or phrase) of the question. *Nōnne* (at the beginning of the sentence) also introduces a question and suggests a positive answer. *Num* (at the beginning of the sentence) expects a negative answer.

A **direct disjunctive question** contains the interrogative particle ***utrum, -ne***, or **no particle** in the first clause and ***an*** or ***anne*** in the second and subsequent clauses. In English, yes-no questions require the auxiliary *do*, subject inversion, interrogative intonation, modal auxiliaries, particles reflecting speaker attitude (*sure, indeed, etc.*), and tag questions.

When the first alternative of a disjunctive question is not explicitly mentioned, ***an*** (at the beginning of the sentence) introduces a very abrupt question.

Tum Ennius: "Quid? Ego non cognoscō vōcem, inquit, tuam?" "'What?' said Ennius then. 'Don't I recognize your voice?'" (Cic. *De Oratore* 2.276)

Putasne satis esse Rōmānīs haec omnia? "Do you think all this is sufficient for the Romans?" (Macrobius *Sat.* 2.2.2)

Nōnne ēmorī per virtūtem praestat? "Isn't it indeed preferable to die with courage?" (Sall. *Cat.* 20.9)

Num negāre audēs? "You would not dare to deny it, would you?" (Cic. *Cat.* 1.8)

*Haec **utrum** tandem lex est **an** legum omnium dissolūtiō?* "After all, is this a law or the destruction of all laws?" (Cic. *Ph.* 1.21)

*Conclāmāvit quid ad sē venīrent. **An** speculandī causā?* "He asked with a shout why they came to him. To spy perhaps?" (Caes. *B.G.* 1.47.6)

229. A **question-word question** is introduced by

a) an **interrogative pronoun** (*quis* 'who', *quid* 'what', *quantus* 'how big', *quālis* 'what kind of', *quot* 'how many', *uter* 'which of two');

b) an **interrogative adverb** (*ubī* 'where', *quō* 'whither', *cūr* 'why', *quōmodo* 'how', etc.).

> ***Quid** ais tū?* "What do you say?" (Plautus *Aul.* 717)
>
> *[Lupus] "**Quārē**" inquit "turbulentam fēcistī mihi aquam bibentī?* "'Why', the wolf asked, 'did you trouble the water while I was drinking?'" (Phaedrus 1.1 *Lupus et agnus* 5–6)

230. With a **rhetorical question** (§ 273c, 454), no answer is expected, either because the answer is evident or because it is impossible to give an answer.

> ***Ubinam** gentium sumus? **Quam** rem pūblicam habēmus? **In quā** urbe vivimus?* "Where in the world are we? What kind of state do we have? In what kind of city do we live?" (Cic. *Cat.* 1.9)

231. In a **deliberative question**, the speaker (first-person singular or plural) is wondering what he/she should do or should have done. A deliberative question about the present is put in the **present subjunctive**; a deliberative question about the past is put in the **imperfect subjunctive**.

The subjunctive is used because the speaker is wondering not about a reality but about a possible action. An infinitive may also be used for this type of sentence.

> *"Icare," dixit, "quā tē regiōne **requīram?**"* "'Icarus,' he said, 'where should I look for you?'" (Ovid *Met.* 8.231–32)
>
> *Non **rogem?** Sine tē igitur **sim?*** "Should I not ask it? Should I then stay without you?" (Cic. *Fam.* 14.4.3)
>
> *Quid **facerem?*** "What should I have done?" (Virg. *Buc.* 1.40)
>
> *Quid enim? **Sedēre** tōtōs diēs in villā?* "So what? Sit for whole days on my farm?" (Cic. *Att.* 12.44.2)

Volitive sentence

232. A **command**, both in Latin and in English, is expressed with a verb in the **imperative mood.** The Latin **present** (or first) **imperative** expects immediate fulfillment. It has second-person **singular** and **plural** forms (§ 80, 86).

In addition to the **present imperative**, Latin also has a **future** (or second) **imperative**, with second- and third-person singular and plural forms. Future imperatives are chiefly used in laws, legal documents, farming instructions, and so on, where the command applies to a future fulfillment.

A passive imperative is only meaningful with deponent verbs or reflexive and reciprocal passives (§ 209). An infinitive may also express an order.

I, lictor, dēligā [eum] ad pālum. "Go, lictor, tie him to the stake." (Livy 8.7.19)

Nostrum dīvellite corpus, leōnēs. "Tear our bodies into pieces, lions." (Ovid *Met.* 4.112–14)

Sī dē mē ipsō plūra dīcere vidēbor, ignoscitōte. "If I give the impression that I am talking quite a lot about myself, [you will] forgive me." (Cic. *Sest.* 31)

Hunc lucum nē quis violātō, neque exvehitō neque exfertō quod lūcī sit. "Let no one violate this grove, nor cart away or carry away what belongs to the grove." (*C.I.L.* 1².366, spelling adapted)

Salictum suō tempore caeditō, glūbitō artēque alligātō; librum conservātō. "Cut willow twigs at the right time, peel them, and tie them tight; save the bark." (Cato *Agr.* 33.5)

Cum pepererunt, tollere substrāmen et recens aliut subicere. "When they have laid their eggs, take the straw away and put fresh straw under them." (Varro *R.R.* 3.9.8)

233. A **prohibition (negative command)** is construed with *nē* + **perfect subjunctive** (without any past or anterior meaning). A prohibition in the imperative does not occur in classical Latin prose, but it does occur in poetry (as in the example from Virgil that follows) and in older Latin.

Sī Bona Fortūna veniat, nē intrōmīseris. "If Good Fortune should come, do not let her in!" (Plautus *Aul.* 100)

Equō nē crēdite, Teucrī. "Do not trust that horse, Trojans." (Virg. *Aen.* 2.48)

234. Periphrastic prohibitions and commands are frequently used in expressions like *nōlī(te)* + **infinitive** 'please do not', *cavē(te)* + **subjunctive** 'beware that you do not', *fac(ite) (ut)* + **subjunctive** 'see that you, please do', and *curā(te) ut* + **subjunctive** 'take care that'. These constructions reflect familiar speech or express softened commands and prohibitions.

Nōlīte existumāre māiōrēs nostrōs armīs rem pūblicam ex parvā magnam fēcisse. "Do not think, I pray, that our ancestors have brought our state from small to great by means of arms." (Sall. *Cat.* 52.19)
Cavē quemquam aliēnum in aedēs intrōmīseris. "Beware you do not let some stranger enter into the house." (Plautus *Aul.* 90)
Fac modo ut veniās. "Only make sure you come." (Cic. *Att.* 3.4)
Cūrā ut valeās. "Take care of your health." (Cic. *Att.* 3.5)

235. An **exhortation** also expresses the will of the speaker, but in a more gentle way than a command or a prohibition. It can occur in all persons. The negation is expressed with *nē*. English translations usually start with the phrase *let me/him/us/them*. Particularly in the second person, the English translation should contain some softening particle reflecting speaker attitude, such as *please* or *only*.

   Hūc coeāmus. "Let us meet here." (Ovid *Met.* 3.386)
   Cētera, quamquam ferenda non sunt, ferāmus. "Although the rest is not bearable, let us bear it anyway." (Cic. *Fam.* 14.4.5)
   Sī est spēs nostrī reditūs, eam confirmēs et rem adiuvēs. "If there is any hope for my return, please confirm it and help our case forward." (Cic. *Fam.* 14.4.3)
   Auxilium petās ab omnibus, etiam ab infimīs. "Only ask for help from anyone, even from the lower classes." (Sall. *Cat.* 44.5)

236. A **wish** or **prayer** is expressed in the **subjunctive** (negation with *nē*). Since a wish is not a real fact, the tenses correspond to those of the potential modality and the contrary-to-fact modality.

   a) If a wish or prayer or malediction is **realizable (in the future)**, it is put in the **present or perfect subjunctive** (without difference in meaning), sometimes introduced by the particle *utinam* or *ut*.

   b) If a wish is **unrealizable now**, it is construed with *utinam* or *ut* + **imperfect subjunctive**; if it is **unrealizable in the past**, *utinam* or *ut* + **pluperfect subjunctive** is used.

   In English, the modal auxiliary *may* is generally used for a wish for the future; such phrases as *if only he were(n't),* or *I wish he were(n't)* are used for the unrealizable wish now; and such phrases as *if only he had (not) been* or *I wish I had (not)* are used for unrealizable wishes in the past.

   Sit tibi terra lēvis. "May earth be light for you." (traditional epitaph)
   Lesbia mē dispeream nisi amat. "May I fall dead if Lesbia does not love me." (Catullus 92.2) (See § 389 on the word order here.)
   Huīc utinam aliquandō gratiam referre possīmus. "May we have the chance to thank him sometime." (Cic. *Fam.* 14.4.2)
   Utinam fortūnā nunc aniīīnā ūterer. "If only I now had the chance to be a duck!" (Plautus *Ru.* 533)
   Utinam minus vītae cupidī fuissēmus. "If only we had enjoyed life less!" (Cic. *Fam.* 14.4.1)

Concession

237. A **concession** occurs as a main clause and is put in the **subjunctive**.

> *Omnia* **possideat,** *non possidet aera Mīnōs.* "Minos may possess everything, he does not possess the air." (Ovid *Met.* 8.187)

Synopsis

238. Synopsis of sentence types (main clauses) and the use of moods

Sentence type	Real	Possible		Contrary to fact	
		Present	**Past**	**Present**	**Past**
Declarative	indicative	present/perfect subjunctive	imperfect subjunctive	imperfect subjunctive	pluperfect subjunctive
Interrogative	indicative	present/perfect subjunctive	imperfect subjunctive	imperfect subjunctive	pluperfect subjunctive
Rhetorical question	indicative	present/perfect subjunctive	imperfect subjunctive	imperfect subjunctive	pluperfect subjunctive

	Realizable		**Unrealizable**	
			Present	**Past**
Wish (volitive)	*(Ut, Utinam +)* present/perfect subjunctive		*Ut, Utinam +* imperfect subjunctive	*Ut, Utinam +* pluperfect subjunctive
Deliberative question	present subjunctive (present)		imperfect subjunctive (past)	
Exhortation (volitive)	present subjunctive		—	
Command (volitive)	imperative (present or future)		—	
Prohibition (volitive)	*nē* + perfect subjunctive		—	
Concession	subjunctive		—	

12
The Subject

Definition

239. **The subject is the first (and sometimes only) obligatory constituent with the predicate (§ 180). It is the constituent with which the predicate agrees** (§ 242). It is a syntactic category in the sentence structure: it has a **function** in the sentence.

240. The subject is often an agent: an animate entity that performs an action (§ 205, 209). However, this semantic role is not an essential characteristic of the subject; there also exist non-agent subjects (§ 205) and patient subjects (§ 206). The subject can also be a thing.

The subject is often the theme of the sentence and for that reason is put at the beginning of the sentence. However, not all subjects are themes. Every constituent can be a theme and occur at the beginning of the sentence. The subject occurs toward the end of the sentence when it is rhematic (§ 383).

Case and agreement

241. The subject stands in the **nominative** in main and dependent clauses with a finite verb and in main clauses with a historical infinitive (§ 225). It stands in the **accusative** in an infinitive clause (§ 266) and in the **ablative** in the ablative absolute (§ 350).

242. The subject governs the **agreement** of the predicate in person, number, gender, and case, if these categories are present in the predicate (§ 195–203). If the nominal part of the predicate is a noun, it has its own gender.

243. **If the subject is a demonstrative, interrogative, or relative pronoun, reverse agreement occurs**: the subject pronoun agrees with the predicate noun (§ 202).

Form of the subject

244. A typical subject has the form of a **noun**. It can be expanded to a **noun phrase** by means of an attribute or an attributive clause (chap. 16). Other possible forms of the subject are a **pronoun**, an **adjective** or **participle** used independently, or a **phrase** with one of these as its head. A subject is often **understood** (ø) because as theme it is already known from the preceding sentence (§ 383). Also, **personal pronouns** of the first and second person are often thematic (known from the speech situation) and thus not expressed in classical Latin, unless there is a reason to mention them.

> *Druidēs ā bellō abesse consuērunt neque tributa ūnā cum reliquīs pendunt.* "The druids usually do not participate in war and do not pay taxes like the others." (Caes. *B.G.* 6.14.1) (In both Latin and English, the subject of *pendunt* 'pay' is understood.)
>
> *Appārent rārī **nantes** in gurgite vastō.* "Here and there swimmers appear in the enormous whirlpool." (Virg. *Aen.* 1.118)

245. The subject can consist of an **infinitive** or **infinitive phrase**. In such a case, the predicate is either a **predicate noun + copula** or an **impersonal verb**. So-called impersonal verbs are *licet* 'it is allowed', *libet* 'it pleases', *decet* 'it suits', *dēdecet* 'it is a disgrace', *placet* 'it pleases', *oportet* 'it is needed', *praestat* 'it is better', *interest/refert* 'it is in the interest', *mē paenitet* 'I regret', *mē pudet* 'I am ashamed', *mē piget* 'it disgusts me, I am sorry'. In English translation, there is often an initial dummy subject (*it*) and a real subject (*to* + infinitive) after the predicate, or there is a gerund as subject before the predicate.

> *Errāre hūmānum est.* "To err is human." Or "It is human to err." (after Hieronymus)
>
> *Perfacile esse **imperiō potīrī**.* "It is very easy to seize power." Or "Seizing power is very easy." (Caes. *B.G.* 1.2.2)
>
> *Placuit **egredī in litus**.* "They decided to go out to the shore." Or "It pleased them to go out to the shore." (Pliny 6.16.17)

246. The subject can consist of a dependent clause in one of several forms:

   a) an **infinitive clause**;

   b) an **indirect question**;

   c) a **dependent clause** introduced by *quod* (cause) with verbs of happening (sometimes such a clause is an epexegetic clause, explaining a demonstrative pronoun that serves as a dummy subject);

   d) a **dependent clause** introduced by *ut* (result) with verbs of happening;

   e) a **dependent clause in the subjunctive without the conjunction** *ut* with the verbs *oportet, licet,* and *necesse est.*

> *Germānōs consuescere Rhēnum transīre* perīculōsum [est]. "That the Germani get accustomed to crossing the Rhine is dangerous." (Caes. *B.G.* 1.33.3)
>
> *Reī pūblicae communisque salūtis [interest] **manūs hostium distinērī**.* "It is in the interest of the state and the common safety that the forces of the enemy be kept apart." (Caes. *B.G.* 2.5.2)

*Incrēdibile memorātū est **quam facile coaluerint**.* "It is incredible to mention how easily they coalesced." (Sall. *Cat.* 6.2)

*Accidit perincommode **quod eum nusquam vīdistī**.* "It happened unfortunately that you did not see him anywhere." (Cic. *Att.* 1.17.2) (The clause with *quod* is not an adverbial clause: *quod* cannot be translated by *because.*)

*Illud mihi occurrit **quod uxor ā Dolābella discessit**.* "It occurred to me that Dolabella's spouse left him." (Cic. *Fam.* 8.6.1)

*Eādem nocte accidit **ut esset plēna luna**.* "In that same night, it happened that the moon was full." (Caes. *B.G.* 4.29.1)

*****Faber haec faciat** oportet.* "A craftsman should do the following." Or "It is needed that . . ." (Cato *Agr.* 14.1)

Remark. For the construction of all these dependent clauses and their sequence of tenses, see § 266–71, 275–80, 347–48.

Predicates without subject

247. A sentence does not contain a subject

a) with verbs expressing a **natural phenomenon**: *pluit* 'it rains', *fulget* 'it lightens', *ningit* 'it snows', *tonat* 'it thunders', *lūcet* 'it is daylight', and so on.

b) with **impersonal verbs expressing a feeling**: *mē miseret* 'I pity', *mē paenitet* 'I am sorry', *mē piget* 'I repent', *mē pudet* 'I am ashamed', *mē taedet* 'I am disgusted', and so on. Usually these verbs have two objects (§ 263). These verbs do have a subject if this subject is a pronoun, an infinitive, or an infinitive phrase (§ 245, 263).

c) with an **impersonal passive** (both of transitive and intransitive verbs): *turbātur* 'there is disturbance', *pugnātur* 'there is fighting, there is a fight, they fight', *ītur* 'one goes, they go' (§ 208).

d) with the **impersonal gerundive (verbal adjective)** (§ 208).

13
The Object

Definition and terminology

248. Whereas the subject is the first obligatory constituent with the predicate, the **object** is **the second or third obligatory sentence constituent with the predicate**. How many objects there are and which cases are used depend on the predicate frame of the active verb (§ 180).

If the action of the verb passes (*transīre*) directly from the subject to an object, this object is called a **direct object** of a **transitive verb**. This obligatory constituent stands in the **accusative** in Latin. Such a direct object has the semantic role of **patient** (or **undergoer**), and, for that reason, can be the subject as patient of the same verb in the **passive voice**.

If such an obligatory constituent (object) without preposition occurs in the genitive, dative, or ablative, it is called an **indirect object**. It does not have the semantic role of patient and cannot be the subject of the passive verb. In such a case, the verb is called **intransitive**.

An active verb expressing the idea of giving, saying, or showing is construed with a direct object as patient and an indirect object as recipient. Such a trivalent verb is transitive because the direct object can be the subject as patient of the passive verb. However, unlike in English, the indirect object cannot be such.

If the object consists not of a noun or noun phrase but of a dependent clause, this obligatory constituent is called an **object clause**.

Predicates with a subject and one object

249. Many predicates have, in addition to their subject, only one object. Often, this is a noun or its equivalent (§ 244). Its form and case can vary a great deal.

With **transitive verbs**, the object stands in the **accusative**. It is the **patient** (or **undergoer**). Such an object as patient can be the subject as patient of the passive verb (§ 147–51, 206).

Barba nōn facit philosophum. "The beard does not make the philosopher." (saying)
Cervus in liquōre vīdit effigiem suam. "A deer saw its own image in the water." (Phaedrus 1.12 *Cervus ad fontem* 3–4)

250. **Intransitive predicates (verbs and adjectives) can have an (indirect) object in the genitive, dative, or ablative.** Depending on the case, such an object is also called a genitive object, a dative object, or an ablative object. Some verbs and adjectives, particularly compound ones, are construed with a **prepositional object**. So *colloqui* 'talk to' is construed with a prepositional object (*cum* + ablative) or a dative object, whereas *loqui* 'speak' has a direct object or is used intransitively.

The semantic role of such objects is not that of patient but the one expressed by the case (§ 125, 136, 138, 162–63). An indirect object or prepositional object cannot be the subject of a passive verb. In the English translation, either of them can be a direct object or a prepositional object.

> *Veteris contuméliae oblīviscī [voluit].* "He wanted to forget the old insult." (Caes. *B.G.* 1.14.3) (gen. object)
>
> *[Sugambrī] magnō pecoris numerō, cūius sunt cupidissimī barbarī, potiuntur.* "The Sugambri get hold of a great number of cattle, for which barbarians are very eager." (Caes. *B.G.* 6.35.6) (abl. object with *potiuntur*, gen. object with *cupidissimī*)
>
> *Multō sanguine ac volneribus ea Poenīs victoria stetit.* "That victory cost the Carthaginians a lot of blood and wounds." (Livy 23.30.2) (abl. object with *stetit*)
>
> *...tamquam respublica pecūniā abundāret.* "...as if the state abounded in money." (Valerius Max. *Mem.* 5.6.8) (abl. object)
>
> *Helvētiī ferē cotidiānīs proeliīs cum Germānīs contendunt.* "The Helvetii fight with the Germani in almost daily battles." (Caes. *B.G.* 1.1.4) (prepositional object)
>
> *[Oppidum] vacuum ab defensōribus esse audiēbat.* "He heard that the town was devoid of defenders." (Caes. *B.G.* 2.12.2) (prepositional object)
>
> *Iuventus plēraque Catilīnae inceptīs favēbat.* "The majority of the youth was in favor of Catiline's plans." (Sall. *Cat.* 17.6) (dat. object)
>
> *Diviciācum atque Haeduōs fīnibus Bellovacōrum appropinquāre cognōverant.* "They had learned that Diviciacus and the Haedui were approaching the territory of the Bellovaci." (Caes. *B.G.* 2.10.5) (dat. object)
>
> *Reliquae [erant] ad navigandum inūtilēs.* "The remaining [ships] were useless for sailing." (Caes. *B.G.* 4.29.3) (prepositional object)
>
> *Sunt nōbīs mītia pōma.* "I have mellow apples." (Virg. *Buc.* 1.80) (dat. object of possessor)

251. The object slot can be filled by a **monologue** (a text in direct speech) or an **infinitive phrase**. For the infinitive clause in indirect speech, see § 261, 273, 284.

> *"Unde venīs?" exclāmat, "Nīl mihi respondēs? Aut dīc aut accipe calcem."* "'Where do you come from?' he shouted. 'Aren't you answering me? Tell me or you get a kick.'" (Iuv. *Sat.* 3.292–95)

Nequeō patī. "I can not stand it anymore." (Plautus *Aul.* 726)
Vincere *scīs, Hannibal,* **victōriā** *ūtī* **nescīs.** "Win, you can, Hannibal, but use your victory, you cannot." (Livy 22.51.4)
Transīre Tiberim et intrāre castra hostium *volō.* "I want to cross the Tiber and enter into the camp of the enemy." (Livy 2.12.5)

252. **Verbs of actual or intellectual perception** (*verba sentiendi*)—such as *sentīre, vidēre, cernere, audīre, conspicere, intellegere,* and *cognoscere*— take an **infinitive clause as object clause**. Unlike the Latin infinitive clause, the English translation uses a conjunction (*that*) to introduce the dependent clause containing a finite verb.

> *Caesar cognōvit* **Vercingetorīgem castra movisse propius Avaricum.** "Caesar learned that Vercingetorix had moved his camp closer to Avaricum." (Caes. *B.G.* 7.18.1)

> **Remark.** Verbs of perception can be construed with an **infinitive clause** or with a **participial clause** as object.

> **Patēre tua consilia** *nōn sentīs?* "That your plans are clear, don't you feel that?" (Cic. *Cat.* 1.1)
> **Uxōrem tuam neque gementem neque plōrantem** *audīvimus.* "We did not hear your wife sigh or wail." (Plautus *Amph.* 1098–99)

> However, there is a significant difference in meaning and a difference in translation between an infinitive clause and a participial clause. Compare *audiō eum venientem*, 'I hear him come,' with *audiō eum venīre*, 'I hear [others say] that he is coming.' See § 253, first example, and § 304, first example.

253. **Verbs of emotion** (*verba affectuum*) are construed with an **object clause**, consisting either of an **infinitive clause**, or of a **clause** introduced by *quod* **+ indicative** for real causes or *quod* **+ subjunctive** for subjective reasons of the subject of the main clause. For the object clause, the English translation uses the conjunction *that*, not *because*, which would introduce an adverbial clause.

> *Gaudē* **quod spectant oculī tē mille loquentem.** "Rejoice that a thousand eyes see you speaking." (Hor. *Epist.* 1.6.19)
> *Līber indoluit* **quod nōn meliōra petisset.** "Bacchus regretted that he [Midas] had not asked for better [according to Bacchus] things." (Ovid *Met.* 11.105)
> *Molestissimē ferō* **quod tē ubī vīsūrus sim nesciō.** "I find it very annoying that I do not know where I will see you." (Cic. *Fam.* 3.6.5)
> *[Nonnullī Gallī]* **populī Rōmānī exercitum hiemāre in Galliā** *molestē ferēbant.* "Some Gauls found it annoying that the army of the Roman people was wintering in Gaul." (Caes. *B.G.* 2.1.3)

254. Some **verbs of will and desire** (*verba volendi*) are construed with an **infinitive clause** as object: *velle, nōlle, mālle; cogere, iubēre, vetāre; cupere, sinere, patī; prohibēre.* The subject of an infinitive clause with these verbs is different from that of the main clause. The infinitive clause is not to be confused with the infinitive or infinitive phrase with some of these verbs of will or desire, as in the last example of § 251.

> *Caesar suīs quoque rēbus eōs timēre voluit.* "Caesar wanted them also to fear for their own possessions." (Caes. *B.G.* 4.16.1)
>
> *Hostēs Lūtēciam incendī iubent.* "The enemies ordered Lutecia to be burned [literally, "that Lutecia be burned"]." (Caes. *B.G.* 7.58.6)
>
> *Caesar Helvētiōs in fīnēs suōs revertī iussit.* "Caesar ordered the Helvetians to return to their own territory." (Caes. *B.G.* 1.28.3)
>
> *[Gracchus] vetābat quemquam cīvem plus quingentīs iūgeribus habēre.* "Gracchus forbade that a citizen have more than five hundred *iūgera.*" (Velleius Paterculus *Hist. Rom.* 2.6.3) (five hundred *iūgera* = ca. 330 acres = ca. 130 hectares).

Remark. The subjects of the last two infinitive clauses in the preceding examples (*Helvētiōs* and *quemquam cīvem*) are sometimes considered objects of the main verb (as the result of a transformation called "subject to object raising"). However, by analogy with the first two sentences, it seems better, at least with respect to Latin, to consider those two constituents subjects of the infinitive clause.

255. Some **verbs of will and desire** (*verba volendi*)—for example, *hortārī, postulāre, monēre, petere, ōrāre, cūrāre, facere* and sometimes *velle, nōlle, mālle,* and so on—take an **object clause of purpose** with *ut/nē* + **subjunctive.** The conjunction *ut* is often omitted. *Ut* in such an object clause is translated by *to,* never by *in order to* (as in an adverbial clause: see § 341).

> *Fac modo ut veniās.* "Only make sure you come." (Cic. *Att.* 3.4)
>
> *Senātus dēcrēvit darent operam consulēs nē quid respūblica dētrīmentī caperet.* "The senate decided that the consuls should pay attention that the State not suffer any damage." (Sall. *Cat.* 29.2) (The object clause of the first degree is not introduced by a conjunction *ut.* This clause in turn contains an object clause of the second degree, which is also an object clause with a verb of will or desire (*verbum volendi*). The second object clause is introduced by *nē.*)
>
> *[Membra conspīrāvērunt] inde nē manūs ad ōs cibum ferrent.* "Therefore, the parts [of the body] agreed that the hands would not bring the food to the mouth." (Livy 2.32.10)
>
> *Id velim sit eīus modī ut rectē spērāre possimus.* "I wish things were such that I could rightly hope." (Cic. *Fam.* 14.4.5)

256. **Verbs of fearing** (*verba timendi*) have **an object clause of purpose** with *nē* or *nē nōn* + **subjunctive.** The conjunction is negative (*nē*) if one fears something, because it is the purpose, intent, or wish that something does

not happen. Compare the French construction, as shown with the first two examples that follow.

> *Timeō nē veniat.* 'I fear that he is coming.' Or 'I fear lest he come.' In French, 'Je crains qu'il **ne** vienne.'
>
> *Timeō nē nōn veniat.* 'I fear that he is not coming.' In French: 'Je crains qu'il **ne** vienne **pas**.'
>
> *Quō factō cum [nōn] timērent nē āversī ab hoste circumvenīrentur, audācius resistere coepērunt.* "As, through that maneuver, they were not afraid to be surrounded by the enemy in the rear, they began to resist more audaciously." (Caes. *B.G.* 2.26.2)

257. **Verbs of hindering** have an **object clause of purpose** with *nē, quōminus*, or *quīn* + subjunctive. These conjunctions contain a negative element because something that was intended to happen does not. *Quōminus* equals *ut eō minus* 'that thereby the less'. This negative aspect does not occur in English translation, which usually has the form *(prevent someone) from* + gerund (with the ending *-ing*).

> *Caesarem deterrēre posse nē māior multitūdō Germānōrum Rhēnum trādūcātur.* "Caesar was able to prevent a greater number of Germani from crossing the Rhine." (Caes. *B.G.* 1.31.16)
>
> *Quid obstat quōminus [deus] sit beātus?* "What is in the way of god's being happy?" (Cic. *N.D.* 1.95)

258. **Verbs of doubt and uncertainty, when negative or interrogative,** are construed with an **object clause of result** with *quīn* + subjunctive.

> *Nōn fuerat mihi dubium quīn tē Tarentī aut Brindisī vīsūrum essem.* "I had not doubted that I was going to see you in Tarentum or Brindisium." (Cic. *Att.* 3.6)
>
> *Neque abest suspiciō quīn ipse sibi mortem cōnscīverit.* "There is a strong suspicion that he committed suicide." (Caes. *B.G.* 1.4.4)
>
> *Facere nōn possum quīn cottidiē ad tē mittam [litterās].* "I cannot help sending a letter to you daily." Or "I cannot do without daily sending a letter to you." (Cic. *Att.* 12.27.2)

259. **Verbs of asking** have as an **object clause** an **indirect question in the subjunctive** (§ 275–80).

> *Puer Papīrius quid māter institisset, quid ipse mātrī dīxisset dēnarrat.* "The boy Papirius told what his mother had insisted on and what he had said to his mother." (A. Gellius *Noctes Att.* 1.23)
>
> *Quaesīvī cognōsceretne signum.* "I asked him if he recognized the seal." (Cic. *Cat.* 3.10)

Predicates with a subject and two objects

260. **Some predicates require** not only a subject and a (direct or indirect) object but also **a third object** (in the acc., gen., dat., or abl.; or a prepositional object; or an object clause). The following table shows a number of possible combinations of objects with some predicates. The complete example sentences follow the table (§ 261–62).

Predicate	1 Subject	2 Object	3 Indirect object	Remarks on 2 and 3
da	∅	*argentum*	*nōbīs*	direct object + indirect object (§ 261)
inquam	*ego*	*"Studēs?"*	*huīc*	direct object (direct question) + indirect object
respondēs	*tū*	*nīl*	*mihi*	direct object + indirect object (§ 261)
respondit	*Caesar*	*sēsē pacem esse factūrum*	*hīs*	object clause + indirect object (§ 261)
docēbō	*ego*	*tē*	*tua fata*	2 accusatives (§ 151)
trādūxit	*Caesar*	*exercitum*	*Axonam*	2 accusatives (§ 150)
condemnō	*ego*	*mē*	*inertiae*	accusative + genitive with judicial verbs (§ 132)
accomodat	*Daedalus*	*ālās*	*umerīs*	accusative + dative with compound verbs (§ 138c)
liberābis	*tū*	*mē*	*magnō metū*	accusative + ablative
prohibēre	*sēsē*	*vim*	*ab oppidīs*	accusative + prepositional object
hortāris	*tū*	*mē*	*ut animō sim magnō*	accusative + object clause (indirect command, § 255)
percontāta est	*māter*	*fīlium*	*quid pătres ēgissent*	accusative + object clause (indirect question, § 259)
persuāsit	*is*	*cīvitātī*	*ut dē fīnibus exīrent*	dative + object clause (indirect command, § 274)

261. **Verbs of saying (*verba declarandi*) and verbs of giving (*verba dandi*) require a subject, a direct object (either a noun phrase or a clause), and also a third obligatory constituent: the indirect object as recipient**—the person to whom the message or the thing is given, said, or shown (§ 137). In English, the indirect object as recipient is recognizable by the preposition *to,* which is omitted if the indirect object precedes the direct object (as in *give something to someone, give someone something*). In Latin (and most Western European languages), the indirect object cannot be the subject of a passive sentence. In English, both the direct and the indirect object of such verbs can be the subject of a passive sentence (as in *something is given to someone, someone is given something*).

> *Da istud argentum **nōbīs**.* "Give that money to us." (Plautus *As.* 692)
> ***Huīc** ego "Studēs?" inquam.* "'Are you a student?' I asked him." (Pliny 4.13.3)
> *Nīl **mihi** respondēs?* "Aren't you answering me?" (Iuv. *Sat.* 3.295)
> ***Hīs** Caesar ita respondit sēsē cum iīs pacem esse factūrum.* "Caesar answered them that he would conclude peace with them." (Caes. *B.G.* 1.14.1–6)

262. The following sentences contain **examples of the two types of objects**, direct and indirect (but the latter not as a recipient). The third obligatory constituent is printed in bold type.

> *Tē **tua fata** docēbō.* "I will tell you your destiny." (Virg. *Aen.* 6.759)
> *[Caesar] **flumen Axonam** exercitum trādūcere mātūrāvit.* "Caesar hurried to bring his army over the river Axona." (Caes. *B.G.* 2.5.4)
> *Iam mē ipse **inertiae nēquitiaeque** condemnō.* "I condemn myself already for idleness and worthlessness." (Cic. *Cat.* 1.4)
> *[Daedalus] ignōtās **umerīs** accomodat ālās.* "Daedalus attached the únknówn wings to the shoulders." (Ovid *Met.* 8.209) (The accents on *únknówn* render the Latin hyperbaton §432.)
> ***Magnō** mē **metū** liberābis.* "You will free me from a great fear." (Cic. *Cat.* 1.10)
> *Ambarrī Caesarem certiōrem faciunt sēsē nōn facile **ab oppidīs** vim hostium prohibēre.* "The Ambarri inform Caesar that they do not easily protect their towns from the violence of the enemy." (Caes. *B.G.* 1.11.4)
> *Tū mē hortāris **ut animō sim magnō**.* "You encourage me to pull myself together." (Cic. *Fam.* 14.4.5)
> *Māter Papīriī puerī percontāta est fīlium **quidnam in senātū pătrēs ēgissent**.* "The mother of young Papirius asked her son what the senators had discussed in the senate." (A. Gellius *Noctes Att.* 1.23)
> *Is cīvitātī persuāsit **ut dē fīnibus suīs exīrent**.* "He persuaded his tribe to leave their own territory." (Caes. *B.G.* 1.2.1)

Predicates without a subject and with two objects

263. Some **impersonal verbs** expressing an emotion (see the list in § 247b) do not have a subject but do **have two objects**: one in the **accusative** for the person having an emotion and one in the **genitive** for the object of the emotion. The expression *opus est alicuī aliquā rē* 'someone needs something' is construed with a person in the dative and a thing in the ablative.

> *Data mercēs est errōris meī magna ut **mē** nōn sōlum pigeat **stultitūdine meae**, sed etiam pudeat.* "I have paid a high price for my mistake, so

that I not only regret my silliness but also am ashamed of it." (Cic. *Dom.* 29)

Remark. These impersonal verbs do have a subject if this subject is a pronoun, an infinitive, or an infinitive phrase (§ 245, 247).

*Ariovistus respondit si **quid** [subject] **ipsī** [dat. object] ā Caesare opus esset, sēsē ad eum ventūrum fuisse.* "Ariovistus answered that if he needed something from Caesar, he would have come to him." (Caes. *B.G.* 1.34.2)

*Mē, mī Pomponī, valde paenitet **vīvere**.* "My dear Pomponius, I intensely regret being alive." (Cic. *Att.* 3.4)

Predicates with various constructions

264. Some verbs have more than one predicate frame (hence different functions and roles), but without much difference in meaning.

> *docēre aliquem litterās* 'teach someone literature'
> *docēre aliquem dē suō adventū* 'inform someone about one's arrival'
>
> *donāre alicuī cīvitātem* 'give citizenship to someone'
> *donāre aliquem cīvitāte* 'bestow citizenship on someone'

265. Some verbs have various predicate frames with differences in meaning. The various constructions and their meaning are listed in the dictionary.

> *Timeō **Danaōs*** "I am afraid of the Greeks." (Virg. *Aen.* 2.49)
> *[Daedalus] **comitī** timet.* "Daedalus is afraid for this companion." (Ovid *Met.* 8.213)
>
> *consulere* (intransitive) 'to deliberate'
> *consulere senātum* 'to consult the senate'
> *consulere rēī pūblicae* 'to look after (the interests of) the state'
> *consulere crūdēliter in victōs* 'take cruel measures against the defeated'
> *consulere ut ...* 'take care that ...'
>
> *Dīcō **eum venīre**.* 'I say he is coming.' (indirect statement in the infinitive clause)
> *Dīcō **ut veniat**.* 'I tell him to come.' (indirect command with *ut* + subjunctive)
> *Dīcō **quis veniat**.* 'I say who is coming.' (indirect question in the subjunctive)

Infinitive clause and sequence of tenses

266. Definition and characteristics. The infinitive clause is a **dependent clause** with the following characteristics.

- **There is no conjunction.**
- **The predicate is an infinitive** (not a finite verb).
- The **subject** and hence also the **predicate** (if declinable) are in the **accusative**.

267. Translation. In English, the infinitive clause as dependent clause is translated in various ways.

   a) If the infinitive clause is an indirect statement with a verb of saying or if it depends on a verb of perceiving, the English subordinate clause contains a finite verb and possibly the conjunction *that*. For examples, see the infinitive clauses in § 252, 261–62, 265, 270, 273, 281–82. On the translation of longer pieces of indirect speech, see § 284. It should be noted that in an infinitive clause, the reflexive pronoun *sē* 'he/she/they' refers to the subject of the main clause. This may not always be clear in the English translation, which uses a personal pronoun (*he/she/they*).
   b) If the infinitive clause is an indirect command, the English translation puts the accusative subject of the Latin infinitive clause in the object form (e.g., *him*) and uses the infinitive (*to* + verb). For examples, see § 254, with remark.

268. Function. The infinitive clause can be the **subject clause** of a predicate noun with *esse* or of so-called impersonal verbs, such as *appāret* 'it becomes clear', *constat* 'it is (well) established', *decet* 'it suits', *libet* 'it pleases', *licet* 'it is allowed', *oportet* 'it ought', *placet* 'it pleases', *praestat* 'it is better', *expedit* 'it is useful', *necesse est* 'it is necessary', and so on. In English, there is a dummy subject (*it*) before that impersonal verb unless a personal verb is used to translate the Latin verb.

> ***Pătrem familiae villam rusticam bene aedificātam habēre* expedit.** "It is expedient that the master of the household have a well-built country farm." Or "It is expedient for the master of the household to have a well-built country farm." (Cato Agr. 3.2)
> ***Ad mortem tē dūcī* iam prīdem oportēbat.** "You should have already been put to death a long time ago." Literally, "It was needed already a long time ago that you be put to death." (Cic. *Cat.* 1.2)
> *Ita fit vērum illud, quod initiō dīxī,* **amīcitiam nisi inter bonōs esse nōn posse.** "So what I said in the beginning becomes true, that friendship can only exist between good people." (Cic. *Amic.* 65)

269. More frequently, the infinitive clause occurs as an **object clause** with

   - *verba declarandi* (verbs of saying, § 261–62);
   - *verba sentiendi* (verbs of perception and thinking, § 252);
   - *verba affectuum* (verbs of emotion, § 253);
   - some *verba volendi* (verbs of will and desire, § 254).

270. Sequence of tenses. The tense of the verb in the infinitive clause expresses a certain relationship with respect to the governing verb. This relationship can be **simultaneous, anterior**, or **posterior**.

The tense of the governing verb plays no role in the Latin infinitive clause or in English constructions with *to* or the gerund, but it does in an English finite clause, as can be seen from the translations in the following table ('think he is in love,' 'thought he was in love'). This phenomenon, the adaptation of the tense of the subordinate verb to a past governing verb, is called **backshift. It only occurs in finite verb forms**, both in English and in Latin (§ 271, 278–80).

Sequence of tenses in the infinitive		
Simultaneity: imperfective infinitive (active/passive)	*Putō eum amāre/ amārī.* *Putābam eum amāre/ amārī.*	'I think (that) he is in love/ is loved.' 'I thought he was in love/ was loved.'
Anteriority: perfective infinitive (active/passive)	*Putō eum amāvisse/ amātum esse.* *Putābam eum amāvisse/ amātum esse.*	'I think he has been in love/ has been loved.' 'I thought he had been in love/ had been loved.'
Posteriority: future infinitive (active/passive)	*Putō eum amātūrum esse/ amātum īrī.* *Putābam eum amātūrum esse/ amātum īrī.*	'I think he will be in love/ will be loved.' 'I thought he would be in love/ would be loved.'

271. Remark. If a verb has no supine and hence no future participle and infinitive, **posteriority** can be expressed by a periphrastic construction with *futūrum esse ut* or *fore ut* + **present subjunctive** or **imperfect subjunctive**. The choice of the latter tense depends on the tense of the governing verb. If this is past, backshift applies to the dependent verb.

> *Spērō fore ut tē paeniteat* ... 'I hope you will regret ...' Literally, 'I hope that it will happen that you regret ...'
> *Spērēbam fore ut tē paenitēret* ... 'I hoped that you would regret ...'

Nominative with an infinitive

272. Some verbs having an infinitive clause as object can occur in a different construction. The subject of the infinitive clause occurs as the subject of the governing verb in the passive. The verb of the infinitive clause remains as an infinitive complement of the passive main verb. This construction is called the **personal passive** or *nominativus cum infinitivo* (*NcI*). The same construction occurs in English.

> *Dīcitur altam coctilibus murīs cinxisse Semīramis urbem.* "Semiramis is said to have surrounded the lofty city with brick walls." (Ovid *Met.* 4.57–58) (The equivalent with an infinitive clause would be *Hominēs*

dīcunt Semīramidem ... cinxisse ..., 'People say that Semiramis has surrounded ...')

Sabīnus iussus arma abicere imperātum facit. "Sabinus, ordered to throw down his arms, obeyed the command." (Caes. *B.G.* 5.37.1) (The corresponding active infinitive clause would be *Ambiorix iussit Sabīnum arma abicere.*)

Postēs radiāre videntur. "The door is seen to be shining." Or "One sees the door shine." (Ovid *Met.* 11.115)

Indirect statement

273. In direct speech, the words are given directly between quotation marks, as they are spoken. In indirect speech, the words spoken depend as an object on a governing verb. **In an indirect statement, those words depend on a verb of saying or thinking.** In Latin, an **indirect statement stands as an infinitive clause** in the following cases.

   a) **Statements**

   Dico me esse atriensem. "I say that I am the steward." (Plautus *As.* 352) (The corresponding direct statement would be *Dico: "Ego sum atriensis,"* 'I say: "I am the steward."')

   b) **Apparent relative clauses** (introduced by a **connecting relative pronoun**: see § 374), which in direct speech are actually independent clauses

   *Caesar vehementer eōs incūsāvit ... **ex quō iūdicārī posse quantum habēret in sē bonī constantia.*** "Caesar accused them violently, [saying] ... that one could judge from that how much good there was in firmness." (Caes. *B.G.* 1.40.1–6) (The corresponding direct statement would be *ex quō iūdicārī potest ...*, 'Thence one can judge ...')

   c) **Rhetorical questions**, which formally look like questions but actually are statements (§ 230, 454)

   Ubī fueris quem nostrum ignōrāre arbitrāris? "Who of us—do you think—does not know where you have been?" (Cic. *Cat.* 1.1) (The direct rhetorical question *Quis nostrum ignōrat ubī fueris?* equals the statement *Nēmō ignōrat ubī fueris ...*, 'Nobody does not know where ...')

Indirect command or prohibition

274. An **indirect command or prohibition** is put in the **subjunctive** with **verbs of will or desire** (*verba volendi*). An indirect command or prohibition is an object clause of purpose construed with *ut/nē* + subjunctive. The conjunction *ut(ī)* is often omitted. For the sequence of tenses, see § 347.

*Albānus exercitus inclāmāvit Curiātiīs **uti opem ferant fratrī**.* "The Alban army shouted to the Curiatii that they should help their brother (or "to help their brother")." (Livy 1.25.9) (The corresponding direct command would be *Opem **ferte** fratrī!* 'Help your brother!')

*Ariovistus postulāvit **nē quem peditem ad conloquium Caesar addūceret**.* "Ariovistus demanded that Caesar bring no infantry to the parley." (Caes. *B.G.* 1.42.4) (The corresponding direct prohibition would be *Nē quem peditem ad conloquium **adduxeris!*** 'Do not bring infantry to the parley!')

Indirect question and sequence of tenses

275. Whereas a direct question is an independent sentence (§ 228–31), **an indirect question is a dependent clause**. As a **subject clause**, it depends on a nominal predicate (§ 246b). More frequently, it depends as an **object clause** on a verb of asking (§ 259–60; 262, next-to-last example).

Just like direct questions, indirect questions are introduced by a **question particle** for **yes-no questions** and by an **interrogative pronoun or adverb** for **question-word questions**. In indirect questions, *nōnne* rarely occurs, while *-ne* and *num* are used without difference in meaning.

276. **An indirect question generally stands in the subjunctive.**

277. The verb of an indirect question has a certain **time relationship** to the governing verb.

    a) The tenses (active and passive) construed on the **imperfective stem** express **simultaneity.**

    b) The tenses construed on the **perfective stem** (active) or formed with the **PPP** express **anteriority.**

    c) The forms of the **periphrastic future** (future active participle + *sim* or *essem:* see § 100) express **posteriority**.

278. The tense of the verb of the indirect question is also determined by the **tense of the governing verb**. After a **present or future governing verb**, the verb of the indirect question stands in the present or perfect. After a **past governing verb** (imperfect, perfect, pluperfect, and sometimes—according to the author's choice—historical present), the verb of the indirect question stands in the imperfect or pluperfect. This **backshift** also applies to English (§ 270–71). See also § 284.

Simultaneity of the indirect question with the governing verb occurs in the following examples:

    *Quid mihi **reddat** ager quaeris* [present]. "You ask what my field yields me." (Mart. *Ep.* 2.38.1)

Quī sim ex eō cognoscēs [future]. "Who I am, you will learn from him." (Sall. *Cat.* 44.5)

Lentulus quaesīvit [past] *ā Gallīs* **quid sibi esset cum īīs**. "Lentulus asked the Gauls what he had to do with them." (Cic. *Cat.* 3.11)

Anteriority of the indirect question to the governing verb occurs in the following examples:

Quid proximā nocte ēgeris, quem nostrum ignōrāre arbitrāris? [present] "What you have done last night, who among us, do you think, does not know that?" (Cic. *Cat.* 1.1)

[Lentulus] quaesīvit [past] *ā Gallīs* **quam ob rem domum suam vēnissent**. "[Lentulus] asked the Gauls why they had come to his house." (Cic. *Cat.* 3.11)

Posteriority of the indirect question to the governing verb occurs in the following examples:

Consīderō [present] *quae condiciō vitae futūra sit.* "I contemplate what our living condition will be." (Sall. *Cat.* 20.6)

[Labienus] litterās Caesarī remittit [historical present taken as past] **quantō cum perīculō legiōnem ex hībernīs ēductūrus esset**. "Labienus answered Caesar by letter how dangerous it would be to lead the legion out of the winter camp." (Caes. *B.G.* 5.47.5)

279. Synopsis of the sequence of tenses in the indirect question

Time relationship of the verb of the indirect question with the governing verb	Tense of the verb of the indirect question	
	Depending on a present or future governing verb	Depending on a past governing verb
Simultaneity	present subjunctive	imperfect subjunctive
Anteriority	perfect subjunctive	pluperfect subjunctive
Posteriority	future active participle + *sim*, etc. (periphrastic future)	future active participle + *essem*, etc. (periphrastic future)

Rogō quis vincat/vincātur. 'I ask who defeats/is defeated.'
Rogāvī quis vinceret/vincerētur. 'I asked who defeated/was defeated.'

Rogō quis vīcerit/victus sit. 'I ask who has defeated/has been defeated.'

Rogāvī quis vīcisset/victus esset. 'I asked who had defeated/had been defeated.'

Rogō quis victūrus sit. 'I ask who will defeat.'
Rogāvī quis victūrus esset. 'I asked who would defeat.'

280. If an indirect question depends on a verbal form that is neither present nor past—that is, infinitive, participle, supine, or gerund—the tense of the indirect question depends on whether the verb governing that tenseless verb form is present or past.

Quibus terrārum militet ōrīs Claudius scīre labōrō. "I am very eager to know on which shores of the world Claudius is campaigning." (Hor. *Epist.* 1.31–32) (The dependent verb *militet* [present subjunctive] is simultaneous with *scīre*. This tenseless infinitive depends on *labōrō*. The tense of *militet* therefore depends on the present *labōrō*. If the main verb were *labōrābam*, then *scīre* would remain unchanged, but the verb of the indirect question would be in the imperfect subjunctive [*militāret*].)

Dependent clause in indirect statement, command, or question

281. **A dependent clause (a dependent clause of the second degree) in indirect speech stands in the subjunctive.** Dependent clauses that in direct speech already stood in the subjunctive remain in the subjunctive. Dependent clauses in the infinitive remain in the infinitive.

*Caesar reperiēbat [Nerviōs] incūsāre reliquōs Belgās, quī sē populō Rōmānō **dedissent**.* "Caesar found out that the Nervii accused the other Belgae who had surrendered to the Roman people." (Caes. *B.G.* 2.15.3–5) (The corresponding direct statement would be *Nerviī incūsābant ... Belgās, quī ... **dederant**.*)

Remark. The sequence of tenses (§ 277–80) is also respected in the preceding example. Since *reperiēbat* is a past tense and *incūsāre* is tenseless (neither present nor past), the verb of the relative clause in the indirect speech is in the pluperfect subjunctive. If the indirect statement were to depend on a present or future verb *reperit/reperiet*, the verb of the relative clause would be in the perfect subjunctive: *Reperit ... incūsāre ... dederint.*

282. Placing dependent clauses in the subjunctive has to do with the fact that such clauses are statements made by the subject of the verb of saying, commanding, or asking, not by the author. The author does not take on the responsibility of that statement but puts it in the subjunctive to attribute it to the speaker/writer, the subject of the governing clause. However, **if, in a text in indirect speech, a dependent clause is the opinion not only of the speaker/writer but also of the author of the work, then such a dependent clause stands in the indicative.**

Catilīna docet [historical present] *sē Manlium praemīsisse ad eam multitūdinem quam ad capiunda arma **parāverat**.* "Catiline informed [them] that he had sent Manlius to that crowd that he had prepared to take arms." (Sall. *Cat.* 27.3) (***Parāverat*** is information given not only by Catiline but also by the author, Sallust, who puts it in the indicative as a real fact.)

283. A dependent clause of the second (or lower) degree occurring in an infinitive clause or a subjunctive clause that is not an indirect statement or indirect question **can be in the subjunctive through attraction of mood.** The **mood** is thus **attracted** by the mood of the governing clause.

> *Huīc quoque accidit ut nōnnūllī milites, quī lignātiōnis mūnitiōnisque causā in silvās discessissent, repentīnō equitum adventū interciperentur.* "It also happened to him that some soldiers who had dispersed to fetch firewood and fortification materials were cut off by the sudden arrival of the horsemen." (Caes. *B.G.* 5.39.2)

Reference in direct and indirect speech

284. In large part, language refers, through words, to the world outside the text. Some deictic (pointing) words, however, point to a (first or second) **person** in a certain **time** and **place**. But the referent of those words can only be determined with respect to the interlocutors. For example, when, in a dialogue, a person A is speaking to a person B, *tū* initially refers to the person B, but in B's answer, *tū* refers to A. When a piece of direct speech is put into indirect speech (or vice versa), some shifts with regard to person, time, and place occur. When a text in the indirect speech is translated into direct speech, one has to take these shifts into account.

Indirect speech	Direct speech
sē 'he/she/they' (referring back to the subject of the governing clause)	*ego* 'I' or *nōs* 'we'
ille, is 'he'	*tū* 'you' or *ille, is* 'he'
tunc, tum 'then'	*nunc* 'now'
ibi, illic 'there'	*hīc* 'here'
pridiē 'the day before'	*herī* 'yesterday'
past tense after a governing past verb	present tense
subjunctive (indirect command)	imperative (command)
subjunctive (indirect question)	indicative (question in reality)

Longer stretches of indirect speech, particularly in the works of historians, usually are translated in English not in the indirect or direct style but in the **semi-direct** or **free indirect style.** The references are the same as in indirect speech, but the successive indirect statements (infinitive clauses), commands (subjunctive or infinitive clauses), and questions (subjunctive) are translated, with the exception of the first one(s), as **main clauses.** Compare the variations in translation style in the following example.

> *[Vercingetorix] peditātū quem anteā habuerat sē fore contentum dīcit, neque fortūnam temptātūrum aut in aciē dīmicātūrum; aequō modo animō suā ipsī frūmenta corrumpant aedificiaque incendant.* (Caes. *B.G.* 7.64.2–3)

Indirect style: "Vercingetorix said that **he would** be happy with the infantry **he had** had at **his** disposal before and that **he would** not try **his** fortune or fight in regular battle order; that for **their** part, **they should** just destroy, with resignation, **their** own crops and burn **their** buildings."

Direct style: "Vercingetorix said: '**I will** be happy with the infantry **I have** had at **my** disposal before and **I will** not try **my** fortune or fight in regular battle order. For **your** part, **you must** just destroy, with resignation, **your** own crops and burn **your** buildings.'"

Free indirect style: "Vercingetorix said that **he would** be happy with the infantry **he had** had at **his** disposal before. **He would** not try **his** fortune or fight in regular battle order. For **their** part, **they should** just destroy, with resignation, **their** own crops and burn **their** buildings."

14
Predicativum

285. Definition. The predicativum is a sentence constituent that expresses the state or function of another sentence constituent in relation to the predicate.

Ibant obscūrī sōlā sub nocte. "They went like shadows through the lonely night." (Virg. *Aen.* 6.268) (The predicativum [predicative apposition] *obscūrī* agrees with the understood plural masculine subject and indicates the state of the men, but it does this in relation to the predicate: it also tells how they went [*ībant*]. Notice that this verse contains a double hypallage [§ 431]. In prose, one might have written, also with a predicative apposition [*sōlī*], *Ibant sōlī obscūrā sub nocte,* 'They went lonely through the obscure night'.)

As the predicativum plays a role with respect to the predicate, it may be **translated** as an adverbial phrase. However, because of its agreement in case with the other constituent it determines, it cannot be **considered** an adverbial phrase in Latin. Because of its agreement with the other sentence constituent, it is sometimes difficult to distinguish a predicativum (e.g., *omnem* in the example that follows) from an attribute.

*Rem **omnem** aperit cūius grātiā mittēbantur; cētera utī factō opus sit, ita agant permittit.* "He [Cicero] explained in broad outline the affair for which they were sent; as for the rest, he allowed them to take action as needed." (Sall. *Cat.* 45.1) (*Rem omnem* cannot be interpreted as 'the whole affair' [noun + attribute], because *cētera,* in the next sentence, refers to the details of the affair.)

A sentence containing a predicativum can be said to contain two predications: one predication expressed by the (main) verbal or nominal predicate and one expressed by **the predicativum as an embedded predication**. In the first example in § 286, the main predication is that the housewives came together; the embedded predication is that the housewives are numerous.

When the predicativum is an obligatory constituent in certain predicate frames, it is a **predicative complement** (§ 181, 184, 288). When it is not obligatory, it is a **predicative apposition** (e.g., *obscūrī* and *omnem* in the preceding examples: see § 289).

286. The predicativum does not have its own case. It modifies another sentence constituent (subject, object, etc.) and agrees with it (though not in gender if it is a noun).

Tum matrōnae ad Veturiam, matrem Coriolānī, Volumniamque ux-
ōrem frequentēs coeunt. "Then, the housewives came together in great
numbers with Veturia, Coriolanus's mother, and Volumnia, his
spouse." (Livy 2.40.1) (*Frequentēs* agrees with *matrōnae* but modifies
both the subject [*matrōnae*] and the predicate [*coeunt*].)
Parentēs eam nōmināvērunt Claudiam. "Her parents called her Clau-
dia." (*C.I.L.* 6.15346) (*Claudiam* has to do and agrees with the direct
object [*eam*] and is the result of *nōmināvērunt.*)
Volturcius postrēmō velutī hostibus sēsē praetōribus dedit. "Finally
Volturcius surrendered to the praetors as to enemies (or "as if they
were enemies")." (Sall. *Cat.* 45.4)

287. The **translation** of a predicativum can take various forms in English, as
may be clear from the translations throughout this chapter. Very often,
English uses *as* (e.g., *as consul, as a boy*). Sometimes, there is no conjunction (with the translations of such verbs as *nōmināre, dīcere,* and *facere*).
Often, there is an adverbial phrase or clause in English. If the predicativum is accompanied by *tamquam, quasi ut, ut, sīcut,* or *velut,* this indicates a comparison and is translated with English *as* or *as if.*

288. The predicativum occurs as an **obligatory predicative complement** with
certain predicates:

– *putāre, existimāre, dūcere, habēre,* and so on 'consider';
– *appellāre, vocāre, dīcere, nōmināre, creāre,* and so on 'name, call,
nominate';
– *facere, reddere,* and so on 'make'.

Omnēs [eum] hostem atque parricīdam vocāre. "They all called
him an enemy and a traitor." (Sall. *Cat.* 31.8)
Haeduōs, fratrēs consanguineōsque ā senātū appellātōs, . . . "The
Haedui, who had been called brothers and kin by the senate, . . ."
(Caes. *B.G.* 1.33.2)

289. The predicative complement is sometimes construed with a prepositional phrase: *aliquem prō amīcō habēre, in numerō (locō) amīcōrum
habēre (dūcere, putāre)* 'consider someone a friend'. For a predicative
complement in the genitive, see § 317, remark c.

290. The following words occur as **non-obligatory predicative appositions**.

a) Nouns indicating an age or function.

[Senex revertī] in pătriam, unde puer profectus sum. "As an old
man I returned to my country from where I had left as a boy."
(Livy 30.30.10)
Quod vispillō facit, fēcerat et medicus. "What he does as an un-
dertaker, he also had done as a doctor." (Mart. *Ep.* 1.47.2)

b) Adjectives of quantity: *ūnus, sōlus, omnis, singulī, ūniversus, tōtus, uterque, crēber, frequens, paucī, plērīque*, and so on.

> *Gallia est **omnis** dīvīsa in partēs trēs.* "Gaul as a whole is divided into three parts." (Caes. *B.G.* 1.1.1)
> *Iuventus **plēraque** Catilīnae inceptīs favēbat.* "The youth for the most part was favorable to Catiline's plans." (Sall. *Cat.* 17.6)

c) Ordinal adjectives indicating number or rank: *prīmus, ultimus, princeps, posterior*, and so on.

> *[Hannibal] **princeps** in proelium ībat, **ultimus** excēdēbat.* "Hannibal always went as the first into the battle and left it as the last." Or "Hannibal always was the first to enter into the battle and the last to leave." (Livy 21.4.8)

d) Adjectives and participles expressing a temporal physical or mental disposition: *absens, praesens, libens, invītus, laetus, maestus, vīvus, sciens, ignārus, aeger, rārus, sērus, nocturnus, tacitus, flens, lacrimans, īrātus*, and so on.

> *En ipse capellas prōtinus **aeger** agō.* "Look, I myself drive my goats forward, sick as I am." (Virg. *Buc.* 1.12–13)
> *Uxor amans **flentem flens** acrius ipsa tenēbat.* "My loving spouse held me crying while she herself was crying even more violently." (Ovid *Tr.* 1.3.17).
> *Ego vivō **miserrimus**.* "I live very miserably." (Cic. *Att.* 3.5)
> *Mīrābar quid **maesta** deōs, Amarylli, vocārēs.* "I was wondering why you, Amaryllis, were calling sadly upon the gods." (Virg. *Buc.* 1.36)

291. Sometimes it is difficult to distinguish among the following predicative constructions:

a) the copula *esse* (which in itself has no meaning) with a predicate noun or adjective;

b) Verbs with meaning—such as *fierī, vidērī, manēre*, or *appārēre*—that can be used independently but that can also have a constituent agreeing with the subject in the nominative (this constituent is sometimes considered a predicate noun or adjective or a predicative apposition);

c) Independent verbs—such as *existere, stāre* (> Spanish *estar*, French *être*), and *vīvere*—that can have a predicative apposition but that are very close to the copula (like *vīvō* in § 290d);

d) independent verbs with a clear case of predicative apposition or predicative complement.

There is thus a gradual progression from the copula *esse*, that has a predicate noun or adjective, to verbs that have a predicative apposition or complement, with some cases in between.

292. Each of the adjectives *summus* 'highest, the highest part of', *īmus* 'lowest, bottom of', and *medius* 'middle, in the middle of' can occur as an **attribute** or as a **predicative apposition**. The translator must analyze the meaning of the text to arrive at the correct interpretation and translation of such an adjective.

> *Mediō ut limite currās moneō.* "I advise you to fly along the middle route." (Ovid *Met.* 8.203–4) (*Medio* functions as an attribute, designating the middle of three possible routes—high, middle, or low.)
>
> *[Daedalus pennās] līnō mediās et cērīs alligat īmās.* "Daedalus bound the feathers together at the middle with flaxen thread and at the bottom with wax." (Ovid *Met.* 8.193) (*Mediās* and *īmās* function as predicative appositions, *mediās* designating not the middlemost feathers but the middle of all feathers, *īmās* designating not the bottommost feathers but the quills of all feathers.)
>
> *Iam summā procul villārum culmina fūmant.* "Already the chimneys of the farms are smoking in the distance." (Virg. *Buc.* 1.82) (*Summā* functions as a predicative apposition, designating not the highest ridges but the highest points of the ridges, i.e., the chimneys.)

15
Adverbials

Definition

293. The **adverbial modifier**, or **circumstantial modifier**, is a non-obligatory constituent in the sentence. It is not a part of the kernel. **Its function is to modify the predicate**. Its form can be a simple adverb, a phrase, or a clause.

Sometimes an adverbial modifier functions on another level in the grammatical hierarchy. On a lower level, it can be the **modifier of an adjective or an adverb**; on a higher level, it can be a **sentence adverbial** (§ 381).

294. The **semantic role** of an adverbial modifier can vary a great deal. It depends on the following factors (if present): the case, the preposition, the meaning of the word, and the meaning of the verb with which the adverbial modifier occurs (§ 187–88). This chapter treats the different semantic roles of the adverbials, as well as their constructions.

295. As to their form, the adverbial modifiers can be classified as follows:
  a) adverbial phrases:
    – adverb and adverb phrase
    – noun and noun phrase
    – prepositional phrase
  b) adverbial clauses:
    – finite clause with conjunction
    – ablative absolute (participial clause)
    – supine and supine clause
    – gerund and gerund clause (the latter is often replaced by a
      noun phrase or prepositional phrase containing a gerundive)

Remark. Some adverbial clauses without finite verb may be so concise that they resemble adverbial phrases (§ 353, 355, 357).

Adverb and adverb phrase

296. The adverb **functions** mostly as an adverbial modifier of the predicate. It has a fixed form (for the morphology, see § 46–51). An adverb may be modified by another adverb: together they form an adverbial phrase. The **semantic role** of an adverb or adverbial phrase is immediately clear from its meaning as given in the dictionary: for example, *miserē* 'in an unhappy way' (**manner**), *fortiter* 'bravely' (**manner**), *diū* 'a long time' (**duration**), *ibī (ubi)* 'there' (**place**), *eō* 'thither' (**direction**), *paulō post* 'a little later' (**time**), *multō aliter* 'in a very different way' (**manner**), and so on.

Noun, noun phrase, and prepositional phrase

297. In this section, the adverbial modifiers are classified according to the **semantic role** they play in relation to the predicate. For each semantic role, the use of the case and the presence or absence of prepositions are mentioned.

298. The **adverbial modifier of place** is generally construed with a **preposition governing the ablative**. It is an answer to the question *ubī?* 'where?' **Countries** and **big islands** (islands having more than one town) also follow this general rule. Prepositions governing the ablative are *in* 'in, on', *sub* 'under, at the foot of', *prō* 'in front of, instead of', and so on. The verb with which an adverbial of place is construed expresses not a motion but a rest.

> *Quod multō aliter fit in Graeciā.* "And this happens in a very different way in Greece." (Nepos *De viris,* proem 7)
> *Nam neque sēdet nisi in interiōre parte aedium.* "For she [the Greek woman] sits only in the inner part of the house." (Nepos *De viris,* proem 7)
> *O quīcumque sub hāc habitātis rūpe, leōnēs!* "Oh whatever lions live at the foot of this rock!" (Ovid *Met.* 4.114)

299. The **adverbial modifier of place** with names of **towns and small islands (of the a- and o-declensions plural and of the third declension)** stands in the **ablative without a preposition**. This is also so for place adverbials with *locō/locīs* accompanied by an attribute and for place adverbials with *tōtus.* The preposition *in* is also used less often in poetry (§ 169).

> *Erat Athēnīs domus spatiōsa sed infāmis.* "Once upon a time, there was in Athens a spacious but infamous house." (Pliny 7.27.5)
> *Aliēnō locō cum equitātū Helvētiōrum proelium committunt.* "On hostile ground, they joined battle with the cavalry of the Helvetii." (Caes. *B.G.* 1.15.2)
> *Vulgō tōtīs castrīs testāmenta obsignābantur.* "In general they were signing and sealing testaments all over the camp." (Caes. *B.G.* 1.39.5)

300. The **adverbial modifier of place** with **names of towns and small islands of the a- and o-declensions singular** stands in the **genitive singular**. This genitive is a fossilized remnant of the old locative ending in *-ī* (§ 19, 30, 133, 305). Real **locatives** (from various declensions) survive in such petrified expressions as *domī* 'at home', *humī* 'on the ground', *rūrī* 'in the countryside', and *domī bellīque, domī militiaeque* 'in times of peace and war'.

Thessalonīcae retentus sum. "I was retained in Thessalonica." (Cic. *Att.* 3.19.1)

Nōs **Brundisiū** *apud M. Laenium Flaccum diēs XIII fuimus.* "We remained thirteen days in Brindisi with Marcus Laenius Flaccus." (Cic. *Fam.* 14.4.2)

Constituēre introīre ad Cicerōnem ac dē imprōvīsō **domī** [loc.] **suae** [gen.] *impārātum confodere.* "They decided to go in to Cicero and to stab him suddenly and unexpectedly in his own house." (Sall. *Cat.* 28.1)

301. The **place adverbial** can also be construed with a **preposition + accusative**, if the preposition always governs the accusative and if the verb expresses not a motion but a rest. (See also the example with *apud* in § 300.)

> **Ad retia** *sedēbam.* "I was sitting near my nets." (Pliny 1.6.1)
> *Omne hoc tempus* **inter pugillārēs ac libellos** *transmīsī.* "All this time I have spent with my writing tablets and booklets." (Pliny 1.6.1)

302. The **adverbial modifier of direction** is construed with a **preposition governing the accusative**. It is an answer to the question *quō?* 'whither?' The preposition is also used with the names of countries and big islands. A direction can be literal (direction) or figurative (purpose).

> **There is no preposition with names of towns and small islands** (§ 153) **or** in such fossilized expressions as *domum* 'home(ward)' and *rūs* 'to the countryside' (§ 305).

> > *Geminās opifex lībrāvit* **in ālās** *ipse suum corpus.* "The technician brought his own body into equilibrium on both wings." (Ovid *Met.* 8.201–2)
> > *Frūmentum in hīs locīs* **in hiemem** *prōvīsum nōn erat.* "In these areas, there was no grain provided for the winter." (Caes. *B.G.* 4.29.4)

303. The **adverbial modifier of separation, origin,** or **descent** usually is construed with a **preposition + ablative**. It answers the question *unde?* 'whence? from where?' The preposition is used for names of countries and big islands. The preposition is missing with names of **towns and small islands** and with the fossilized expressions *domō* 'from home', *rūre* 'from the countryside', and *humō* 'from the ground'.

> *Ipse retrō* **ab urbe** *castra mōvit.* "He himself moved his camp away from the city." (Livy 2.40.10)
> *Catilīna,* **nōbilī genere** *nātus, fuit magnā vī.* "Catiline, born of a noble family, was very strong." (Sall. *Cat.* 5.1)
> **Dyrrachiō** *sum profectus.* "I set out from Dyrrachium." (Cic. *Att.* 4.1.4)
> *Tollit* **humō** *saxum.* "He took a stone from the ground." (Ovid *Met.* 11.110)

304. The **adverbial modifier of "by which way"** is usually construed with *per* **+ accusative**. It answers the question *quā?* 'by which way?' If this adverbial contains the name of a **road, bridge, port, sea**, and so on and an attribute, it is usually put (as an adverbial modifier of means: see § 156, 175, 315) in the **ablative without a preposition**.

Narcissum per dēvia lustra vagantem vīdit. "She saw Narcissus wandering through remote woods." (Ovid *Met.* 3.370–71)

Paucī incertīs itineribus per silvās ad T. Labienum in hiberna perveniunt. "A few made their way, by uncertain routes, through the woods to T. Labienus at his winter camp." (Caes. *B.G.* 5.37.7)

Lupus Esquilīnā Portā ingressus, Tuscō vīcō atque inde Cermalō per portam Capēnam prope intactus ēvāserat. "A wolf had entered through the Porta Esquilina; via the Tuscus neighborhood and, from there, via the Cermalus neighborhood, it had escaped almost unharmed through the Porta Capena." (Livy 33.26.8–9)

305. Synopsis of the spatial adverbial modifiers

Semantic role + interrogative adverb	General rule	Towns and small islands without preposition		Domus, rūs	Adverbs
Place: *ubī?* 'where?'	*in, sub* + ablative other preposition + own case	genitive in a- and o-declensions singular	ablative elsewhere	locative: *domī, rūrī, humī, domī militiaeque*	*ibī (ibi), hīc, istīc, illīc*
Direction: *quō?* 'whither?'	*in* + accusative *ad* + accusative	accusative		*domum, rūs*	*eō, hūc, istūc, illūc/illō*
Separation: *unde?* 'whence?'	*ā, ab* + ablative *ē, ex* + ablative	ablative		*domō, rūre, humō*	*inde, hinc, istinc, illinc*
Road by which: *quā?* 'by which way?'	*per* + accusative	ablative: *ponte, portā, marī, viā,* etc. + adjective		—	*eā, hāc, istāc, illāc*

Remarks. The spatial meaning of the great number of adverbs (in the last column of the preceding table) is in the ending. In each row in the preceding table, the last syllable of the adverb (and sometimes also of the case ending, in the other columns) contains the typical sound of the interrogative adverb:

- in the row **'place'**, the sound *ī* of the locative as in *ubī;*
- in the row **'direction'**, the sound *ō/ū* as in *quō;*
- in the row **'separation'**, the sound *n* as in *unde;*
- in the row **'by which way'**, the sound *ā* as in *quā.*

306. The **adverbial modifier of time** is usually expressed by *in* + **ablative**, if the noun by itself does not express a time and is not accompanied by an attribute (§ 170).

Sī regum atque imperātōrum animī virtus in pāce ita ut in bellō valēret, aequābilius atque constantius sēsē rēs hūmānae habērent. "If the moral values of kings and generals in time of peace were as in wartime, human affairs would be more just and stable." (Sall. *Cat.* 2.3)

307. The **time adverbial** is often put in the **ablative without a preposition**, if the noun itself already indicates a time or is accompanied by an attribute (§ 170). *Vesperī* 'in the evening' is an old locative (§ 25h).

> *Quaeris quamadmodum in Tuscīs diem **aestāte** dispōnam.* "You ask me how I organize my day [on the farm] in Etruria in the summer." (Pliny 9.36.1)
>
> *Repetō noctem, **quā** tot mihi cāra relīquī.* "I recall the night in which I left so much that is dear to me." (Ovid *Tr.* 1.3.3)
>
> ***Prīmā lūce** ex castrīs proficiscuntur.* "At dawn they set out from the camp." (Caes. *B.G.* 5.31.6)

308. The **days of the calendar** are indicated by reference to **three fixed days in the month**. The other days are given by counting back from these fixed days, whereby also the first and the last day are counted. The fixed days are

- *Kalendae, -ārum* 'the Kalends' = the first day of each month;
- *Nōnae, -ārum* 'the Nones' = the seventh day of March, May, July, and October and the fifth day of the other months (actually, the ninth day before the Ides);
- *Idus, -uum* (f.) 'the Ides' = the fifteenth of March, May, July, and October and the thirteenth of the other months.

The months (adjectives with understood *mensis*) are called *Iānuārius, Februārius, Martius, Aprīlis, Māius, Iūnius, Quintīlis* (later *Iūlius*), *Sextīlis* (later *Augustus*), *September, Octōber, November,* and *December.* Until 153 B.C., March was the first month of the year in which the army, under the protection of Mars, could start its campaigns. This explains the names, based on numbers, assigned to the months from *Quintīlis* (fifth, now seventh month) through *December* (tenth, now twelfth month).

> ***Kalendīs Iānuāriīs** "On January 1." (Cic. *Att.* 1.12.4)
>
> *Brundisium vēnī **Nōnīs Sextīlibus**.* "I arrived in Brundisium on August 5." (Cic. *Att.* 4.1.4)
>
> *Marcellīnō et Philippō consulibus **Nōnīs Aprīlibus** mihi est senātus adsensus, ut dē agrō Campānō frequentī senātu **Idibus Māiīs** referretur.* "Under the consulate of Marcellinus and Philippus on the fifth of April, the senate agreed with me that a proposal about the Campanian territory would be introduced in the full senate on May 15." (Cic. *Fam.* 1.9.8)
>
> ***Ante diem XII Kalendās Decembrēs** Milō ante mediam noctem cum manū magnā in campum vēnit.* "On November 20 [= the twelfth day before the first of December] Milo went before midnight with a large gang to the Campus Martius." (Cic. *Att.* 4.3.4)
>
> *D. **pr. K. Iūn.** [= Data prīdiē Kalendās Iūniās] Athēnīs.* "Given on the thirty-first of May [= the day before June 1] in Athens." (Cic. *Fam.* 4.12.3)

Pr. Nōn. Sext. Dyrrachiō sum profectus. "On August 4 [= the day before August 5] I set out from Dyrrachium." (Cic. *Att.* 4.1.4)
Abs tē proximās litterās habēbam Ephesō a. d. V Idūs Sextīl. datās. "The
most recent letter I have from you is dated in Ephesus on the ninth of
August [= five days before August 13]." (Cic. *Att.* 4.18.5)

Remark. Instead of *quintō diē ante Idūs Sextīlēs,* Romans usually said
quintō Idūs Sextīlēs or *ante diem quintum Idūs Sextīlēs* (in abbreviation,
a. d. V Id. Sext), as in the last example above.

309. All the time adverbials discussed in § 306–8 are answers to the question
quandō? 'when?' Other time adverbials answer such questions as *how
long before? how long after? how much earlier? how long ago? within how
much time?* The answers can be put in the **ablative** with the adverbs *ante*
or *post* or can be given with the prepositions *ante, post,* or *intra* + **accusative.** Such questions as *since when?* and *till when?* are answered by constructions with *ab* + **ablative** (separation) and *ad* + **accusative** (direction).

Paucīs post diebus exclāmat Nāsīca domī nōn esse. "A few days later,
Nasica shouted that he was not home." (Cic. *De oratore* 276)
... sē illā ipsā nocte paulō ante lūcem mē interfectūrōs esse. "... that later
that same night, a little before dawn, they would kill me." (Cic. *Cat.* 1.9)
*Nam hōc tōtō proeliō, cum ab hōrā septimā ad vesperum pugnātum sit,
āversum hostem vidēre nēmō potuit.* "For in this entire battle—though
the fighting went on from the seventh hour until evening—nobody
could see an enemy flee." (Caes. *B.G.* 1.26.2)
Agitabātur magis magisque in diēs animus ferox. "His fierce mind was
agitated more and more from day to day." (Sall. *Cat.* 5.7)

310. The **adverbial modifier of duration (extension in time)** answers the question
how long? It stands in the accusative or is construed with *per* + **accusative.**

Per continuōs diēs nimis imperat vōcī. "For days on end, he required
too much from his voice." (Pliny 5.19.6)
Hīc iam ter centum tōtōs regnābitur annōs gente sub Hectoreā. "Here,
then, for a full three hundred years shall the kingdom endure under
Hector's family." (Virg. *Aen.* 1.272–73) (A literal translation by an impersonal passive does not work in English.)

311. The **adverbial modifier of distance or measure (extension in space)** is put
in the **accusative** to indicate the distance, the road covered, the height,
the depth, the length, or the width, particularly with the adjectives
longus, lātus, and so on.

Fīnēs in longitūdinem mīlia passuum ducenta quadrāgintā patēbant.
"Their territory extended for 240 miles in length." (Caes. *B.G.* 1.2.5)

Remark. The adverbial modifier of distance or measure can also be
put in the ablative (§ 165). Not the case but the meaning of the verb is
important.

312. The **adverbial modifier of cause or reason** often stands in the **ablative**. Despite frequent translation with the preposition *by* in English (*metū* 'by fear', *īrā* 'by anger'), this semantic role is to be distinguished in Latin from the adverbial modifier of agent (§ 313): the cause adverbial never takes the preposition *a(b)* + **ablative**, does not refer to a living being, and can also occur with an active verb. It can also be translated with other prepositions (*because of, through,* etc.).

> *Terra **marmoreō** est candida facta **gelū**.* "The earth has become white with the marble frost." (Ovid *Tr.* 3.10.10)
> ***Mōbilitāte et lēvitāte animī** novīs imperiīs studēbant.* "Because of their fickleness and frivolity, they supported a change of government." (Caes. *B.G.* 2.1.3)

> **Remarks.** Other constructions use prepositional phrases, each with its own case: *e(x)/de* + ablative, *ob/propter* + accusative, genitive + *causā/ grātiā.* If *causā/grātiā* is construed with a gerund and a direct object (or a gerundive construction: see § 357), the whole construction is more like a concise adverbial clause.

> *Id mihi **duābus dē causīs** instituisse videntur.* "It seems to me that they have instituted this for two reasons." (Caes. *B.G.* 6.14.4)
> *Diviciācus **auxiliī petendī causā** Rōmam profectus infectā rē redierat.* "Diviciacus had left for Rome in order to ask for help, but he had returned without achieving his purpose." (Caes. *B.G.* 6.12.5)

313. The **adverbial modifier of agent**, constructed with *a(b)* + **ablative**, indicates the **living being** (human, animal, personified force) that performs the action of a **passive verb**. The agent phrase is often omitted for various reasons (§ 207).

> *Omnia aut scripta esse **ā tuīs** arbitror aut etiam nuntiīs ac rūmōre perlata.* "Everything either has been written by your people—I think—or has also reached me through messages and rumors." (Cic. *Att.* 4.1.4) (Only *ā tuīs* is an agent phrase.)

314. The **adverbial modifier of accompaniment** is construed with *cum* + **ablative**. The preposition *cum* means '(together) with', never 'by means of'.

> *Cotta pugnans interficitur **cum maximā parte militum**.* "Cotta was killed in the battle, with the greatest part of his soldiers." (Caes. *B.G.* 5.37.4)

315. The **adverbial modifier of means** stands in the **ablative**. Also persons, particularly military, can be considered a means and stand in the ablative. For non-military people, *per* + **accusative** is mostly used.

> *Amor non est medicābilis **herbīs**.* "Love is not curable with herbs." (Ovid *Her.* 5.149)
> *[Catilīna] opportūna loca **armātīs hominibus** obsidēre.* "Catiline occupied strategic places with armed men." (Sall. *Cat.* 27.2)

*Coniūrātiōnis principes convocat **per M. Porcium Laecam**.* "He called a meeting of the captains of the conspiracy through M. Porcius Laeca." (Sall. *Cat.* 27.3)

*Partem finitimī agrī **per vim** occupātam [possident].* "They possess a part of the neighboring territory that they had occupied by force." (Caes. *B.G.* 6.12.4)

316. The **adverbial modifier of manner** stands in the **ablative** or sometimes in a prepositional phrase with *cum* **+ ablative**.

> *Ibat illa **lentō gradū**.* "The ghost walked with slow step." (Pliny 7.27.9)
> *Omne hoc tempus **iūcundissimā quiēte** transmīsī.* "All this time I spent in the most pleasant rest." (Pliny 9.6.1)
> *Face rem hanc **cum curā** gerās.* "Make sure you carry out my instruction with care." (Plautus *Persa* 198)

317. The **adverbial modifier of price** or **value** stands in the **ablative** both for definite and indefinite price. However, **comparatives** (*plūris, minōris*) and **correlatives** (*tantī, quantī*) stand in the genitive. Indefinite expressions (negative polarity items)—such as *nihili* (also ablative *nihilo*) 'not anything', *non floccī* 'not a bit, not a straw, not a brass farthing', *non naucī* 'not a trifle,'—stand in the genitive.

> *Conduxit **nōn magnō** domum.* "He rented a house for a low price." (Cic. *Cael.* 18)
> *Emit [hortos] **tantī, quantī** Pythius voluit.* "He bought the gardens for as much as Pythius wanted." (Cic. *Off.* 3.59)
> *Agedum, sūme hoc tisanārium orīzae. — **Quantī** emptae? — **Parvō**. — **Quantī** ergō? — **Octussibus**.* "Come on, take this rice gruel. — Bought for how much? — Little. — So, for how much? — Eight *asses.*" (Hor. *Sat.* 2.3.155–56)

Remarks

a) The constituent of price or value is an obligatory **object** with some verbs, such as *(con)stāre* 'cost' (§ 163; 250, third example).

b) In such expressions as *est tantī* 'is worth so much', the genitive is not an adverbial but part of the **predicate** (§ 135).

c) In the expression *nōn habeō naucī eum* 'I do not count him worth a tuppence', the genitive *naucī* is a **predicative complement** (§ 288–89)

318. The **adverbial modifier of comparison (second member with a comparative)** can be construed in two ways. The English translation always resembles the second construction.

a) The oldest construction is only used when the comparative adjective stands in the nominative or accusative. In this construction, the second member of the comparison stands—mostly before the comparative—in the **ablative**, as the member "from which" (separation) the comparison starts or is seen (see the first example in § 318b). The use of the ablative as second member of the comparison is also possible with an adverb in the comparative.

b) The more recent and more frequently used construction is the one with **quam + the same case or function as the first member of the comparison** (or the nominative as the subject of an understood *esse*). The construction with *quam* is also used if the ablative would be ambiguous. After *amplius, longius, minus,* and *plūs,* the conjunction *quam* is often omitted before adverbials of measure or distance, without affecting the case of such modifiers.

> *Dē imprōvīsō celeriusque* **omnium opiniōne** *[vēnit].* "He arrived unexpectedly and faster than everyone thought." (Caes. *B.G.* 2.3.1)
> *Lūce sunt clāriōra nōbīs tua consilia omnia.* "Clearer than the daylight are for us all your plans." (Cic. *Cat.* 1.6)
> *Oh!* **Melle dulcī** *dulcior mihi tū es.* "Oh! Sweeter than sweet honey are you to me." (Plautus *As.* 614)
> *Potius in suīs* **quam in aliēnīs finibus** *[dēcertant].* "They'd rather decide the issue in their own territory than in other people's." (Caes. *B.G.* 2.10.4)
> *Ubī aut iūcundius morārentur* **quam in pătriā** *aut pudicius continērentur* **quam sub oculīs parentum** *aut minōre sumptū* **quam domī?** "Where could they stay more pleasantly than in their hometown? Or where could they be kept more decently under control than under their parents' eyes? Or with less expense than at home?" (Pliny 4.13.4)
> *Rōmānī sociīque* **paulō plūs sescentī** *cecidērunt.* "A few more than six hundred Romans and allies fell." (Livy 39.31.15)

Remark. A comparative in itself has an intensive meaning, such as 'more than normal', 'more than is fitting', 'more than you would expect'. Therefore, it is not always followed by a second member of the comparison. In English translation, such intensifying adverbs as *too* and *rather* can be used.

> *Puer quīdam audentior cēterīs* **in ulteriōra** *tendēbat.* "A boy who was more daring than the others went rather far [or "farther than others"]." (Pliny 9.33.4)

319. The **adverbial modifier of restriction or limitation** stands in the **ablative**. It limits the validity of the statement. (The statement is only true with respect to the word in the ablative.) The **supine in -ū** (ablative) is also used with adjectives for this restriction (see § 171).

> *Nescīō ut* **mōribus** *sint vostrae.* "I do not know how your women are as far as their behavior goes." (Plautus *Most.* 708–9)
> *Hī omnēs* **linguā, institūtis, legibus** *inter sē differunt.* "All these peoples

differ among themselves with respect to language, institutions, and laws." (Caes. *B.G.* 1.1.2)

Horrendum dictū. "It is horrible to say." (Virg. *Aen.* 8.565)

320. The **adverbial modifier of respect** (or so-called **Greek accusative**) indicates in which respect a statement is true. It stands in the **accusative** and usually refers to a part of the body. Under the influence of Greek, it occurs chiefly in poetry.

> *Hannibal femur trāgulā graviter ictus cecidit.* "Hannibal was seriously wounded in the thigh by a javelin and fell down." (Livy 21.7.10)
>
> *Quid rīdētis?* "What are you laughing at?" Or "Why are you laughing?" (Plautus *Aul.* 718)
>
> *Saepēs Hyblaeīs apibus flōrem dēpasta salictī . . .* "A willow hedge whose catkins have been sucked out [literally, "a hedge sucked out with respect to its catkins"] by Hybla bees . . ." (Virg. *Buc.* 1.53–54)

321. The **adverbial modifier of degree** (also called the **adverbial accusative**: see § 157) indicates to which degree a statement is true. This adverbial occurs sometimes as a noun in the **accusative** but more frequently as a neuter adjective or pronoun in the **accusative**. Those forms are often felt more as an adverb than as an independently used adjective or pronoun. Examples are *multum* 'for the most part', *parum* 'little', *nihil* 'no, in no way', *summum* 'at the most', and the expressions as in *magnam partem* 'for a great deal', *id genus* 'of this kind', and *id aetātis* 'of that age'.

> *Nihilne tē urbis vigiliae mōvērunt?* "Aren't you moved at all by the night watches of the city?" (Cic. *Cat.* 1.1)
>
> *Adloquor extrēmum maestōs amīcōs.* "For the last time, I speak to my sad friends." (Ovid *Tr.* 1.3.15)

322. The **adverbial modifier of advantage or disadvantage** stands in the **dative** (*dativus commodi et incommodi:* see § 139). It indicates the person in whose honor, interest, advantage, or pleasure (or the reverse) the action takes place.

> *Unicus anser erat, quem dīs hospitibus dominī mactāre parābant.* "There was only one goose the inhabitants of house wanted to sacrifice for their divine guests." (Ovid *Met.* 8.684)
>
> *Sentiō quam malē scrībam, licet mihi bonum animum faciās.* "I feel how badly I am writing, although you cheer me up [literally, "although you create a positive spirit for me"]." (Pliny 7.30.4)

With a gerundive + *esse*, the **adverbial modifier of the person involved** is put in the **dative** (see § 141). The dative indicates for whom the obligation expressed by the gerundive holds. Occasionally, the dative with a PPP also indicates **for whom** a situation or state exists or the perfective action is over and done.

*Faciundum est **mihi** illud fierī.* "I have to make sure that that happens." (Plautus *Amph.* 891)

***Mihi** consilium captum iam diu est.* "As far as I am concerned [or 'For me'], the decision has been taken already a long time ago." (Cic. *Fam.* 5.16.2)

See also the last example in § 440, where ***Hyblaeïs apibus*** 'Hybla bees' are involved in the sucked (catkins of the) hedges.

323. The **adverbial modifier of purpose** stands in the **dative** with such verbs as *mittere, relinquere,* and *venīre.* It frequently occurs in combination with a dative object (§ 138) or with an adverbial modifier of advantage (§ 139, 322). For the dative of purpose as part of the predicate with *esse,* see § 143, 204a.

> *Submittit cohortēs equitibus **subsidiō**.* "He sent his cohorts to help his horsemen." (Caes. *B.G.* 5.58.5) (dat. object + purpose adverbial)
>
> *Caesar omnem equitātum **auxiliō** suīs misit.* "Caesar sent his whole cavalry to the rescue of his men." (Caes. *B.G.* 4.37.2) (purpose adverbial + adverbial of advantage)

Remark. In poetry, such a purpose modifier is also used for a place to where someone is going. It is then also called a modifier of direction.

> *Facilis descensus **Avernō**.* "The way down to the Avernus is easy." (Virg. *Aen.* 6.126)

324. The **adverbial modifier of point of view** stands in the **dative**. It indicates for whom the statement is true.

> *Sita Anticyra est in Locride laevā parte **sinum Corinthiacum intrantī**.* "Anticyra is located in Locris at the left-hand side for him who enters the Corinthian Gulf." (Livy 26.26.2)

325. Some constructions resemble each other so much that there can be doubt as to which of the many semantic roles is expressed or, for the ablative, even which of the three original cases (locative, ablative, instrumental) is meant. Furthermore, some constructions are idiomatic expressions that have no English counterpart. The problem is still worse in poetry, because of the frequent omission of prepositions. In any case, the English translation should be correct English.

> *ex **equō** pugnāre* 'fight on horseback' (origin/place)
> *currū vehī* 'travel by car' (means/place)
> *unā ex parte* 'on the one hand' (origin/place)
> *superiōribus proeliīs exercitātī* 'trained in earlier battles' (place/means)
> *ex meīs litterīs cognoscere* 'learn from my letter' (origin/means)
> *cognōvī litterīs frătris* 'I have learned through my brother's letter' (means)

*inclūdere aliquem **carcere*** 'keep someone in prison' (means/place)
*inclūdere **in cellā*** 'keep in the cellar' (place)
*inclūdere **in equum Troianum*** 'enclose in the Trojan horse' (direction)
***in furtō** aut **ex aliquā noxiā** sunt comprehensī.* 'They were arrested on
the basis of theft or some other fault.' (place/origin)
*pendēre **dē rūpe*** 'cling to the rocky cliffs' (origin/place)
*compōnī **tumulō eōdem*** 'be buried in the same grave' (place/means;
used by the poet Ovid)
*Ibam forte **Viā Sacrā**.* 'I was walking along/on the Via Sacra.' (road
by which to somewhere/place on which; used by the poet Horace)

Seven finite clauses with conjunction

Time

326. The **adverbial clause of time** generally stands in the **indicative** because it
usually communicates when a **factual event** takes place. It is introduced
by a **subordinating conjunction** of time. Some conjunctions (e.g., *dum*
'while', *postquam* 'after') are construed with a tense that does not necessarily correspond to the tense in English.

Some conjunctions can occur with a verb in the **subjunctive**, if the action of the main clause takes place with the **purpose or intention** of doing
something before or until a certain time.

327. Conjunctions of time

Conjunction	Meaning	Mode	Tense	Remark
cum, ut, ubī	'when'	indicative	mostly perfect	*cum temporale*
cum prīmum, ut prīmum, ubī prīmum	'as soon as'		also historical present also future perfect	
dum	'while'	indicative	present	simultaneity
dum, dōnec, quoad, quamdiu	'as long as'	indicative		
dum, dōnec, quoad	'until'	indicative		fact
		subjunctive		purpose, expectation
postquam	'after'	indicative	perfect (seldom histor- ical present)	anteriority
antequam, priusquam	"before (he did)"	indicative	perfect	fact
	"before (he could)"	subjunctive		purpose, expectation
cum	'when'	subjunctive	imperfect: simultaneity pluperfect: anteriority	*cum historicum* circumstances: time + cause

*Nam color in pōmō est, **ubī permātūruit**, āter.* "For the color on the fruit, when it has ripened, is black." (Ovid *Met.* 4.165)

***Dum loquimur**, fūgerit invida aetās.* "While we talk, envious time will have fled." (Hor. *Carm.* 1.11.7–8)

***Postquam suōs cognōvit amōrēs**, percutit indignōs lacertōs.* "After she had recognized her love, she smote her innocent arms." (Ovid *Met.* 4.137–38)

*[Germanī] nōn **prius** fugere destitērunt, **quam ad flūmen Rhēnum pervēnērunt**.* "The Germans did not stop their flight until they reached the Rhine." (Caes. *B.G.* 1.53.1) (fact: indicative)

*Caesar, **priusquam sē hostēs ex fugā reciperent**, in fīnēs Suessiōnum exercitum duxit.* "Before the enemy could recuperate from the flight, Caesar led his army to the territory of the Suessiones." (Caes. *B.G.* 2.12.1) (intention: subjunctive)

***Cum Caesar in Galliam vēnit**, alterīus factiōnis principēs erant Haeduī, alterīus Sequanī.* "When Caesar came to Gaul, the Haeduans were the leaders of one faction, the Sequani of the other." (Caes. *B.G.* 6.12.1) (*cum temporale*)

*Quōrum dē nātūrā mōribusque Caesar **cum quaereret**, sīc reperiēbat.* "When Caesar inquired about their nature and customs, he got the following information." (Caes. *B.G.* 2.15.3) (*cum historicum*)

328. Remarks

a) ***Cum inversum.*** Sometimes the time clause with *cum* + indicative (often with *repente* or *subitō*), though subordinate, contains the principal idea, whereas the grammatical main clause (often with *iam, adhūc, nondum,* or *vix*) only gives the time or circumstance. The main and subordinate clause thus contain each the opposite (***inversum***) of what the speaker or author considers to be the main and subordinate idea.

> *Iam Iūnōnia laevā parte Samos, dextrā Lebinthos erat, **cum puer audācī coepit gaudēre volātū**.* "Samos of Juno was already on their left side and Lebinthos on their right, when the boy began to enjoy his audacious flight." (Ovid *Met.* 8.220–23)
>
> *Nondum Hannibal ē castrīs exierat, **cum pugnantium clamōrem audīvit**.* "Hannibal had not yet left the camp, when he heard the shouting of the fighters." (Livy 27.42.1)

b) The conjunction *cum* 'whenever', expresses a repeated action and is called a ***cum iterativum***. *Cum* 'whereas' expresses a contradistinction and is called a ***cum adversativum***.

Cause and reason

329. The **adverbial clause of cause and reason** generally stands in the **indicative**, because it usually communicates a **real fact**.

It is put in the **subjunctive** after *cum causale*. A **subjunctive** is also used after *quod* and other conjunctions, if the speaker/writer presents the reason not as his/her own but as that of someone else. It is then the **subjective reason** of that person. However, as that reason does not depend on a verb of saying or telling (*verbum dicendi*), it is **covert indirect speech**.

Moreover, if one gives a reason that is not a reason (a **non-reason**), the subordinate clause (usually with *quod*) stands in the **subjunctive**. The real reason follows (usually with *quia*) in the indicative.

330. Conjunctions of cause and reason

Conjunction	Meaning	Mode	Tense	Remark
quia, quod, proptereā quod	'because'	indicative		real fact
		subjunctive		non-reason subjective reason
quoniam	'since'	indicative		
cum	'as, because'	subjunctive		*cum causale*
cum	'when'	subjunctive	imperfect: simultaneity pluperfect: anteriority	*cum historicum* circumstances: time + reason

*Hōrum omnium fortissimī sunt Belgae, **proptereā quod ā cultū prōvinciae longissimē absunt**.* "Of all these peoples, the Belgae are the fiercest, because they are the farthest removed from the culture of the [Roman] Province." (Caes. *B.G.* 1.1.3)

*Brūtus terram osculō contigit, **scīlicet quod ea commūnis māter omnium mortalium esset***. "Brutus touched the earth with a kiss, evidently because she was [according to him] the common mother of all mortals." (Livy 1.56.12) (*Quod* introduces the covert indirect speech or subjective reason of Brutus, not of Livy)

*Pugilēs in iactandis caestibus ingemescunt, **nōn quod doleant animove succumbant, sed quia profundenda vōce omne corpus intenditur venitque plāga vehementior**.* "Boxers groan in swinging their boxing gloves, not because of any pain they might have or because they are losing heart, but because when they bring forth a deep sigh, their whole body gets tense, and their blow strikes home more violently." (Cic. *Tusc.* 2.56)

*Quae **cum** ita **sint**, Catilīna, perge quō coepisti.* "Things being as they are, Catiline, go on to where you started to go." (Cic. *Cat.* 1.10)

Concession

331. The **adverbial clause of concession** can be construed with a great number of subordinating conjunctions, each governing its own mode. In the main clause, the adverb *tamen* occurs frequently.

332. The conjunctions of concession

Conjunction	Meaning	Mode	Remark
quamquam *etsī, tametsī, etiam sī*	'although, even if'	mostly indicative subjunctive for possible and contrary-to-fact condition	The real condition is more common.
licet, ut	'although'	subjunctive	*Licet* originally is a verb.
cum	'even if'	subjunctive	*cum concessivum*
quamvīs	'however'	subjunctive	with adjectives and adverbs, participles and ablative absolutes

Etsī ab hoste ea dicēbantur, tamen nōn neglegenda existimābant. "Although these words were spoken by an enemy, they nevertheless thought that they should not disregard them." (Caes. *B.G.* 5.28.1)
Terrās licet et undās obstruat, at caelum certē patet. "Let him obstruct land and waves, but heaven surely lies open." (Ovid *Met.* 8.185–86)
Quamvīs multa meīs exīret victima saeptīs, nōn umquam gravis aere domum mihi dextra redībat. "However many sacrificial victims left my sheepfold, I never returned home my hands full of money." (Virg. *Buc.* 1.33–34)

Comparison

333. The **adverbial clause of comparison** stands in the **indicative** if the comparison is **real**. The **apparent comparison** stands in the **subjunctive**.

334. The conjunctions of comparison

Conjunction	Meaning	Mode	Remark
(sīc)ut, (sīc)uti	'as', 'according to'	indicative	real comparison The demonstrative *sīc* or *ita* often occurs in the main clause (§ 49, table).
quasi, ut sī, velut sī, tamquam sī, tamquam	'as if'	subjunctive	apparent comparison: no reality
quam	'than'	indicative	after a comparative (inequality)
ac, atque *ac, atque* *nisi*	'as' 'than' 'than'	indicative	after *idem, similis, pariter,* etc. after *alius, aliter,* etc. after *non alius, non aliter,* etc.

*Ille meās errāre bovēs, **ut cernis**, permīsit.* "He allowed my cows to wander around, as you see." (Virg. *Buc.* 1.9–10)
*Fīlius dēcessit, parentibus nōn minus ob alia cārus, **quam quod fīlius erat.** *"The son died. His parents loved him not less for other reasons than because he was their son." (Pliny 3.16.3)
*Siccīs oculīs, compositō vultū redībat, **tamquam orbitātem forīs relīquisset.***

"Eyes dry and face composed, she returned inside, as if she had left her childlessness outside." (Pliny 3.16.5)

*Quī aliā ratiōne **ac reliquī Gallī** bellum gerere coepērunt.* "They started to wage war according to a different tactic than the other Gauls." (Caes. *B.G.* 3.28.1)

Condition

335. The **adverbial clause of condition** is more closely connected with the main clause than are the other adverbial clauses. In the case of the adverbial clause of condition, the main clause is a consequence of the stated condition. The verb of the dependent clause is usually in the same mode as the verb of the main clause (§ 224, 227; but see also § 338).

336. In Latin, there are **three possible modalities** for the relation of the verb to fact: it can be **real, possible,** or **contrary to fact.** However, the relation between the verb of the dependent clause and the verb of the main clause is not the same in these three cases. When the relation is **real (simple condition)**, the speaker/writer does not present the actions of the main and dependent verbs as real but presents the relation between the two verbs as real. When the relation to fact is **possible (potential condition)**, the speaker/writer presents each of the verbs as possible. When the relation is **unreal (contrary-to-fact condition)**, the speaker/writer presents each of the verbs as contrary to fact or counterfactual.

337. **The conjunctions of condition**

Conjunction	Meaning	Mode + Tense		Translation
sī *nisi (= nī)* *sī nōn* *sīn*	'if' 'unless' 'if not' 'if however'	real:	indicative	indicative
		possible:	subjunctive present/ perfect	'should, could'
		contrary to fact:	subjunctive imperfect: present	past and 'would'
			subjunctive pluperfect: past	past perfect and 'would have'
sīve … sīve, *seu … seu*	'whether … or'	same as above can also connect two nouns		
dum, modo, *dummodo*	'if only, pro- vided that'	subjunctive		

*Sī id facis, hodiē postrēmum mē **vidēs.*** "If you do that, today is the last day you see me." (Ter. *And.* 322) (What is real here is not *facis* and *vidēs* but the relation between both.)

Possīs ignāvus habērī, ad cēnam sī intestātus eās. "You would be considered as indolent, should you go for dinner without making your will." (Iuv. *Sat.* 3.272–74)

Sī vēlōcitāte equōrum traherentur, esset ratiō nōnnulla. "If they were attracted by the speed of the horses, there would be some reason [to go to the races]." (Pliny 9.6.2) (contrary-to-fact condition in the present) *Quās ego expectassem Brundisiī, sī esset licitum per nautās.* "I would have waited for those letters in Brundisium, if the boatmen had allowed it." (Cic. *Fam.* 14.4.5) (contrary-to-fact condition in the past)

338. Difference in tense and modality. While having the same modality, the dependent clause and the main clause can have a different tense, because they occur at different moments (see examples in § 222 and 227). But, although it is not very frequent, the modality of the dependent clause and the main clause can differ. In such a case, the difference is very expressive and strongly emphasized. An expressive translation is needed.

> *Tū quingentōs simul, **nī hebes machaera foret** [contrary to fact], **ūnō ictū occīderas** [real].* "If your sword were not blunt, you would **certainly** have killed five hundred men at once." (Plautus *Miles* 52–53)
> *Sī in mediō certāmine hic color illūc, ille hūc transferātur [possible], studium favorque transībit [real].* "If, in the middle of the race, this color would go there and that color here, then the enthusiasm and support will **definitely** shift as well." (Pliny 9.6.2)

339. Remarks

a) Some verbs expressing a modality (e.g., *posse* 'can', *debēre* 'must') can occur in the indicative: *possum* 'I should be able', *dēbeō* 'I should', *melius est* 'it might be better', *decet* 'it would be decent'. English uses another modality (§ 225).

b) If *sī* means 'whenever', it is a conjunction of time governing the indicative.

c) If *sī* means 'to see if, in case that', it introduces an indirect question in the subjunctive. The dependent clause is then an object clause depending on a verb, such as *exspectāre* 'wait to see if', *temptāre* 'try out if', or *cōnārī* 'try if'.

d) *Sī nōn* and, above all, *sī minus* are often used, as in English, without a verb and mean 'if not'.

e) *Nisi* negates the whole dependent clause. *Sī nōn* negates one word (even the verb) in the dependent clause.

f) A negative main clause is followed by *nisi*.

g) In the expressions *quod sī* and *quod nisī*, the relative *quod* is a connecting relative pronoun (§ 374) meaning 'in this respect'. It need not be translated.

h) *Sīn, sīn autem* 'but if, if however' occurs in opposition to a previous condition.

Purpose

340. The **final adverbial clause (purpose clause)** always stands in the **subjunctive**. It states not a real fact but an intention, an expectation, a will.

341. The conjunctions of purpose

Conjunction	Meaning	Mode	Tense
ut *nē* *neu, neve*	'in order that, to' 'in order that not, lest' 'and that . . . not'	subjunctive	present: after a present or future governing verb
quō (= ut eō) *quō* + comparative	'that thereby' 'in order that more . . .'		imperfect: after a past verb

> *[Horātius] ergō **ut sēgregāret pugnam eōrum**, capessit fugam.* "In order to split up the fight with them, Horatius took to flight." (Livy 1.25.7)
>
> *Docet quantō opere intersit manūs hostium distinērī, **nē cum tantā multitūdine ūnō tempore conflīgendum sit**.* "He shows how important it is to keep the enemy's forces apart, in order not to be obliged to fight against such a great number at the same time." (Caes. *B.G.* 2.5.2) (*Conflīgendum sit* is a present subjunctive and is thus simultaneous with its governing verb, *distinērī*. *Distinērī* itself is neither present nor past and therefore does not govern the tense [present or imperfect] of *conflīgendum sit*. But *distinērī* is governed by the present verb *intersit*. Therefore, *conflīgendum sit* is present. See § 278–80 on the sequence of the tenses.)
>
> *Sinum ad īma crūra dēduxit, **quō honestius caderet**.* "He drew the folds of his toga to the lower part of his legs in order to fall more decently." (Suetonius *Caes.* 82.2)

342. Remark. The purpose conjunctions *quīn* and *quōminus* (as well as *ut* and *nē*) can occur in object clauses (§ 255–57). In this case, they are translated by *that, to,* or the omission of a conjunction, never by *in order that.*

Result

343. The **adverbial consecutive clause (result clause)** stands in the **subjunctive**. Since the result can be not only accidental but also an intended result, the consecutive clause and the final clause closely resemble each other. Both clauses use the same positive conjunction (*ut*) and the subjunctive mode. Only their negative clause is usually distinct (final *nē* and consecutive *ut nōn*).

Consecutive clauses are often the result of an action or event that has reached a certain degree or has happened in a certain way. Therefore, the subordinating conjunction and dependent clause are often preceded in the main clause by a demonstrative pronoun or adverb indicating such a degree or manner. The degree is indicated by *adeō/tam* 'such', *tālis* 'such a', *tantus* 'so great', *tantum* 'so much, only', *totiens* 'so often'. The manner is indicated by *ita/sīc* 'so, in that way', *eiusmodī* 'of that kind', and so on.

344. Conjunctions of result

Conjunction	Meaning	Mode	Tense
ut *ut nōn*	'(so) that' '(so) that not'	subjunctive	present: after a present or future governing verb
quīn (after a negative main clause)	'(so) that not'		imperfect: after a past verb

*Nam pōnit in ordine pennās, **ut clīvō crēvisse putēs**.* "For he puts the feathers in a row so that you might think they have grown on a slope." (Ovid *Met.* 8.189–91)

*Ariovistus tantam arrogantiam sumpserat, **ut ferendus nōn vidērētur**.* "Ariovistus had become so arrogant that he seemed unbearable." (Caes. *B.G.* 1.33.5)

Remark. If *ut* occurs as a conjunction of a subject clause (§ 246) or an object clause (§ 255), it is translated by *that*. For *quīn* in an object clause, see § 257–58.

Synopsis of the use of the conjunction *cum*

345.

Semantic role	Meaning	Mode	Tense
cum temporale (time)	'when'	indicative	
cum historicum (time + cause)	'when'	subjunctive	imperfect: simultaneity pluperfect: anteriority
cum causale (cause)	'since, as'	subjunctive	
cum concessivum (concession)	'although'	subjunctive	
cum inversum (time)	'when'	indicative	perfect/historical present
cum iterativum (time)	'whenever'	indicative	
cum adversativum (time/ opposition)	'whereas'	subjunctive	

Synopsis of the use of the conjunction *ut*

346.

Semantic role	Meaning	Mode
Time	'when'	indicative
Comparison	'as'	indicative
Purpose	'to, in order to'	subjunctive
Result	'(so) that'	subjunctive
Concession	'even if'	subjunctive

Sequence of tenses in the subjunctive

347. The **rules of the sequence of tenses (relative time)** in finite clauses are the same as those for indirect questions (§ 277–80).

> **Final clauses**, by their very nature, refer to the future, but the conjunction *ut/nē* itself makes this clear. Therefore, the verb is put in the present or imperfect.

> **Posteriority** with the periphrastic future (*-ūrus sim/essem*) rarely occurs.

348. When an adverbial clause together with its governing clause constitutes an **indirect statement** or an **indirect question**, the adverbial clause (a dependent clause of the second degree) is put in the **subjunctive**, because it is part of the statement or question of somebody other than the author (§ 281–82). The tense of this adverbial clause also depends, via its governing verb (dependent clause of the first degree), on the tense of the next higher verb in the grammatical hierarchy, usually the main verb. Dependent adverbial clauses that already stand in the subjunctive remain in the subjunctive. The tenses of the contrary-to-fact condition and the deliberative question remain as they are, irrespective of the tense of the new governing (main) verb.

Even if such an adverbial clause and its governing clause do not occur in indirect speech but depend on a verb in the infinitive or subjunctive, the dependent clause may be put in the **subjunctive** by **modal attraction** (§ 283). Compare the following quote from Caesar and possible variations.

> *Ad haec Ariovistus respondit Haeduōs sibi,* **quoniam bellī fortūnam temptassent ac superātī essent,** *stīpendiāriōs esse factōs.* "To this Ariovistus answered that since the Haedui had tried their luck in war and had been overcome, they had become tributary to him." (Caes. *B.G.* 1.36.1–3) **(Indirect speech after a past main verb)**

> *Ad haec Ariovistus respondet Haeduōs sibi,* **quoniam bellī fortūnam temptāverint ac superātī sint,** *stīpendiāriōs esse factōs.* 'To this Ariovistus answers that since the Haedui have tried their luck in war and have been overcome, they have become tributary to him.' **(Indirect speech after a present [or future] main verb)**

> *Ad haec Ariovistus respondit:* '*Haeduī mihi,* **quoniam bellī fortūnam temptāvērunt ac superātī sunt,** *stīpendiāriī factī sunt.*' "To this Ariovistus answered: 'Since the Haedui have tried their luck in war and have been overcome, they have become tributary to me.'" **(Direct speech)**

Ablative absolute

349. The **ablative absolute** (*ablativus absolutus*) is a **concise adverbial clause**. It has the same function in the sentence as an adverbial clause with a conjunction and a finite verb. But as to its form, it is much more concise.

Sometimes it is even hard to distinguish from an adverbial phrase (§ 353). Not only is the ablative absolute very short, but it does not have a conjunction, and instead of a finite verb with many grammatical categories, it has a participle, an adjective, or a noun as its predicate. Precisely because of its conciseness, it can easily be inserted into a Latin sentence to express an additional, subordinated idea.

This construction hardly has an equivalent in spoken English. A similar construction in English is the participial clause or phrase, as in *The city being burned, everybody fled.* In this case, the participial clause or phrase could be replaced by a "regular" adverbial clause with a conjunction and a finite verb: *Because/when the city had been burned, everybody fled.*

350. **The characteristics of an ablative absolute are**
   a) **there is no conjunction** (but see § 354c);
   b) **the predicate is** not a finite verb but:
      – **a participle (IAP, PPP**, rarely **FAP) or**
      – **an adjective or noun** (without copula *esse*);
   c) **the subject and the predicate stand in the ablative**;
   d) **the subject usually does not occur in the main clause, either as a subject or in another function.**

The **function** of the ablative absolute is a concise **adverbial clause.**

The **semantic role** can be **time, cause, concession, or condition**. Because there is generally no conjunction (for an exception, see § 354c), this role can only be deduced from the context.

351. The **relative time (sequence of tenses)** expressed by the participle is
   a) **IAP, simultaneous** with the governing verb;
   b) **PPP, anterior** to the governing verb (occasionally, the result of the action is still present at the time of the action of the governing verb);
   c) **FAP, posterior** to the governing verb.

352. **The translation of an ablative absolute rarely consists of a participial clause in English.** The various possible constructions, some more stilted than others, include
   a) **a participial clause;**
   b) **an adverbial clause** with a finite verb and a conjunction of time, cause, concession, or condition;
   c) **an adverbial phrase** with a preposition and a deverbative noun or a gerund (ending in *-ing*). The preposition expresses time, cause, concession, or condition.
   d) **an independent clause** (in this case, it might be useful to add a connecting adverb expressing time, cause, concession, or condition in the next main clause).

Because Latin lacks an active perfective participle, the PPP may conveniently be rendered actively in certain sentences (see the translations b–d of the second example that follows).

In the following examples, the letters of the translations correspond to the letters of the possible constructions in the preceding list.

> ***Foedere ictō*** *trigeminī arma capiunt.* (Livy 1.25.1)
> a) "An agreement being reached, the triplets took up their arms."
> b) "When an agreement had been reached, the triplets took up their arms."
> c) "After reaching an agreement, the triplets took up their arms."
> d) "An agreement was reached and [**then**] the triplets took up their arms."

> *Notārium vocō et,* ***diē admissō***, *quae formāveram dictō.* (Pliny 9.36.2)
> a) "I call my secretary and, daylight having been let in, I dictate what I had thought out."
> b) "I call my secretary and, when daylight has been let in, I dictate . . ." Or "I call my secretary and, when I have let in the daylight, I dictate . . ."
> c) "I call my secretary and, after letting in daylight, I dictate . . ."
> d) "I call my secretary, let the daylight in, and [**then**] dictate . . ." (This translation is the farthest removed in structure from the Latin original but is flowing English. As the original sentence is also flowing Latin, this last translation may be the best equivalent of the Latin style.)

> ***Metū nondum positō*** *illa redit.* (Ovid *Met.* 4.128–29)
> a) "Her fear not yet being over, she returns."
> b) "Although her fear is not yet over, she returns."
> c) "Despite her fear not yet being over, she returns."
> d) "Her fear is not yet over, **but** she returns."

353. The **length of the ablative absolute** and **the length of the whole Latin sentence** influence the choice of the construction in the translation.

An ablative absolute is usually very short, consisting of a subject and a predicate. Sometimes it can hardly be distinguished from an adverbial phrase. In such a case, the English translation will also contain an adverbial phrase, rather than a subordinate clause.

> *Diviciācus* ***infectā rē*** *redierat.* "Diviciacus had returned empty-handed (or "with nothing achieved")." (Caes. *B.G.* 6.12.5)
> ***Mē duce*** *carpe viam.* "Take the road under my guidance [literally, "while I am your guide," without a copula in Latin]." (Ovid *Met.* 8.208)
> *Siccīs oculīs,* ***vultū compositō***, *redibat.* "With dry eyes and her face composed, she went back." (Pliny 3.16.5)

Sometimes the ablative absolute is somewhat more complicated, contains a dependent clause, or occurs as a dependent clause of the third, fourth, or greater degree. In such a case, one might avoid translating the ablative absolute by an adverbial dependent clause in English and, rather, use an independent clause. In the examples that follow, translations containing constructions a–c from the list in § 352 would be, if not impossible, at least harsh. Here, between the example translations with constructions b and d, construction d (an independent clause) allows the clearest English translation.

*Versūs quidem meōs cantat etiamque format cithārā, **nōn artifice aliquō docente, sed amōre, quī magister est optimus**.* (Pliny 4.19.4)
b) "She even sings my verses and accompanies them on her lute, while not some artist is teaching her, but love, who is the best teacher."
d) "She even sings my verses and accompanies them on her lute. Not some artist is teaching her, but love, who is the best teacher."

*Laetīque interdum nuntiī vulgābantur, dōnec **prōvīsīs quae tempus monēbat** simul excessisse Augustum et rērum potīrī Nerōnem fāma eadem tulit.* (Tac. *Ann.* 1.5.6)
b) "And from time to time cheerful communiqués were published, until, after precautionary measures that the circumstances suggested were taken, one and the same notice announced that Augustus had died and that the power was in the hands of Tiberius Nero."
d) "And from time to time cheerful communiqués were published and precautionary measures were taken, as the circumstances suggested. At last, one and the same notice announced that Augustus had died and that the power was in the hands of Tiberius Nero."

354. Remarks

a) The ablative absolute is said to be absolute or free or independent from the rest of the sentence. However, this is only true from a morphological point of view: indeed, there is no agreement with another sentence constituent (as there is with a participium coniunctum: see § 359–63) and no conjunction. But syntactically and semantically, the ablative absolute is a part of the sentence, with a function and semantic role in that sentence. Therefore, the label *absolute* is not appropriate for this participial clause.

b) The subject of the ablative absolute is sometimes lacking in archaic formulas, such as *auspicātō* 'after taking auspices', *intestātō* 'without making a will', *vadātō* 'after having given bail', and *consultō* 'deliberately'.

c) Tacitus sometimes uses a conjunction with the ablative absolute: *Aliī, **quamvis effugiō patente**, interiēre,* "Some died, although an escape was open" (*Ann.* 15.38.7).

d) Occasionally Caesar refers explicitly to the ablative absolute by repeating its subject in the main clause: *Obsidibus imperātīs centum, hōs Haeduīs custōdiendōs trādit,* "He required a hundred hostages and handed them over to the custody of the Haedui" (*B.G.* 6.4.4).

Supine in -*um*

355. The **supine in -*um*** (§ 73, 76, 78, 88) is a noun in the accusative derived from a verb. **It functions as a concise adverbial clause of purpose with verbs of motion.** It is concise because it lacks a conjunction, an overt subject, and a finite verb form and because it rarely has other constituents. It may be called a clause (rather than a phrase) because it can have an object.

> *Lūsum it Maecēnas, dormitum ego Vergiliusque.* "Maecenas goes to play; I and Virgil go to sleep." (Hor. *Sat.* 1.5.48)
> *Constituēre sīcutī salūtātum introīre ad Cicerōnem.* "They decided to enter Cicero's house as if they were going to greet him [or "as for a morning call"]." (Sall. *Cat.* 28.1)
> *Legātōs ad Iugurtham dē iniūriīs questum mīsit.* "He sent ambassadors to Jugurtha to complain about the injustices." (Sall. *Iug.* 21.5)

Gerund phrase and gerundive construction

356. The **gerund is a noun derived from a verb.** It does not exist in the nominative and is not used as a subject or direct object in the accusative. For those two functions, the infinitive is used.

The gerund still has verbal properties and can have an adverb or object.

The genitive is used as an attribute with nouns (§ 131, 365) and can occur as the object of certain adjectives (§ 132).

The dative, the accusative after prepositions, or the ablative can also function as an adverbial phrase or clause. Also, the **genitive +** *causā or grātiā* 'because of, in order to' is an adverbial phrase or clause. Just like the ablative absolute and the supine in -*um*, the gerund can be considered either as a phrase or as a concise clause.

> *Plūrimus hīc aeger moritur vigilandō.* "Many a sick person dies here for lack of sleep." (Iuv. *Sat.* 3.232)
> *Ante domandum ingentēs tollent animōs.* "Before the horses are broken, they will show great spirit." (Virg. *Geo.* 3.206–7)
> *Incendium in ēdita adsurgens et rursus inferiōra populandō anteiit remedia.* "By climbing up to the higher places and once more destroying the lower parts, the fire outstripped the firefighting." (Tac. *Ann.* 15.38.4)
> (The IAP phrase and gerund phrase form a variation: see § 462.)

357. **Instead of a gerund accompanied by a direct object in the accusative, Latin authors usually employ a gerundive construction.** In the example from Tacitus in § 356, this is not the case (see the remarks in the present section), but it is the general rule. In such a phrase with a gerundive construction,

a) the noun that would be the direct object of the gerund (an active verbal noun) takes the case of that gerund and is the head noun of the gerundive construction;
b) the place of the gerund is taken by the gerundive (a verbal adjective), which agrees with the noun in gender, number, and case.

Compare the following gerundive constructions from Caesar and Sallust with the accompanying constructions of gerund + direct object. In both cases, the best translation follows the construction with a gerund rather than the gerundive construction.

Gerundive construction: *Diviciācus* **auxiliū petendī causā** *profectus [est]*. "Diviciacus left because of the help [that was] to be asked." (Caes. *B.G.* 6.12.5)

Gerund + direct object: *Diviciācus* **auxilium petendī causā** *profectus [est]*. 'Diviciacus left in order to ask for help.' (*Auxilium* is a direct object of *petendī*.)

In the gerundive construction:

1) *auxilium* takes the genitive and depends on *causā;*
2) instead of the gerund *petendī*, the gerundive (adjective) is used; it agrees in gender, number, and case with *auxiliū*, which is neuter singular genitive.

Good translation: 'Diviciacus left in order to ask for help.' (The translation uses the construction with a gerund rather than the gerundive construction.)

Gerundive construction: . . . *dīvitiās, quās profundant* **in montibus coaequandīs**. '. . . wealth, which they squander in mountains that have to be leveled.' (Sall. *Cat.* 20.11)

Construction with gerund + direct object: . . . *dīvitiās, quās profundant in montēs coaequandō*. '. . . wealth, which they squander in leveling mountains.'

In the gerundive construction,

1) instead of the direct object *montēs*, there is *montibus* after *in;*
2) instead of the gerund *coaequandō*, there is the gerundive, which in gender, number, and case agrees with *montibus.*

Good translation: '. . . wealth, which they squander in leveling mountains.'

The **gerundive construction** is also used if the gerund + its direct object is not an adverbial phrase but an attributive construction, as in the following example from Pliny. Again the best translation follows the construction with a gerund.

Gerundive construction: . . . *necessitās* **agrōrum locandōrum** *molesta*. '. . . the annoying need of the grounds [that have] to be leased.' (Pliny

7.30.3) (*Agrōrum* is the head of the attributive construction with *necessitas.*)

Construction with gerund + direct object: ... *necessitās agrōs locandī molesta.* '... the annoying need to lease grounds.' [*Locandī* is the head of the attributive construction with *necessitās.*)

Good translation: '... the annoying need to lease grounds.'

Remarks

a) If the gerundive construction would result in several endings in *-ōrum* or *-ārum* as in *agrōrum bonōrum locandōrum*, it is often avoided for reasons of euphony.

b) It is not used with plural neuter adjectives or neuter pronouns only (without a noun), as can be seen in the example from Tacitus in § 356.

16
The Attribute

Level and definition

358. From the preceding chapters, it appears that the number of sentence constituents is limited (§ 184). However, a sentence may be very long. The reason is, first and foremost, that some sentence constituents consist of a dependent clause (subject, object, adverbial: cf. clauses 1 and 3 in § 190).

Secondly, a sentence constituent often does not consist of one word. Many sentences do not look like Sallust's sentence *Curius properē per Fulviam Cicerōnī dolum ēnuntiat,* "Curius then hastily reported the trap via Fulvia to Cicero" (*Cat.* 28.2: see § 190). In Sallust's original Latin sentence, the direct object (*dolum* 'trap') is modified by a relative clause (*qui parābātur* 'that was being prepared'). The direct object consists not of one single noun but of a longer noun phrase. (See clause 2 in § 190.) The head of the sentence constituent is thus modified with one or more **attributes** (either **words, phrases**, or **clauses**). Such an attribute itself is not a sentence constituent but a part of the sentence constituent. It functions on a **lower level** in the grammatical hierarchy.

An attribute can occur with nouns or with adjectives and pronouns used independently (i.e., unaccompanied by a noun). If an attribute is a clause, it contains in turn some of the constituents mentioned in chapters 11–15, which in turn contain further constituents, and so on. In theory, the total sentence could become interminably long. In practice, however, there are limits to the human processing capacity, so that the length of the sentence stays within certain limits. But those limits may be broader in literary Latin than in contemporary English.

The term **attribute** (used alone or in the terms *attributive phrase* and *attributive clause*) is thus the name of the **function within the noun phrase**. The word it modifies is the **head** of the phrase. The **forms** the attribute may take (determiner, qualifying adjective, attributive phrase, attributive clause, etc.) are described in this chapter.

Agreeing attributes

359. A noun can be modified by an attribute that agrees with that noun in gender, number, and case. When one attribute modifies several nouns, it may agree with the nearest one. The parts of speech that can be used attributively and that can agree are

a) a determiner limiting the phrase or the noun phrase: numerals and demonstrative, possessive, indefinite, and interrogative adjectives (there is no article in Latin);

b) a descriptive adjective;

c) a participle (participium coniunctum) or a participial phrase;

d) a gerundive (a verbal adjective: see § 357).

> *Quod rogīs superest, **ūnā** requiescit in urnā.* "What remains over from the funeral pyre now rests in one urn." (Ovid *Met.* 4.166)
>
> *Satis domī salūtātōrum **tālium** habeō.* "At home I have enough such salutators." (Macrobius *Sat.* 2.4.30)
>
> *[Druidēs] rēbus **dīvīnīs** intersunt.* "The druids occupy themselves with religious matters." (Caes. *B.G.* 6.13.4)
>
> *Quod ad mē saepe scripsistī dē **nostrō** amīcō **plācandō**, fēcī et expertus sum omnia, sed **mīrandum** in modum est animō **abaliēnātō**.* "You have often written to me about quieting our friend [or "about our friend to be quieted"]. I did and tried everything, but to an extraordinary degree, he is estranged." (Cic. *Att.* 1.3.3)
>
> *Semper honōs nōmenque **tuum** laudēsque manēbunt.* "Your honor and name and fame will always remain." (Virg. *Aen.* 1.610) (The neuter pronoun *tuum* determines a masculine, a neuter [*nōmen*], and a feminine noun.)

360. When an adjective or participle is not accompanied by a noun, it is called an **independently used adjective or participle**. There is no point in referring to an understood noun. The adjective or participle takes the **function of the noun phrase**.

> *Vastus animus **immoderāta, incrēdibilia, nimis alta** semper cupiēbat.* "His ambitious mind always desired the excessive, the incredible, the overlofty." (Sall. *Cat.* 5.5) (The adjectives form an object cluster.)
>
> *Quis fallere possit **amantem**?* "Who could deceive an enamored woman?" (Virg. *Aen.* 4.296)

Remark. Determiners, adjectives, and participles are used independently in the example immediately preceeding (*amantem*) and in that immediately following (*suōs*). But independent *complexus* in the nominative in the following example is not the subject but a predicative apposition.

> ***Complexus** suōs dimittit.* "With an embrace, he [Coriolanus] sends his relatives away." (Livy 2.40.10)

361. A participle (or participial phrase) expresses a certain **relative time** with respect to the governing verb. An imperfective active participle (IAP) expresses a simultaneity, a perfective passive participle (PPP) an anteriority, and a future active participle (FAP) a posteriority.

Indūcēbat etiam equitātum frēnīs, ephippīs praefulgentem. "He [Anti-ochus] also exhibited his cavalry, shining with bridles and saddles." (A. Gellius *Noctes Att.* 5.5) (simultaneity)

Poenus [ēlūdit] ignāviam militum pretiōsē armātōrum. "The Carthaginian made fun of the cowardice of the soldiers armed in costly fashion." (A. Gellius *Noctes Att.* 5.5) (anteriority)

Avē, Caesar, moritūrī tē salūtant. "Hail, Cesar, those who are going to die greet you." (Suetonius *Claudius* 21.13) (posteriority)

362. **Some translations of participles are better than others.** This depends to a high degree on the complexity of the Latin sentence. If the participle is not accompanied by objects or adverbials, an English construction from the top of the following list will be preferred. The more complex the participial phrase and/or the sentence is, the lower on the list one will find the adequate construction for the translation. Translators should listen to their intuition.

The possible constructions for translating a participle include

a) an English participle before the head;
b) an English participle after the head;
c) a relative clause;
d) an adverbial clause;
e) an adverbial phrase;
f) an independent clause, in which case an additional adverb of time, reason, and so on may be desirable.

Remark. Regarding possibilities d, e, and f, the semantic role and hence the English conjunction, preposition, or adverb can only be deduced from the context (see § 350).

The letters distinguishing each of the translations of the following examples correspond to the numbers in the preceding list.

[Cervus] vēnantum subitō vocibus conterritus per campum fugere coepit. (Phaedrus 1.12 *Cervus ad fontem* 7–8)

a) "The by the voices of the hunters suddenly terrified deer began to flee through the field" (unacceptably stilted translation). Or "Suddenly terrified by the voices of the hunters, the deer began to flee through the field."

b) "The deer, suddenly terrified by the voices of the hunters, began to flee . . ."

c) "The deer that was suddenly terrified by the voices of the hunters began to flee . . ."

d) "As the deer was suddenly terrified by the voices of the hunters, it began to flee . . ."

e) "By sudden fear of the voices of the hunters, the deer began to flee . . ."

f) "The deer was suddenly terrified by the voices of the hunters and **thus** began to flee . . ."

Persaepe interrogantī quid ageret puer, respondēbat: "Bene quiēvit." (Pliny 3.16.4)

a) No such translation is possible.

b) "To her husband, very often asking how the boy was doing, she answered, 'He slept well.'" (This translation is quite impossible without adding the noun *husband.*)

c) "To her husband, who very often asked how the boy was doing, she answered, . . ."

d) "Because he very often asked how the boy was doing, she answered him, . . ."

e) "To his repeated question how the boy was doing, she answered, . . ."

f) "He asked her very often how the boy was doing. She answered him, . . ."

Id oppidum **in campō situm** *magis opere quam nātūrā munītum erat,* **nullīus idōneae reī egens, armīs virīsque opulentum.** (Sall. *Iug.* 57.1)

a) "Located in a plain, this town was rather protected by entrenchments than by nature: it was not short of resources, and it was rich in arms and man power." (The last two attributive phrases, being too far from their head [*oppidum*], can only be translated by independent sentences [construction f].)

b) "This town, located in a plain, was rather protected . . ."

c) "This town, which was located in a plain, was rather protected . . ."

d) "Since this town was located in a plain, it was rather protected . . ."

e) "Because of its location in a plain, this town was rather protected . . ."

f) "This town was located in a plain, and **therefore** it was rather protected . . ."

Dominant participle

363. Syntactically speaking, an attributive participle modifies its head noun. But **as far as content is concerned, the participle may express the leading idea and thus be the dominant element in the phrase.** This meaning has to be rendered correctly in English.

Fugiens Pompeius hominēs movet. "The flight of Pompey disturbs the people." (Cic. *Att.* 7.11.4) (Not the head [*Pompeius*] but the participle [*fugiens*] expresses the main idea.)

Ab urbe **conditā.** "Since the foundation of Rome."

Occīsus *dictātor Caesar aliīs pessimum, aliīs pulcherrimum facinus [vidētur].* "The murder of the dictator Caesar seems to some the worst deed, to others the most beautiful." (Tac. *Ann.* 1.8.8)

Apposition

364. An **apposition** is a special case of an attribute. **It is a noun that modifies another noun or pronoun and agrees with it** (usually only) in case. Both parts of the noun phrase, head and apposition, are usually interchangeable. If one of the two is lacking, the sentence remains grammatical. In the translation, the apposition is put between commas. See also § 131.

> *Placuit igitur orātōrem ad plebem mittī Menēnium Agrippam, facundum virum.* "They decided thus to send as spokesman to the plebeians Menenius Agrippa, an eloquent man." (Livy 2.32.8)
>
> *Gallōs ab Aquitāniā Garunna flūmen dividit.* "The Gauls are separated from Aquitania by the river Garonne." (Caes. *B.G.* 1.1.2)

Noun in the genitive

365. **The head of a noun phrase can be modified by a noun or a noun phrase in the genitive.** The exact semantic relationships between the attribute and the head are explained in § 126–31.

> *Magna praemia coniūrātiōnis docēre.* "He showed them the great rewards of the conspiracy." (Sall. *Cat.* 17.1) (possessive gen.: see § 126)
>
> *In potestāte sunt servī dominōrum.* "Slaves are in the power of their masters." (Gaius *Inst.* 1.52) (subjective gen.: see § 128)
>
> *Hunc lubidō maxuma invāserat reī pūblicae capiundae.* "He was overtaken by the desire to commit a coup d'état." (Sall. *Cat.* 5.6) (objective gen. [see § 129] with gerundive construction [see § 357])
>
> *Nam neque sedet nisi in interiōre parte aedium.* "For she sits only in the inner part of the house." (Nepos *De virīs,* proem 7) (partitive gen.: see § 127)
>
> *Oratiōnem hūiuscemodī habuit.* "He held a speech of the following kind." (Sall. *Cat.* 20.1) (descriptive gen.: see § 130)
>
> *Aliīs ego tē virtūtibus continentiae, gravitātis, iustitiae, fideī ceterīs omnibus, consulātū et omnī honōre semper dignissimum iūdicāvī.* "It is because of all your other virtues of self-control, earnestness, justice, and loyalty that I have always deemed you very worthy of the consulate and every public office." (Cic. *Mur.* 23) (explanatory gen.: see § 131)

Remark. A personal pronoun in the genitive is not used as a possessive or subjective genitive. It is replaced by a possessive pronoun.

> *Accēdit hīs studium litterārum* [objective gen.]*, quod ex meī* [objective gen.] *cāritāte concēpit. Meōs* [possessive pronoun] *libellōs habet, lectitat, ēdiscit etiam.* "Add to this her interest in literature, which she conceived out of love for me. She has my booklets, reads them continuously, and even learns them by heart." (Pliny 4.19.2)

Other attributes

366. Nouns can be modified by other attributes that, because of their form and/or case, resemble adverbial modifiers. But as they modify a noun, they are attributes. See § 127, remark; § 177.

> *At pater infēlix, **nec iam** pater "Icare," dixit, "ubī es?"* "But the unhappy father, no longer a father, said, 'Icarus, where are you?'" (Ovid *Met.* 8.231–32) (adverb as attribute)
>
> *Quid dīcam dē pietāte **in matrem**, līberālitāte **in sorōrēs**, bonitāte **in suōs**, iustitia **in omnēs**?* "What should I say about his love for his mother, his generosity toward his sisters, his goodness toward his people, his justice with all?" (Cic. *Amic.* 11) (prepositional phrase instead of an objective gen. as attribute)
>
> *Inducebat currus **cum falcibus**.* "He exhibited his chariots with scythes." (A. Gellius *Noctes Att.* 5.5) (prepositional phrase as attribute)
>
> ***Satuī** sēmen mūtuum dederit nēminī.* "Let he lend sowing-seed to nobody." (Cato *Agr.* 5.3) (dat. attribute)
>
> *Triumvirātum **reī pūblicae constituendae** per decem annōs administrāvit.* "For ten years he headed the Commission of Three for the Restoration of the State." (Suetonius *Aug.* 27.1) (noun phrase with an attributive gerundive construction in the dat.]
>
> *... ista **turpiculō** puella **nāsō**.* "That girl with her somewhat ugly nose." (Catullus 41.3) (descriptive abl.: see § 177)

Relative clause

367. **A relative clause is introduced by a relative pronoun** (*qui, quae, quod* 'who, that, which'; *quantus* '(so great) as'; *quālis* '(such) as'; etc.) **or a relative adverb** (*ubī* 'where', *unde* 'from where', *quō* 'to where', *quā* 'along which', *quotiens* '(as often) as', *quōmodo* 'just as', etc.). **The relative pronoun or adverb has its own function in the relative clause.**

The relative clause as a whole is an attributive clause modifiying a noun or pronoun in the governing clause. This (pro)noun is the antecedent. When there is no antecedent, the relative clause as a whole has the function that otherwise the whole (pro)noun phrase (the antecedent and the relative clause) would have: subject, object, or adverbial phrase.

368. **The relative pronoun agrees with its antecedent (the head of the noun phrase) in gender and number. It does not agree in case, because it has its own function in the relative clause.** The indeclinable relative adverb functions as an adverbial in the relative clause.

> *Manlius Gallum, **quī in summō constituerat**, dēturbat.* "Manlius threw down the Gaul who had taken a stand on the top." (Livy 5.47.4)
>
> *Longās nāvēs, **quibus** Caesar exercitum transportāverat **quāsque in aridum subduxerat**, aestus complēverat.* "The war vessels in which Cae-

sar had transported his army and that he had pulled on the shore had been filled by the flood." (Caes. *B.G.* 4.29.2)

Nōn habēbam locum **ubī prō meō iūre diūtius esse possem** *quam fundum Siccae.* "I do not have a place where, in my juridical status, I could stay longer than the estate of Sicca." (Cic. *Att.* 3.2) (*Habebam* is an epistolary imperfect: see § 215.)

369. The place of the antecedent (the term is from *ante* + *cēdere* 'to go before') **is normally before the relative clause**, as in the examples in § 368.

Sometimes the antecedent follows the relative clause (as does *tempus* in the example in § 406). This happens chiefly when the relative clause refers to a general category (often with the indefinite relative pronoun *quisquis* or *quīcumque:* see § 67), often in juridical texts. **A pronoun antecedent is sometimes understood**, particularly when it would have the same case as the relative pronoun. Absence of the antecedent implies indefiniteness of the relative clause.

> *Villula tectum praebuit et parochī* **quae dēbent** *ligna salemque.* "A small farm provided us with shelter and the purveyors with the firewood and salt they owe us." (Hor. *Sat.* 1.5.45–46)
>
> **Quibus ita est interdictum,** *hī numerō impiōrum ac scelerātōrum habentur.* "Those who have thus been banished are considered impious and criminals." (Caes. *B.G.* 6.13.7)
>
> **Quī mancipia vendunt,** *nātiōnem cūiusque in venditiōne prōnuntiāre dēbent.* "Those who sell [= whoever sells] slaves must declare publicly the nationality of each one at the sale." (Ulpianus *Ad edictum aed. cur.* 1, *D.* 21.1.31) (The whole relative clause is the subject of *dēbent; quī* is the subject of the relative clause.)
>
> **Quisquis amat,** *valeat. Pereat* **quī nescit amāre.** *Bis tantō pereat* **quisquis amāre vetat.** "Whoever is in love, may he be well off. May he perish who does not know how to be in love. Twice over may he perish who forbids being in love." (graffito, *C.I.L.* 4.4091)

Sometimes the antecedent occurs not in the main clause but in the middle of the relative clause, in the same case as the relative pronoun. Sometimes (as *quibus itineribus* in the second example in § 394) the antecedent is repeated in the relative clause. (This is the formal style of government and law.)

> *Post mē erat Aegīna, ante mē Megara, dextrā Pīraeus, sinistrā Corinthus,* **quae oppida quōdam tempore florentissima fuērunt.** "Behind me lay Aegina, before me Megara, on the right Pireaus, and on the left Corinth, towns that at some time had been very flourishing." (Cic. *Fam.* 4.5.4) (*Oppida* actually is an apposition to the names of the four towns; it is the antecedent of *quae* and normally would precede it.)
>
> *Licēre illīs* **quāscumque in partēs velint** *sine metū proficiscī.* "They are

allowed to leave without fear, in whatever direction they may want." (Caes. *B.G.* 5.41.6)

370. A relative clause mostly refers to a reality and stands in the **indicative**, as in most of the examples in § 369. However, a **potential condition** and a **contrary-to-fact condition** stand in the **subjunctive**. See the relative clause in the second example in § 226, and see the last example in § 368.

371. The relative clause stands in the **subjunctive** if it has the semantic role of **cause, purpose, consequence, or condition** or if it is a **restrictive** clause. The subjunctive is also used in such turns of phrase (expressing a characteristic) as *sunt quī* 'there are people who (are so that they)', *nōn est quod* 'there is no reason why', and *nōn habeō quod* 'I have nothing to'.

> *Titurius, quī nihil ante **prōvīdisset**, trepidāre.* "Titurius, who [= because he] before had taken no precautions, bustled around." (Caes. *B.G.* 5.33.1)
> *Repertī sunt duo equitēs Rōmānī, quī tē istā cūrā **līberārent**.* "There were found two Roman knights who were going to free you from that worry." (Cic. *Cat.* 1.9) (*Quī = ut*, indicating purpose.)
> *Nōn est quod **contemnās** hoc studendī genus.* "There is no reason for you to think light of this kind of literary activity." (Pliny 1.6.2)
> *Nōn edepol ego tē, **quod sciam**, umquam ante hunc diem vīdī.* "By Pollux, as far as I know, I have never seen you before this day." (Plautus *Men.* 500–501)

372. The relative clause also stands in the **subjunctive** if it occurs in an **indirect speech (statement, question, or command)** (see the examples in § 281–82 and the last example in § 369). The **subjunctive** is also used by **modal attraction** in relative clauses that depend on infinitives and subjunctives and form an integral part of the thought (see the example in § 283).

373. **A complex relative clause** occurs when a relative pronoun has a function in a clause depending on the relative clause. The dependent clause may be an infinitive clause, an adverbial clause, an indirect question, or another relative clause. Such a complex relative clause may create some problems in translation. The problem consists in the fact that the relative pronoun, which technically connects the relative clause—the dependent clause of the first degree—to the antecedent, only has a syntactic function in the dependent clause of the second degree. The relative pronoun may be translated twice, or some other construction has to be found in English. Compare the alternative translations provided in the examples that follow.

> *[Caesar] certior fīēbat omnēs Belgās, **quam** tertiam esse Galliae partem dīxerāmus, coniūrāre.* "Caesar was informed that all the Belgae, **about whom** we had said that **they** constituted the third part of Gaul, were

conspiring." (Caes. *B.G.* 2.1.1) (*Quam,* here first translated "about whom," connects the clause with *dīxerāmus* to *Belgās;* translated second as "they," *quam* is the subject of the infinitive clause with *esse.*)

"Caesar was informed that all Belgae, **who**—as we had said—constituted the third part of Gaul, were conspiring."

"Caesar was informed that all Belgae were conspiring. We had said that **they** constituted the third part of Gaul."

In rē familiārī, **quae** *quemadmodum frācta, dissipāta, dīrepta sit nōn ignōrās, valdē labōrāmus.* (Cic. *Att.* 4.1.3) (*Quae* introduces the relative clause with *ignōrās,* but it only functions as a subject in the indirect question *quemadmodum . . . sit.*)

"With respect to our family property, **about which** you know all too well how **it** has been broken up, scattered, and plundered, we are in great pains."

"With respect to our family property, we are in great pains. You know all to well how **it** has been broken up, scattered, and plundered."

374. **The connecting relative pronoun** serves to connect a new sentence to the previous one as a whole or to one element in it. As a thematic element (§ 383), it stands at the beginning of the sentence, even before a possible subordinating conjunction. Despite appearance, it introduces an independent clause or sentence, as can be deduced from the fact that such a relative clause occurs as an infinitive clause in indirect speech (§ 273b). The connecting relative pronoun may conveniently be translated by a coordinating conjunction and a demonstrative or personal pronoun. Thus, *quī = et is.* See § 339g.

Eōrum fīnēs Nerviī attingēbant. **Quōrum** *dē nātūrā mōribusque Caesar cum quaereret, sīc reperiēbat.* "Their neighbors were the Nervii. When Caesar inquired about their nature and customs, he found the following." (Caes. *B.G.* 2.15.2)

Eōrum obsidēs esse apud Ariovistum ac Sequanōs intellegēbat. **Quod** *turpissimum sibi et reī pūblicae esse arbitrābātur.* "He understood that their hostages were kept by Ariovistus and the Sequani. And this was—he thought—very disgraceful for him and the state." (Caes. *B.G.* 1.33.2)

Quā *dē causā . . .* "And for that reason . . ." (stereotyped phrase)

Quod *erat dēmonstrandum.* "Which had to be proven." (traditional closing sentence of the proof of a theorem)

PART 5

Textlinguistics

17
Context

Text in context

375. Although the sentence is a very important meaningful unit, it does not stand on its own. It is only meaningful in the wider context of which it is part.

    a) The sentence has to be understood in its **immediate context** of the paragraph, the chapter, and the work (poem, speech, novel, play, law, etc.).

    b) This larger unit is in turn embedded in the larger context of the **speech act** in which the **speaker/author** communicates it to the **addressee/reader**.

    c) The speech act itself is situated in the still wider context of the **world** around the speaker/author and addressee/reader: **place, time, and circumstances**.

    d) When we consider other **contact factors**—such as distance, language used, oral versus written text, and so on—it is clear that communication is a complex event.

The word *context* is used here for various levels above or around the sentence, just as there are various layers around the heart of an onion. This complex situation can be captured graphically in the following scheme.

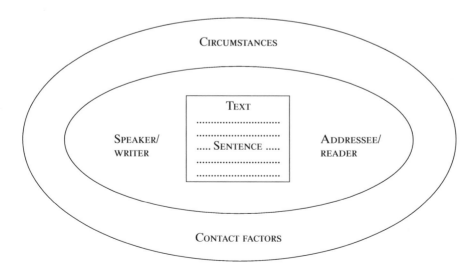

376. A text is shaped by many factors, such as **kind of Latin** used (classical written literary Latin or spoken Latin), **register** (grandiloquent, poetic, formal, familiar, childish, vulgar, etc.), and **(literary) genre** (epic, lyric, tragedy, comedy, satire, history, law, etc.). Also, **circumstances** (time, place), the **intention** of the speaker/author, and the **expectation** of the addressee have their influence on the text. All these factors are involved in the vocabulary, phonology, morphology, syntax, semantics, and style of the example texts discussed in this section.

Phonology and spelling. The patrician family of the **Claudiī** writes and pronounces its name with the diphthong *au*. But P. **Clōdius** Pulcher, belonging to the political party of the *populares,* prefers the pronunciation and spelling with *o*.

The historian Sallust, with his literary intentions, uses words in the "old" spelling (*maxumus, capiundus, honōs, dīvorsus*), whereas Caesar, who intends to create an objective non-literary impression, avoids such a spelling.

The graffito published as *C.I.L.* 4.4091, quoted and translated in § 369, is a perfect distichon (§ 475). The hexameter ends with the first *amare*, but the distichon is written on the wall in Pompeii not in two but in three lines. Its original author is unknown. This distichon has become a common piece of doggerel. It is also found written in eight lines with the following pronunciation and spelling: *Quisquis ama, valia. Peria quī nosci amāre. Bis tantī peria quisquis amāre vota* (*C.I.L.* 4.1173).

Morphology. The epitaph of L. Cornelius Scipio from the third century B.C. tells us, *Hic cēpit Corsica Aleriaque urbe,* "He took Corsica and the city of Aleria" (*C.I.L.* 1².9). In classical Latin, the last three words of this epitaph would have ended with an *m* (§ 2), indicating the accusative (i.e., *Corsicam Aleriamque urbem*). That these words are direct objects is obvious not from the case endings but from the predicate frame of *capere*, which requires a subject and a direct object.

Syntax. Trimalchio, a rich braggart of vulgar descent, says, *Scīs enim* **quod** *epulum dedī bīnōs dēnāriōs,* "You know indeed that I have given a great dinner at two denarii per person" (Petronius *Sat.* 71.9). Instead of an indirect statement with *quod*, an infinitive clause would have been used in classical Latin.

Style. Caesar, a matter-of-fact author, mentions dawn with two words: *Prīmā lūce ex castrīs proficiscuntur,* "At dawn they left the camp" (*B.G.* 5.31.6). But the poet Ovid, a *poeta doctus,* refers to dawn by means of a more lofty periphrasis in hexameters:

> *Postera nocturnōs Aurōra remōverat ignēs*
> *solque pruīnōsās radiīs siccāverat herbās,*
> *ad solitum coiēre locum.*

"Later—Aurora had chased the nighttime stars and the sun had dried the dew-laden grass—they met at their usual place" (Ovid, *Met.* 4.81–83).

Satire on lofty style. In a satirical mixture of prose and poetry, Seneca (*Apoc.* 2.2–4) describes first the autumn in six lofty verses, only to correct himself immediately:

Putō magis intellēgī sī dixerō: "Mensis erat Octōber, diēs III Idūs Octōbrēs," "I think I shall be better understood if I say: 'It was the month October, October 13.'" He then does the opposite changing his plain mention of the hour into three lofty hexameters.

... Inter sextam et septimam [hōram] erat. "Nimis rustice! Adquiescunt omnēs poetae, nōn contentī ortūs et occāsūs dēscrībere, ut etiam medium diem inquiētent: tū sīc transībis hōram tam bonam?"

Iam medium currū Phoebus dīviserat orbem
et propior noctī fessās quatiēbat habēnās,
oblīquō flexam dēdūcens trāmite lūcem.

"It was between the sixth and the seventh hour. 'Hey bumpkin! All poets, not content to describe the rise and the setting of the sun, find pleasure in disturbing also the middle of the day: are you going to overlook so nice an hour?'

Yet Phoebus in his chariot had divided his orbit in two
and, nearer to the night, was shaking the weary reins,
bringing the slanting light along his downhill slope."

377. **Elements from the non-verbal context** may be essential for the understanding of the text.

Dagania viv[a] sibi et M. Aur[eliō] victōrī vet[erānō] leg[iōnis] p[rīmae] co[n]iūgī fēcit. "Dagania made [this grave monument] during her life for herself and her husband Marcus Aurelius, victorious veteran of the First Legion." (epitaph from Cologne, *C.I.L.* 13.2.2.8279) (The direct object has to be inferred from the gravestone on which the text is chiseled.)

Em, hocine volēbas? "There you are, is it this that you wanted?" (Plautus *Most.* 9) (This text can only be understood if one knows that the comedian speaking here gives the other a box on the ears.)

Functions in the text

378. **Some words function not in the sentence but on a higher level in the text.** Even if such a word occurs in the middle of the sentence, it is not a sentence constituent.

379. A word or phrase in the **vocative** has an **appeal function** in the text as a whole (speech or letter). It serves to draw the attention of the addressee/reader to what is said in the following sentences, but it is not a statement, question, command, prohibition, wish, or exhortation (§ 225– 38). Neither does it function as part of the sentence next to it (§ 184–86). For an example, see § 124.

380. A text may be interrupted by **emotional elements** whereby the speaker/writer shows his/her interest, concern, or sympathy. The following words or constructions can be used:

a) **an exclamation in the vocative, dative, or accusative**, sometimes accompanied by an interjection, such as *heu, ō,* or *prō* (§ 124, 145, 160);

b) **an interjection**, often with onomatopoeic effect: *ō* 'oh', *hem* 'eh?', *vae, heu* 'alas', *heus* 'ho, hallo', *ōhē* 'stop, enough', *iō* 'hurrah', 'oh', *immō* 'yes indeed, yes even, no on the contrary';

c) **an interjection** derived from a noun or verb: *age, agedum* 'come on', *sīs (= sī vīs)* 'please', *apage* (Greek ἄπαγε) 'go away', *en* 'look', *ecce* 'see', *meherc(u)le* 'by Hercules', *edepol* 'by Pollux';

d) the *dativus ethicus*: *mihi, tibi* (§ 144).

381. A sentence can be accompanied by a **sentence adverbial** (an adverb, an adverb phrase, or an adverbial clause). Such a sentence adverbial does not modify the predicate of the sentence but **constitutes a comment (parenthesis) about the sentence as a whole**. The sentence and the comment together are called a hyper-sentence.

> *Opportūnē complūrēs pătrēs audiēbant.* "Fortunately, several fathers were listening." (Pliny 4.13.4) (The adverb *opportūnē* is not an adverbial with *audiēbant* but is a judgment of the speaker about the fact that the fathers were listening. Therefore, the translation of this hyper-sentence is not "Several fathers were listening in a fortunate way" but "It was very lucky that several fathers were listening".)
>
> *Nē longum sit, Quirītēs, tabellās prōferrī iussimus.* "To be short, Roman citizens, we ordered the tablets to be brought forward." (Cic. *Cat.* 3.10) (In this hyper-sentence, the clause *nē longum sit* is not a purpose clause with the predicate *iussimus* or *prōferrī* but a comment of the speaker about his own account of the events, which he wants to be short.)

18

Word Order

Communicative perspective: theme-rheme

382. The place of the constituents in the sentence is not determined by their function (subject, object, adverbial, etc.). Wherever the constituents are placed, their syntactic function is clear from their endings and the sentence structure (§ 184–86). Nevertheless, the constituents do not occur at random in the sentence. In the communication, the speaker/writer provides, on the one hand, elements already known to the addressee/reader and, on the other hand, elements that help move the communication forward. These elements require not a syntactic structure but a **communicative organization**.

383. Theme-rheme. A sentence is always about some subject matter, not a subject in the syntactic meaning, but the **subject talked about**, or **theme**. This matter consists of **information known or supposed to be known to the addressee/reader**. This information must be given in order to know what the rest of the sentence is all about. The theme is not so important informationwise, but it is the indispensable anchor for connecting the sentence to the preceding context. The theme provides text cohesion. It makes sure that what is said in the sentence is about something.

About this theme at the beginning of the sentence, **something is said** in the **second part of the sentence**. This part is the **rheme** (Greek ῥῆμα 'saying, verb, predicate'). The rheme is the section that pushes the communication forward: it offers relevant information. This (usually new) information is needed to communicate something. Without it, the sentence would provide only something the addressee/reader already knows; repeating only the theme would make no sense.

In his *Metamorphoses* (8.159–68), Ovid narrates how Daedalus (on Crete in exile from Athens) builds a labyrinth for the Minotaur. Then follows the story of Theseus killing the Minotaur and fleeing with Ariadne from Crete (vv. 169–82). The next verses read as follows:

> *Daedalus intereā Crētēn longumque perōsus*
> *exsilium tactus locī nātālis amōre*
> *clausus erat pelagō. "Terrās licet, inquit, et undās*
> *obstruat, at caelum certē patet. Ibimus illāc."*
> "In the meantime Daedalus, detesting Crete and his long exile, and touched by nostalgia, was closed off by the sea. 'Let Minos obstruct

land and sea,' he said, 'but heaven certainly lies open. We'll go that way.'" (Ovid *Met.* 8.183–86)

In verse 183 the poet refers to the earlier themes of the Daedalus narrative: Daedalus and *intereā* (the intervening story) about Theseus and Ariadne. The reference to these two themes does not teach us anything, as they are known from the preceding context, but at the beginning of the sentence, they do provide two anchors to connect the new story to what the reader/listener knows. In the rest of the sentence, we receive more news about Daedalus's state of mind (detestation, nostalgia) and his isolation on the island: this is the information, the rheme, that pushes the sentence further and creates a dynamic process in the narrative. Among these new elements (rhemes), some are more relevant than others. Daedalus's state of mind certainly is useful new information explaining the reasons for his plans, but the major point (the rheme proper) is that Daedalus is cut off from his homeland by the sea. This information and particularly the last word in *clausus erat pelagō* is going to bring us to the metamorphosis of people flying through the air. In the next sentence, Daedalus goes on saying that nothing can be done by land or by sea but that the air is open. Also in this sentence, the first part about land and sea is more or less given (Crete is an island), but the rheme *caelum* and the rheme proper *patet* are pushing the narrative forward. The poet has thus created some perspective in his communication: the sentence basically goes from theme (starting point, known, supposed to be known) to rheme (new, most relevant).

The rheme thus has a greater **communicative dynamism** in the sentence than does the theme: after hearing/reading the theme, one learns something more about that theme. Through the **communicative perspective** given by the speaker/writer to the sentence, **the sentence constituents are thus ordered according to their degree of communicative dynamism, with the theme (or themes) at the beginning and the rheme (or rhemes) at the end.** If there are several themes or several rhemes, one of them usually is the **theme proper (Tp)** or the **rheme proper (Rp)**, respectively. The other themes and rhemes occur between those two. The principle of word order—or, rather, of the order of the sentence constituents (irrespective of their syntactic function)—is thus

$$\text{Tp} - \text{T} - \ldots - \text{R} - \text{Rp}$$

The information does not necessarily need to be new in order to be rhematic: an "old acquaintance" could also be the most relevant element (rheme), as are *vōbīs* in the first example in § 203, *nōbīs* in the first example in § 261, *nōbīs* in the second example in § 389, *tē* in the first example in § 390, and *pedēs* in the first example in § 394. Through their final position in the English translation, these words automatically receive full emphasis when read aloud.

Normal word order in the sentence

384. **In the normal order of the sentence constituents, the theme occurs at the beginning.** Themes make the connection with elements from the speech act or from the preceding context. The speaker/writer starts with what the addressee/reader already knows and gives further information about it. Being so well known, **some themes are not even mentioned but are understood from the context.**

Typical themes are

a) **the speaker** and **the addressee** in a dialogue (§ 387a–c).
b) **an element from the preceding sentence.** The rheme of one sentence is often the theme of the following sentence. It is often taken up as a synonym or pronoun, or else it is understood (§ 387d [*id*], g–h).
c) **an element that is supposed to be known or that is self-evident from the context,** even if it has not been mentioned ("the house and the roads" in the last example in § 391).
d) **a new theme** that, without introductory sentence, stands at the beginning of a sentence (*Caesarī* in § 387d and *Gallia* in § 387g1). Sometimes it occurs as a *nominativus pendens* (dangling nominative), somewhat loose from the sentence, but it is then taken up again by a pronoun in the appropriate case (§ 387e–f).
e) **a setting element of place or time.** These elements are needed in order to situate the rest of the sentence (§ 387h1). Without that indication, misunderstandings could occur. For instance, the sentence *On September 11 the president died* would be misunderstood or not understood by a reader today if the sentence did not start with the correct setting elements, that is, *In Santiago de Chile, on September 11, 1973 . . .* A setting element by itself is not dynamic in the communication, hence it has a thematic character and is placed at the beginning of the sentence. (If those elements were to occur at the end of the sentence, as a rheme, the sentence might be a student's answer to a history teacher's question about the theme "the death of a president.")

385. **Jurists and historians (particularly Caesar and Sallust) have a tendency to put the verb at the end,** irrespective of its degree of communicative dynamism (§ 387h3–6, 8), *esse* often excepted (§ 387h1–2, 7, 9). The place of the verb thus does not conform to the ideal distribution of the constituents in the sentence according to their degree of communicative dynamism. In these authors, the rheme stands right before the verb. (In other authors, the verb does not occur as systematically at the end of the sentence.) The pattern of the order of the sentence constituents in these authors is thus

$$\text{Tp} - \text{T} - \ldots - \text{R} - \text{Rp}, \text{Verb}$$

386. The communicative perspective (and hence the order of constituents) of the Latin sentence has to be preserved as much as possible in the English translation. If necessary, the Latin syntactic structure should give way to another English construction that permits saving the original communicative perspective. Turning an active sentence into a passive one may be a handy solution, as appears from certain translations (§ 387g2–4, 6).

387. Examples and Commentary. In the example sentences in this section, the bold type indicates the theme(s) (T). The rheme(s) (R) are printed in regular type.

a) *Exī, inquam, age, exī!* "Get out, I say, come on, get out!" (Plautus *Aul.* 40)

In the preceding first line of their dialogue, both the speaker and the addressee are known themes to each other and are not even mentioned. Relevant information about *ego* and *tū* (understood) is given by the rhemes *exī* and *inquam.*

b) *Sunt **nōbīs** mītia pōma, castaneae mollēs et pressī cōpia lactis.* "I have ripe apples, soft chestnuts, and plenty of cheese." (Virg. *Buc.* 1.80–81)

With the preceding sentence, Tityrus invites Meliboeus to pass the night with him. At the beginning of the sentence stands the semantically very weak "presentative verb" *sunt* 'there are' (§ 394). Then follows the theme *nōbīs* 'we/I' (the well-known speaker). At the end is the rheme, the three very informative subjects.

c) ***Ego** cum **tē** quaererem, ancillae tuae crēdidī . . . **Tū mihi** nōn crēdis ipsī?* "When I asked for you, I believed your maidservant . . . You do not believe me in person?" (Cic. *De oratore.* 2.276)

Ego, tē, tū, and *mihi* are partners in the preceding dialogue and hence are themes. They are expressed here (cf. § 54e) because they are in contrast. The other elements in the first sentence are new information and thus rhematic. The rheme (*crēdidī*) from the first sentence becomes a theme in the second sentence. New and very informative is now the negation *nōn* (a strong rhematizer for the otherwise thematic element *crēdis*). In the object *mihi ipsī,* the personal pronoun *mihi* is thematic. Within this pronoun phrase, *ipsī* strongly emphasizes *mihi,* hence it is positioned in a hyperbaton (§ 432) and in a conspicuous place, at end of the sentence.

d) ***Caesarī** cum id nuntiātum esset, eōs per prōvinciam nostram iter facere cōnārī, mātūrat ab urbe proficisci.* "When this was reported to Caesar—that is, that they were trying to travel through our province—he hastened to leave Rome." (Caes. *B.G.* 1.7.1)

In this sentence, Caesar is mentioned for the first time in his book as a new theme, the theme proper. The preceding chapters by Caesar dealt with the emigration plans of the Helvetians (here, the theme *id* is once more summarized in the infinitive clause *eōs . . . cōnārī*, because otherwise *id* could refer to a particular minor detail in the preceding sentence). As *Caesarī* is the theme of the dependent clause and of the main clause (and also of the passage that starts here and actually of Caesar's whole book), this theme stands at the very beginning of the sentence, before the conjunction *cum*. This theme is the indirect object in the dependent clause and the subject of the main clause. This very conspicuous new theme could be introduced more explicitly in English as follows: "Now, turning to Caesar, when this was reported to him, he . . ."

e) *Sed **urbāna plēbēs, ea** vērō praeceps erat dē multīs causīs.* "But the city masses, yes, they were very eager for many reasons." (Sall. *Cat.* 37.4)

In the preceding sentence is a case of the *nominativus pendens* as a new theme, taken up by *ea,* theme and subject.

f) ***Mercātor Siculus, cuī erant geminī fīliī, eī** surreptō alterō mors obūgit.* "A Sicilian merchant who had twin sons—he lost one of them through a kidnapping and later died." (Plautus *Men.,* arg. 1–2)

In the preceding sentence is a case of the *nominativus pendens* (with relative clause) as theme, taken up as theme by the dative object *ei.*

g) The following segmented example is from a continuous passage by Caesar (*B.G.* 1.1.1–3).

> 1) ***Gallia** est omnis dīvīsa in partēs trēs.* "Gaul [T, not mentioned before, but the reader understands that at the beginning of a book, this is the theme proper of the book, the chapter, and the sentence] as a whole is divided [R] into three parts [Rp]."
> 2) ***Unam partem** incolunt Belgae,* "One part [the Rp of the preceding sentence is now the T of this sentence] is inhabited [R, in English in the passive so that "one part" can be at the beginning in the translation] by the Belgae [Rp, with a different function in Latin than in English],"
> 3) ***aliam** Aquitānī,* "the other [T] by the Aquitani [Rp],"
> 4) ***tertiam** quī ipsōrum linguā Celtae, nostrā Gallī appellantur.* "the third [T] by those who are called in their own language Celts and in our language Gauls [Rp]."
> 5) ***Hī omnēs** linguā, institūtīs, lēgibus inter sē differunt.* "All these peoples [T, known from segments 2–4] differ [R, sentence-final in Caesar's original (§ 385)] among themselves in language, institutions, and laws [three-part Rp]."
> 6) ***Gallōs ab Aquitānīs** Garunna flūmen, **ā Belgīs** Matrona et Sequana dīvīdit.* "The Gauls [Tp, known from segment 4, translated

as the subject in English because it is easier to put it at the beginning] are separated [R, sentence-final in Caesar's original] from the Aquitani [T] by the river Garonne [Rp], from the Belgae [T] by the Marne and the Seine [Rp]."

7) *Hōrum omnium fortissimī sunt Belgae.* "The bravest [R, new idea] of all those peoples [initial T, summary of rhemes in segments 2–4] are the Belgae [Rp; although mentioned before, they are singled out and specifically mentioned as the bravest. Notice the intonation of the English sentence, when read aloud with high pitch on the rheme and the rheme proper.]."

Segments 2–4 and 6 of the preceding example could be translated in the active voice, but in that case, the object themes "one part," "the second," "the third," "Gauls," and "Aquitani" would occur at the end of the sentence, and the subject rhemes "Belgae," "Aquitani," "those who . . . ," and "Marne and Seine" would occur at the beginning. This would be contrary to the communicative theme-rheme perspective. English tends to make of the subject the theme, hence the English passive construction is employed in translation in these examples. In Latin, the coincidence between theme and subject is less frequent.

h) The following segmented example is from a continuous passage by Caesar (*B.G.* 6.13.1–8).

1) *In omnī Galliā eōrum hominum quī aliquō sunt numerō atque honōre genera sunt duo . . .* "In the whole of Gaul [T], there are two classes [Rp, almost impossible to put at the end] of people who are of some rank and honor [R] . . ."

2) *Dē hīs duōbus generibus alterum est druidum, alterum equitum.* "Of those classes, one [T, Rp in the preceding sentence] is that of the druids [R], the other [T] that of the knights [R]."

3) *Illī rēbus dīvīnīs intersunt,* "The first ones [T, pronoun = druids] are involved [R, sentence-final in Caesar's original] in religious matters [Rp];"

4) *sacrificia pūblica ac prīvāta prōcūrant,* "they [T, understood] take care [R, sentence-final in Caesar's original] of public and private sacrifices [Rp];"

5) *religiōnēs interpretantur.* "they [T, understood] explain [R, sentence-final in Caesar's original] religious ceremonies [Rp]."

6) *Ad hōs magnus adulescentium numerus disciplīnae causā concurrit,* "To these [druids, Tp], a great number of youth [R] flock together [R, sentence-final in Caesar's original] for instruction [Rp],"

7) *magnōque hī sunt apud eōs honōre.* "and these [Tp] stand with them [the students, second T] in great honor" [Rp, emphasized by the hyperbaton: see § 432].

8) *Nam ferē dē omnibus contrōversiīs pūblicīs prīvātīsque*

constituunt . . . "For they [T, understood] decide [R, sentence-final in Caesar's original] almost all public and private disputes [Rp] . . ."

9) **Hīs autem omnibus druidibus** *praeest ūnus, quī summam inter eōs habet auctōritātem.* "At the head of all these druids [T, taken up again as a full noun phrase after a seven-line excursus about the sub-theme of punishments and punished people], there is [R] one who has the highest authority among them [Rp]."

The preceding nine segments contain eleven themes (two each in segments 2 and 7). Five have the function of subject (the subject in segments 3 and 7 and the understood subject in segments 4–5 and 8), two are a part of the predicate (segment 2), one is an object in the dative (segment 9), and three are adverbials (segments 1 and 6–7).

388. **The communicative perspective given to the sentence by the author has its importance for the correct interpretation and translation of the text.** Each of the next two examples contains a predicate (*mittere*), a subject, a direct object, an adverbial complement of direction, and an adverbial clause of purpose. The verb in both sentences is clause-final (not sentence-final), irrespective of its degree of communicative dynamism. The subject in both cases is thematic. The three other constituents are rhematic in both sentences: they provide completely new information. In both sentences, the final clause is the rheme proper, the most weighty element. **In the first sentence, the adverbial complement** (at the end of the main clause) **is more relevant for the information than is the direct object**, as appears from the adverbial clause in the first example following (with *eō dēprecātōre* taking up *Dumnorīgem*). **In the second example following, the direct object** (at the end of the main clause) **is more relevant than the adverbial complement**, as appears from the following dependent final clause (the message of the *nuntiōs*, an indirect prohibition).

The context of the first example is that the Helvetii want to emigrate through the territory of the Sequani but cannot force their way through on their own.

Legātōs ad Dumnorīgem Haeduum mittunt, ut eō dēprecātōre ā Sequanīs impetrārent. "They [understood T] sent delegates to the Haeduan Dumnorix, in order to obtain permission from the Sequani at his intercession." (Caes. *B.G.* 1.9.2)

After Caesar's victory, the surviving Helvetii have fled to the Lingones. Caesar does not have time to follow them immediately.

Caesar ad Lingōnās litterās nuntiōsque mīsit, ne eōs frūmentō nēve aliā rē iuvārent. "Caesar [T] sent the Lingones a letter and messengers, [saying] that they should not help them with grain or other supplies." (Caes. *B.G.* 1.26.6)

389. **Prolepsis** is a phenomenon based on the communicative perspective in the sentence. In a case of prolepsis, the subject of the dependent clause is shifted to the front (Greek πρόληψις *pro-lepsis*) as a constituent (often direct object) of the main clause. Sometimes it is fronted in the nominative. **Prolepsis occurs if the dependent clause is rhematic but its subject is thematic. Such a thematic element fits better into the communicative organization of the sentence if it occurs more to the front of the sentence, according to its low degree of communicative dynamism.** In English translation, such a prolepsis usually cannot be rendered, because the English would be too awkward. Too much emphasis would fall on that thematic element, which is exactly what the Latin construction wants to avoid. The weight should be carried by the rhematic dependent clause.

In an example from the comedy *Aulularia,* the miser Euclio has hidden a pot with gold. The public knows this, but his maidservant Staphyla does not. Euclio says (to the public), *Nimis ego **hanc** metuō malē nē mihi ex insidiīs verba imprūdentī duit neu persentiscat **aurum** ubi'st absconditum,* "I am terribly afraid that behind the scenes she might fool me if I do not take care and that she might smell whére the gold is hídden." (Plautus *Aul.* 61–63). Here, *hanc* 'her' (i.e., Staphyla) is the theme and direct object of *metuō,* but the translation "I am afraid of her" would emphasize "her" too much. Staphyla is also the subject of *duit (= det),* but as a theme, this subject is not in accordance with the rhematic character of that dependent clause. The same holds for the thematic *aurum,* here the direct object of *persentiscat,* but also the understood subject of *absconditum est.* The translation, therefore, is not: ". . . where the góld is hidden" but ". . . whére the gold is hídden." (In the translation, the accent marks indicate emphasis so as to render the rheme(s).)

In a second example, Tityrus has spoken earlier with much enthusiasm about a god who has provided him with a life free of care. Meliboeus complains about his own misfortune. He ends, *Sed tamen, **iste deus** quī sit, da, Tītyre, nōbīs,* "But, to come back to that god of yours, who he is, Tityrus, tell it to mé" (Virg. *Buc.* 1.18). Here, the thematic *iste deus* is taken to the front outside the rhematic indirect question *quī sit;* then follow the rhematic imperative *da* and the rheme proper *nōbīs.* Although this pronoun refers to a partner in the dialogue, it is nevertheless rhematic (unlike *nōbīs* in § 387b): it is important for Meliboeus that finally hé gets to know that god.

A third example comes from Catullus 92.2: ***Lesbia mē** dispeream nīsī amat.* "As for Lesbia and me, may I fall dead if she doesn't love me." Here, the thematic subject *Lesbia* and object *mē* of the otherwise rhematic dependent clause *nisi amat* are moved forward.

Emotive and special word order

390. The **theme-rheme** scheme (or the **theme-rheme, verb** scheme in such authors as Caesar) is the normal communicative organization of the sentence. But sometimes the speaker/writer **emotionally starts with what he/she considers most important and utters the rheme proper first**, only to add later the theme (or themes)—which of course is (or are) also needed in order to know what the rheme is all about. The **emotive word order is thus**

$$R - T$$

Two examples are instructive. The first is an epigram, a distich from Martial.

*Quid **mihi** reddat ager quaeris, Line, Nōmentānus.*
*Hoc **mihi reddit ager**: tē, Line, nōn videō.*
"What my field in Nomentum yields me, you ask, Linus. This my field yields me: I do not see yóu, Linus." (Mart. *Ep.* 2.38)

Here, themes in the first sentence are the speaker (*mihi*) and the addressee (understood *tū*). All the rest is rhematic. (About *quid,* see § 392.) In the second, largely parallel sentence, the three bold constituents are thematic because they are known from the preceding verse. The first word uttered by the poet is *hoc*, something that was sticking in his throat: this is the emotive rheme. In the last sentence, this *hoc* is explained, also with an emotive rheme proper (*tē*) at the beginning.

In the second example, Pliny argues that most people go to the circus races out of interest not in the speed of the horses or the dexterity of the charioteers but in the color of the tunic of their favorite drivers.

*Nunc favent pannō, pannum **amant**.* "Now they favor a piece of cloth, a piece of clóth they love!" (Pliny 9.6.2)

In the first sentence of this example, *favent* is rhematic, but *pannō* is clearly the rheme proper. In the second sentence, all three constituents (understood subject, object, and predicate) are known, but the scornful writer once again wants to berate that colored piece of cloth, which he therefore puts at the beginning of the sentence as an emotive rheme. The rhematic character of this constituent could also be rendered emphatically in an English cleft sentence: "It is a piece of cloth they love!" Pliny's two sentences, with T-R and R-T, form a nice chiasmus (§ 418), both in the syntactic and in the communicative structure.

Both the normal and the emotive word order sometimes play a role in certain figures of speech (§ 410, 418, 432, 442, 453).

391. Sometimes the normal and the emotive word order occur together in the same sentence. In such a **special order**, the sentence contains successively a rheme, then one or more themes, and then one or more rhemes (including the rheme proper). In both translations that follow, the first rheme is highlighted by a cleft construction, and the passive is used in order to leave the theme (object in Latin, subject in English) in the beginning of the sentence, after the initial emotive rheme. Both English sentences end with the rhemes proper.

> *Nimium diū tē imperātōrem tua illa Manliāna castra dēsīderant.* "It is all too long [R] that you [T] as general [R] are expected [R] by that famous camp of your Manlius [Rp]!" (Cic. *Cat.* 1.10)

In the second example, the context (Tac. *Ann.* 1.5.5) is that "Tiberius is suddenly called by urgent letter from his mother [Livia]. It is not known whether he found Augustus (in the villa) near Nola still alive or dead." *Acribus namque custōdiīs domum et viās saepserat Līvia.* 'For it was with fierce sentries [R, strengthened by the hyperbaton and therefore translated by means of a cleft sentence: see § 432] that the house and the roads [T, to be inferred from the fact that Augustus is dying in his villa near Nola] had been sealed off [R] by Livia [Rp].' (Tac. *Ann.* 1.5.6) In this case, a translation in the passive brings the name *Livia* to the rhematic end position also in English. Tacitus wants to suggest that Livia, the rheme proper, may be responsible for Augustus' death. She is also the understood agent of the verbs *vulgabantur* and *provisis* in the sentence from Tacitus, quoted in § 353, which immediately follows the sentence about Livia, discussed here.

392. **In a question, the interrogative pronoun or interrogative adverb, or the word with the question particle -*ne*, stands at the beginning of the sentence as a stereotyped emotive rheme.**

> *Quemadmodum in urbe potuisti?* "How [R] could [R] you [T] [enjoy quietly your time] [T, understood from the preceding sentence (quoted in § 316)] in Rome [R]?" (Pliny 9.6.1)
> *Malusne ego sum?* "Am I [T] bad [R]?" (Plautus *Persa* 371)

See also the example in § 409 and the first example in § 428.

Place of the verb

393. **The place of the verb can vary a great deal. First, there is the strong tendency of the verb to occur at the end of the sentence in certain authors:** legal texts, Caesar, Sallust, and other historians (§ 385).

394. **In other authors, particularly in poetry, the verb is not confined to the final position,** as can be seen in many examples (see, e.g., § 432, 475). Often, particularly in Plautus, its position is **also determined by its degree of communicative dynamism**: it fits into the theme-rheme scheme (see also the last example, from Tacitus, in § 391).

In an instructive example from Plautus, Harpax has described someone with red hair, a fat belly, big feet, and so on. Ballio reacts: *Perdidistī,
ut nōmināvistī pedēs. Pseudolus fuit ipsus,* "You killed me, when you [T]
mentioned [T] the feet [Rp]. It was Pseudolus himself" (Plautus *Pseud.*
1220–21). Here, the verb does not occupy the stereotyped final position
as in Caesar, because in Plautus it is sensitive to its degree of communicative dynamism. The verb *nōmināvistī* is thematic, for that is exactly
what Harpax has been doing. Also, the feet have been mentioned in the
preceding sentence, but they are singled out by Ballio as the most relevant—the most weighty—element (Rp). The verb would be final if it
were the rheme (proper).

**The communicative perspective is particularly observed, even in Cae-
sar, with presentative verbs, verbs indicating that somebody or something
is somewhere or is arriving on the scene.** These verbs have a relatively
low degree of communicative dynamism. Important is not so much the
presence or the arrival but who or what is present or arrives. Presentative verbs are never final: they are initial or occur after a possible theme;
the rhematic subject follows the verb.

Erant omnīnō itinera duo, quibus itineribus domō exīre possent.
"There were in total two roads along which they could leave their
homeland." (Caes. *B.G.* 1.6.1) (*Erant* is a weak presentative verb with
a rhematic subject. Notice the repetition of the antecedent within the
relative clause [§ 369].)
In an example from Sallust, Catiline has called conspirators to a
meeting.
Eō convēnēre P. Lentulus Sūra, P. Autrōnius, L. Cassius, etc. "There [=
at the meeting, T] arrived [weak R] P. Lentulus Sura, P. Autronius, L.
Cassius, and so on [Rp]." (Sall. *Cat.* 17.3)
See also the second example in § 443 (*Hīc est sepulchrum . . .*) and the
example from Ovid in § 422 (T-weak R [*vēnit*]-Rp). For an initial presentative verb in Virgil, see § 387b (*sunt*).

395. **A verb in the beginning of the sentence has a special significance in all authors. It indicates velocity or agitation.** Even Caesar writes reports about
a swift action with verbs in initial position or **in an alternating initial and
final position.**

Conticuēre omnēs. "Silent were they all." (Virg. *Aen.* 2.1)
*Agitābātur magis magisque in diēs animus ferox inopiā reī familiāris et
conscientiā scelerum.* "More and more from day to day his fierce mind
was shaken by poverty and the conscience of his crimes." (Sall. *Cat.* 5.7)
> *Est mollēs flamma medullās*
> *intereā et tacitum vivit sub pectore vulnus.*
> *Uritur infēlix Dīdō tōtāque vagātur*
> *urbe furens.*

"Fire devours her tender marrow meanwhile and silent lives her wound deep in her heart. Desperate Dido burns and, raging, she roams through the entire city." (Virg. *Aen.* 4.66–69) (Not one of the four verbs is final in these dramatic hexameters.)

Caesar . . . nuntium . . . ad Crassum **mittit** *. . .* **Iubet** *mediā nocte legiōnem proficiscī celeriterque ad sē venīre.* **Exit** *cum nuntiō Crassus. Alterum ad Fabium legātum* **mittit** *. . .* **Scrībit** *Labiēnō . . .* "Caesar sends [final] a messenger to Crassus. He orders [initial] the legion to leave at midnight and to come quickly back to him. Off goes [initial] Crassus with the messenger. He sends [final] another [messenger] to his commander Fabius. He writes [initial] to Labienus . . ." (Caes. *B.G.* 5.46.1–4)

19
Stylistics

Introduction

396. Language is a complex communication system, consisting, on the one hand, of vocabulary and, on the other hand, of grammatical subsystems (phonology, morphology, syntax, semantics, pragmatics, etc.). Not all people use this system of systems in the same way. To voice their ideas and feelings in an expressive way and to draw the attention to their speech or writing, they use all kinds of creative means whereby they differentiate themselves from others. These means are studied in one of those subsystems; **stylistics**, which deals with stylistic means based on sounds, rhythm, choice of vocabulary, placement of words, sentence construction, versification, and so on. These stylistic ornaments or **figures of speech** increase the sensation of beauty or the **aesthetic pleasure** when one reads or listens to a text. Some matter-of-fact authors may not make much use of those figures of speech. But in artistic prose, particularly in rhetoric and in poetry, writers will do their utmost to express themselves in a creative and elegant way. Some figures of speech occur in both prose and poetry, others only in poetry.

Rhetorical period

397. Although authors sometimes like to express themselves in vivid, short sentences with quick and surprising turns, they also often strive for a more **connected style with longer sentences containing a complete thought process**. Such a complete thought process is found in the rhetorical period. **A rhetorical period is a well-proportioned sentence of a certain length where several clauses are connected to the main clause and where rhythm and equilibrium provide a certain stateliness.** *Period* (Greek περίοδος) means 'cycle'. A rhetorical period in the strict sense of the word begins with the subject, encircles the dependent clauses, and rounds up with the rest of the main clause(s). In many periods, however, the subject of the main clause does not stand at the beginning.

398. A **rhetorical period** consists of two parts: first, a **protasis** 'preceding stretching', or the preparatory part, which has a rising intonation until the climax; and second, an **apodosis** 'restitution, rendering', or the conclusion or answer to the protasis, with descending intonation.

In a **historical period** (narrating), the protasis contains the causes and the chronological preparation, and the apodosis gives the events of the story.

In a **rhetorical period** (arguing), the protasis contains various considerations and arguments (cause, condition, etc.), and the apodosis gives the main idea or the thesis of the orator.

399. The **equilibrium** in the period is attained by the fact that the protasis and the apodosis have roughly the same number of clauses of similar length. (See also § 436, on the isocolon.)

400. In the Latin sentence, **rhythm** is obtained not by the alternation of stressed and non-stressed syllables, as in English, but by the alternation of long and short syllables. Particularly for the end of the sentence, its **clausula**, certain rules and patterns are preferred over others. A sentence should not end like a dactylic hexameter (§ 466), with a dactyl and a trochee (§ 465). Preferred clausulae are of the type *iactābĭt aūdācĭā*, with two cretics (long + short + long)*; patiēntĭā nōstrā*, with a cretic and a spondee (long + long, § 465); *ōptĭmūm iūdĭcārĕm*, with a cretic and two trochees (long + short); or *ēssĕ vĭdĕātŭr*, with a paeon (long + short + short + short) and a trochee. These paradigm clausulae are from famous speeches of Cicero. The first and the second one occur at the end of sentences quoted in § 454, the last one in § 402.

401. **Example 1**: Cicero Pro *Milone* 24. Bold type indicates clause markers and predicates.

> *P. Clōdius*
>> ***cum statuisset** omnī scelere in praetūrā vexāre rem pūblicam,*
>> ***vidēretque***
>>> *ita **tracta esse** comitia annō superiōre,*
>>>> ***ut** nōn multōs mensēs praetūram gerere **posset**,*
>>> ***quī** nōn honōris gradum **spectāret** ut cēterī,*
>>> ***sed et** L. Paulum collegam effugere **vellet**, singulārī virtūte cīvem,*
>>> ***et** annum integrum ad dīlacerandam rem pūblicam **quaereret**,*
>> *subitō **relīquit** annum suum,*
>> ***sēsēque** in proximum **transtulit**,*
>>> *nōn, **ut fit**, religiōne aliquā*
>>> *sed **ut habēret**,*
>>>> ***quod** ipse **dicēbat**,*
>>> *ad praetūram gerendam,*
>>>> ***hoc est** ad evertendam rem pūblicam,*
>>> *plēnum annum atque integrum.*

"As P. Clodius had decided to harm the state during his praetorship through all kind of crimes, and as he saw that the elections of the year before had been drawn out so that he would not be able to conduct his praetorship for many months, and as he did not look to a position of honor like the others, and as he both wanted to avoid L. Paulus, a citizen of particular virtue, as colleague and looked for an entire year to tear the state to pieces [climax], he suddenly abandoned his year and advanced his candidacy to the next one, not, as it happens, for some religious reason, but in order to have, as he himself said, for the conduct of his praetorship—that is, for turning the state upside down—a full and complete year."

In this example, the theme and subject of the main and dependent clauses stands at the beginning. The protasis contains seven dependent clauses, six of which have a finite verb. The apodosis contains six clauses: two main and four dependent clauses. It would be possible to translate this Latin period in a smooth, but less grandiloquent, style through some eight English sentences and a few dependent clauses.

402. Example 2: Cicero *In Catilinam* 1.32. Bold type indicates clause markers, accusative subjects, and predicates.

> *Polliceor hoc vōbīs, pătres conscriptī,*
> > *tantam in nōbīs consulibus fore dīligentiam,*
> > *tantam in vōbīs auctōritātem,*
> > *tantam in equitibus Rōmānīs virtūtem,*
> > *tantam in omnibus bonīs consensiōnem,*
> > > *ut Catilīnae profectiōne*
> > > > *omnia patefacta,*
> > > > *illustrāta,*
> > > > *oppressa,*
> > > > *vindicāta esse*
> > > *videātis.*

"I promise you, senators, that there will be such vigilance in us consuls, such authority in you, such courage in the Roman knights, and such concord among all good citizens [climax] that through Catiline's departure you will see all the plotting being unveiled, divulged, suppressed, and punished."

In this example, the protasis contains one main clause with a finite verb and four infinitive clauses with a common *fore*. The apodosis contains four infinitive clauses with a common *esse* and one clause with a finite verb.

Figures of speech

403. General remarks. Many of the figures of speech mentioned below co-occur with other figures. The more figures there are, the more refined or mannered the literary work is. Latin authors pay great technical care to their oeuvre.

By using figures of speech, Latin poets can place certain words at particular places where they fit into the meter. Nevertheless, one should not explain too easily the occurrence of a figure of speech as *metri causa,* or because of meter. The poet uses figures of speech not to patch together a verse that fits in with the meter but to render in an expressive way his/her feelings or thoughts.

404. Allegory: a sustained comparison or metaphor (expressing a truth or generalization).

> *O nāvis, referent in mare tē novī fluctūs.*
> "O ship, new waves will take you to the sea." (Hor. *Carm.* 1.14.1–2)
> (The complete ode of twenty lines is an allegory about the ship of state.)

405. Alliteration: two or more succeeding words begin with the same sound(s).

> *Magnō mē metū līberābis.* "You will free me from a great fear." (Cic. *Cat.* 1.10)
> *Vī victa vis.* "Violence has been overcome by violence." (Cic. *Mil.* 30)

406. Anacoluthon (the Greek term translates 'not following'): syntactical inconsistency, especially the inadvertent or intended shift from one construction, left incomplete, to another. See also *nominativus pendens* at § 384d.

> *Nam nōs omnēs quibus est alicunde aliquis obiectus labōs,*
> *omne quod est intereā tempus prius quam id rescītumst lucrost.*
> "For we all who are blocked by some hardship from somewhere—
> all the time that lies between before we find it out, is gain." (Ter. *Hec.* 286–87)

407. Anaphora (the term translates 'reference': see § 57): repetition of the same word (or other words referring to the same person or thing) at the beginning of several sentences.

> *Mille domōs adiēre locum requiemque petentēs,*
> *mille domōs clausēre serae.*
> "A thousand houses they approached looking for a quiet place, a thousand houses were locked with bolts." (Ovid *Met.* 8.628–29)

408. Anastrophe or **postposition**: inversion of the usual syntactic order of preposition and noun phrase, an archaic postpositioning of the preposition after the noun (§ 117). The preposition stands between the adjective and the noun or even after the noun (phrase). Except for some stereotyped formulas in prose, such as *quam ob rem* 'for that reason', anastrophe occurs chiefly in poetry.

*Inde latet silvīs nullōque **in** monte vidētur.*
"Since then she hides in the woods and is nowhere seen in the mountains." (Ovid *Met.* 3.400)

*. . . sī nōn tanta quiēs īret frigusque calōremque **inter.***
". . . if there did not come such a quiet period between the cold and the heat." (Virg. *Geo.* 2.344–45)

409. Anticlimax: a succession of words or phrases each expressing something smaller (either in length or in content).

Ubinam gentium sumus? Quam rem pūblicam habēmus? In quā urbe vīvimus? "Where in the world are we? What kind of state do we have? In what kind of city do we live?" (Cic. *Cat.* 1.9) (This anticlimax is followed by the climax quoted in § 419. Such a combination in itself constitutes a beautiful figure of speech.)

See the example of an anticlimax in length quoted in § 471.

410. Antithesis: strong contrast between words, phrases, or longer stretches of text. An antithesis often occurs in combination with an oxymoron, a chiasmus, or parallelism.

*Thāis habet **nigrōs, niveōs** Laecania dentēs.*
*Quae ratiō est? **Emptōs** haec habet, illa **suōs.***
"Thais has black teeth, Laecania snow-white ones. What is the reason? The latter has bought teeth, the former her own." (Mart. *Ep.* 5.43) (Notice also the two or even three chiasmi.)

*Ita variē per omnem exercitum **laetitia, maeror, luctus** atque **gaudia** agitābantur.* "So by turns there reigned joy and sorrow, mourning and delight throughout the entire army." (Sall. *Cat.* 61.9) (Notice also the chiasmus.)

411. Archaism: use of obsolete or old-fashioned language (in spelling, vocabulary, morphology, style, etc.), often for a stylistic reason, such as stateliness.

. . . lubidō maxuma reī pūblicae capiundae, . . . pessuma ad divorsa inter sē mala. ". . . a very strong desire to perpetrate a coup d'état, . . . very great evils of opposite character." (Sall. *Cat.* 5.6–8) (old spelling)
Flavam modo pollice cēram mollībat. "Then he softened the yellow wax with his thumb." (Ovid *Met.* 8.199) (The imperfect in classical Latin is *molliēbat.*)
*Multīs et magnīs **tempestātibus** vōs cognōvī.* "Through many important occasions, I have learned to know you." (Sall. *Cat.* 20.3) (*Tempestās = tempus;* in classical Latin, *tempestās* means 'storm'.)

412. Archaic second position in the sentence: the placing of certain words not at the beginning of the sentence but in second position. Enclitic words

(words without independent stress and leaning in pronunciation against a preceding word) never stand at the beginning of the sentence. This is the case for some particles and conjunctions, such as *autem, enim, quidem, tamen, vērō, -que, -ve,* and *-ne.* However, there is a **literary tendency** to extend this old tradition to other words that can occur in first position (*nam, namque, et, igitur, quī,* etc.). Putting these words in second or later position in the sentence is an archaism in poetry.

> *Hīc inter densās corylōs modo **namque** gemellōs relīquit.*
> "For here between the dense hazels she [the goat] recently left her twins behind." (Virg. *Buc.* 1.14–15)

See also the second example (with *āles, . . . **quae***) in § 432.

413. **Assonance**: repetition of sounds in several successive syllables of one or more words.

> *Percutit indignōs clārō plangōre lacertōs.*
> "She beat her guiltless arms with loud lamentation." (Ovid *Met.* 4.138)

See also the nasals in the fourth example in § 432.

414. **Asymmetry**: see variation (§ 462).

415. **Asyndeton**: absence of conjunctions in a series of coordinate words, phrases, or clauses. An asyndeton often expresses close connection or speed.

> *Vēnī, vīdī, vīcī.* "I came, I saw, I conquered." (Suetonius *Caes.* 1.37.4)
> *Onerāvī rursum vīnum, lardum, fabam, sēplasium, mancipia.* "Again I took in cargo of wine, bacon, beans, perfumes, slaves." (Petronius *Sat.* 76)

See also the examples of such clauses in § 436.

416. **Brachylogy** (the term translates 'short speech'): a condensed expression. An omission of a word that (often in another form) occurs elsewhere in the sentence. A special case of brachylogy is gapping (§ 424).

> *Vestītus nihil inter aequālēs excellens.* "His clothing did not stand out at all against [the clothing of] his equals." (Livy 21.4.8)

417. **Caesural rhyme**: terminal consonance in one word at the end of the first hemistich (just before the caesura) and another word at the end of the verse.

> *Prospiciens summā ‖ placidum caput extulit undā.*
> "Looking out, he raised his calm head above the surface of the waves." (Virg. *Aen.* 1.127) (caesural rhyme + scheme *abBA* [§ 432]

+ stately hyperbaton of the waves + the calm head in between those waves + dactylic verb occupying the fifth foot)

418. **Chiasmus** (named in reference to the Greek letter chi [χ]): the crosswise arrangement of contrasted pairs; the inversion of syntactic and/or lexical elements in the second of two juxtaposed phrases or clauses.

Satis ēloquentiae, sapientiae parum. "Enough eloquence, [but] little wisdom." (Sall. *Cat.* 5.4)

See also examples in § 410.

419. **Climax** or **gradation**: the arrangement of a number of phrases or sentences in an ascending order of increasing rhetorical forcefulness. The increase may be due to the length of the elements and/or to their content.

Hīc, hīc sunt . . . quī dē nostrō omnium interitū, quī dē hūius urbis atque adeō dē orbis terrārum exitiō cōgitent. "Here, here are people who contemplate the death of us all, who contemplate the destruction of this city and even of the whole world." (Cic. *Cat.* 1.9)

420. **Ellipsis**: the omission of one or more words that are obviously understood and must be supplied to make the construction grammatically complete. Particularly the copula and auxiliary *esse* are often omitted, but also omitted often are *dīcere, loquī, agere,* and *facere.*

L. Pisōnem legātum Tigurinī eōdem proeliō quō Cassium interfēcerant. "The Tigurini had killed the lieutenant L. Piso in the same battle in which [they had killed] Cassius." (Caes. *B.G.* 1.12.7)
C. Plīnius Cornēliō Tacitō S. [*S. = salūtem dat*] "Gaius Plinius greets his friend Cornelius Tacitus." (Pliny 1.6.1)
Tellus ā nōmine dicta [= *dicta est*] *sepultī.* "The land is named after the one buried there." (Ovid *Met.* 8.235)
Sīc Vēnus. 'Thus [spoke] Venus.' (Virg. *Aen.* 1.325)

421. **Enjambment**: the running over of a sentence from one line of a verse to another so that closely related words fall in different lines; one leg (French *jambe*) of the sentence stands in the next line. The sentence does not come to a rest at the end of the line but runs on and creates a certain velocity or unrest. The word on the next line often receives special emphasis.

Vix spēs ipse suōs animō capit, aurea fingens
omnia.
"His mind could hardly grasp its own expectations, making gold of everything." (Ovid *Met.* 11.118–19)

422. **Epitheton ornans** or **stock ornamental epithet**: an adjective or phrase often accompanying the name of a person or thing by fixed association.

It is used even when not relevant or appropriate for its specific context. Examples are *Iūnōnia Samos* 'Samos consecrated to Juno', *pius Aenēas* 'the conscientious Aeneas', *ātra mors* 'dismal death', *almus ager* 'the nourishing field'.

> *Cumque parente vēnit Atlantiadēs positīs cādūcifer ālīs.* "And together with his father went Atlas's grandson, the herald's staff-bearer without his wings." (Ovid *Met.* 8.626–27) (Mercury travels incognito without his wings and of course also without his staff.)

423. **Euphemism**: agreeable or inoffensive expression as a substitution for one that is harsh, unpleasant, or taboo.

> *Persequar **exstinctum**.* "I will follow you in your death." (Ovid *Met.* 4.151) (*Exstinguere* 'extinguish' = 'kill'.)
> *[Allobrogēs] nuper **pacātī** erant.* "The Allobroges had recently been pacified." (Caesar *B.G.* 1.6.2) (*Pacāre* 'pacify' = 'subdue'.)

424. **Gapping** or **conjunction reduction**: a special case of brachylogy. **Gapping is the omission of all but one occurrence of an identical verb in conjoined sentences that differ in at least two of their constituents.** In general, if the conjoined sentences are **verb final, the gap occurs to the left (backward to the beginning of the sentence**; that is, the verb [or verbs] of the first sentence(s) is [or are] omitted, and the last verb is expressed); **if the verb is not in final position, the gap occurs to the right (forward to the end of the sentence**; that is, the first verb is expressed, and the following verb [or verbs] is [or are] omitted). Exceptions to this general rule chiefly occur in poetry, for various stylistic reasons. Gapping seems to contribute to the cohesion between the conjoined sentences and to render the conjunction a somewhat superfluous cohesive device. Hence, a high ratio of asyndetons occurs with gapping.

> *Haec oculīs, haec pectore tōtō **haeret**.* "She [Dido] clung [to him] with her eyes, she [clung to him] with her whole heart." (Virg. *Aen.* 1.717–18) (The sentence-final verb *haeret* gaps to the left, or backward to the beginning of the sentence.)
> *Iam intellegēs multō mē **vigilāre** acrius ad salūtem quam tē ad perniciem reī pūblicae.* "You [Catiline] will already understand that I [Cicero] look much more carefully after the interest of the state than you [do] after its destruction." (Cic. *Cat.* 1.8) (The non-final verb *vigilāre* gaps to the right, or forward to the end of the sentence.)

In examples 2 and 4 in § 387g, the non-final *incolunt* gaps forward, and the final *appellantur* gaps backward. In example 6 in § 387g, the final *dīvīdit* gaps backward. In the example in § 419, the final *cōgitent* gaps backward. In the example in § 410, the non-final *habet* gaps forward; the second *habet* is final but nevertheless gaps forward, presumably to obtain a final *suōs*, the point of the epigram.

425. Gradation: see climax.

426. Grecism: a feature of a Greek word, phrase, or construction occurring in Latin, usually to create an artistic or learned impression.

> *Nec te spectāre **Boōten** aut **Helicen** iubeō.* "I order you not to look to Boötes or the Great Bear." (Ovid *Met.* 8.206–7) (Two Greek words occur here, both with the Greek accusative ending.)

427. Hendiadys (Greek ἕν διὰ δυοῖν 'one by two'): expression of an idea by two conjoined nouns instead of by a noun and an adjective.

> *Haeduōs **in servitūte atque in diciōne** vidēbat Germānōrum tenērī.* "He saw that the Haedui were kept in slavery and the sway [or "in servile sway" or "in submissive slavery"] of the Germani." (Caes. *B.G.* 1.33.2)

> For further examples, see § 407 (*locum requiemque*) and 435 (*furōrem ac tēla*).

428. Hiatus: the occurrence of two vowel sounds, one at the end of a word and one at the beginning of the following word. Poets generally avoid hiatus by means of an elision (§ 468). However, it is sometimes used on purpose before a caesura (marked by two vertical lines in the following examples) to bring out a word very clearly, with emphatic monosyllabic words, in exclamations, or in enumerations where every word is pronounced separately with utmost pleasure.

> *Quid struit? Aut quā **spē** ‖ **inimīcā** in gente morātur?* "What is he planning? Or with what hope does he loiter among a hostile nation?" (Virg. *Aen.* 4.235) (There are hiatus and a caesura after *spē* and an elision in *inimīcā* before *in*.)
> *Vidēre, ‖ amplectī, ‖ ausculārī, ‖ alloquī.* "Looking, embracing, kissing, chatting." (Plautus *Merc.* 745)

429. Homeric comparison or **epic simile**: an extended simile running to several lines and used typically in epic poetry to intensify the heroic stature of the subject and to serve as decoration. Many elements in the long description of the picturesque nature scene are not involved in the comparison: the second part of the simile is relatively short.

> *Utque lēvēs stipulae demptīs adolentur aristīs,*
> *ut facibus saepēs ardent, quās forte viātor*
> *vel nimis admōvit vel iam sub lūce relīquit,*
> *sīc deus in flammās abiit, sīc pectore tōtō*
> *ūritur et sterilem spērandō nutrit amōrem.*
> "As light blades of straw are kindled after reaping the ears of corn, as hedges keep simmering with burning wood that a traveler happened to put too close or left behind at dawn, so was the god ignited

in flames, so did he burn in all his heart, and nourished a fruitless love on hope." (Ovid *Met.* 1.492–96)

430. Homoeoteleuton: the occurrence of the same word endings, usually close together, but sometimes at the end of succeeding verses, sentences, or constituents. This can happen by chance or be done for rhythmical effect.

> ... *omnia patefacta, illustrāta, oppressa, vindicāta esse* ... "... that everything is revealed, made clear, suppressed, and punished ..." (Cic. *Cat.* 1.32) (See § 402.)

See also the example of repetition in § 453.

431. Hypallage (the Greek term translates 'interchange'): the agreement of an adjective with a noun when it actually refers to (and often occurs next to) another noun that has to do with the first one.

> *Dapēs **avidō** convellere dente parābat.* "He got ready to tear the food to pieces with greedy teeth." (Ovid *Met.* 11.123) (Greedy refers not to the teeth but to Midas.)
> *Sīc aquilam pennā fugiunt **trepidante** columbae.* "So with trembling wings the doves fled from the eagle." (Ovid *Met.* 1.506)

432. Hyperbaton or **disjunction**: the separation of words that syntactically belong together. One word has "stepped over" (Greek ὑπερβαίνω) some other words. Usually a noun and an adjective are involved, sometimes a noun and its attributive genitive. This figure emphasizes one of the two words, usually the first, which is most often an adjective. The further apart the words are, the stronger the emphasis is. Hyperbata are very difficult to reflect or translate into English. One can resort to a repetition, a cleft sentence, an emphatic particle, accent marks, and so on.

Very often, the separation of two words also indicates **visually** that something is **very long or wide**. In some cases, the adjective and the noun even occur in different verses.

In **prose**, the emphasized word of the hyperbaton stands at the beginning or the end of the clause.

In **poetry**, one word of a hyperbaton is often followed by a pause as it occurs before the caesura. In poetry also, double and crossed hyperbata occur with the following **schemes** (whereby a capital letter indicates a noun, the corresponding small letter its attributive adjective):

   a) one word (adjective *a*) stands before the caesura, the other (noun *A*) at the end of the verse (see also the caesural rhyme in § 417);
   b) a **golden verse** contains two crossed hyperbata, ***abAB***;
   c) a **silver verse** contains two hyperbata with the verb in the middle, ***ab-v-BA***;
   d) a **bronze verse** contains one or two hyperbata with the scheme ***abBA***.

[Helvētiī] **angustōs** *sē* **finēs** *habēre arbitrābāntur.* "The Helvetii judged that they possessed an all too limited territory." (Caes. *B.G.* 1.2.5) (The hyperbaton emphasizes the adjective *angustōs.* Because the hyperbaton is very small, there is also visually little space for the Helvetii [*sē*] between the adjective and the noun.)

> ... *velut āles, ab* **altō**
> *quae teneram prōlem prōduxit in aera* **nīdō.**

"... as a bird that from her high, high nest leads her tender young into the air." (Ovid *Met.* 8.213–14) (This very wide hyperbaton is located in two different verses. For the archaic place of *quae,* see § 412.)

> ... *et* **ignōtās** ‖ *umerīs accomodat* **ālās.**

"... and he attached the stránge wings to [his boy's] shoulders." (Ovid *Met.* 8.209)

Silvestrem tenuī ‖ **mūsam** *meditāris* **avēnā.**
"On your fine reed you practice a rural melody." (Virgil *Buc.* 1.2) (The scheme is *abAB*; notice also the humming assonance through the many nasal sounds.)

Ultima Cūmaei ‖ *vēnit iam* **carminis aetās.**
"The last epoch of the prophecy from Cumae has already come." (Virgil *Buc.* 4.4) (*ab-v-BA*)

> *Illīus* **āram**
> *saepe* **tener nostrīs** ‖ *ab* **ovīlibus** *imbuet* **agnus.**

"His altar will often be drenched by [the blood of] a tender lamb from our sheep fold." (Virgil *Buc.* 1.7–8) (*abBA*)

433. Hyperbole: extravagant exaggeration, sometimes ironic or comic.

Mille domōs *adiēre.* "A thousand houses they visited." (Ovid *Met.* 8.628)

434. Hysteron proteron: reversal of the natural or (chrono)logical order.

Moriāmus *et in media arma* **ruāmur.** "Let us die and rush into the middle of the turmoil of battle." (Virg. *Aen.* 2.353)
Neque ego Erotiō **dedī** *nec pallam* **surrupuī.** "And I did not give the robe to Erotium, nor did I steal it [from my wife]." (Plautus *Men.* 509–10)

435. Irony: humor, ridicule, or light sarcasm intended to imply the opposite of the literal sense of the words.

Nōs autem fortēs virī satis facere reī pūblicae vidēmur, sī istīus furōrem ac tēla vītāmus. "But we, courageous men, seem to do enough for the state if we avoid the furious arms of that fellow." (Cic. *Cat.* 1.2)

436. Isocolon: a sentence consisting of a number of members (larger than a phrase, but smaller than a sentence) of approximately equal length. Isocolons often occur in rhetorical periods, as in § 402 (two tetracolons). The names for two, three, four, or more colons are **bicolon, tricolon, tetracolon**, and so on.

> *Maecēnās atavīs // ēdite regibus, . . .* "Maecenas, high descendent of royal ancestors, . . ." (Hor. *Carm.* 1.1.1) (bicolon)

In the next verses, two shepherds sing in dialogue about their love: the first one for his girlfriend, the second for his boyfriend.

> *Triste lupus stabulīs, mātūrīs frūgibus imbrēs,*
> *arboribus ventī, nōbīs Amaryllidis īrae.*
> *—Dulce satis umor, dēpulsīs arbutus haedīs,*
> *lenta salix fētō pecorī, mihi sōlus Amyntas.*
> "Baneful to the fold is the wolf, to the ripe harvest the rains,
> to the trees the winds, and to me Amaryllis's bursts of anger.
> —Sweet to the sowings is the moisture, to the new-weaned kids
>   the strawberry tree,
> to the pregnant flock the flexible willow, and to me Amyntas alone.'
> (Virg. *Buc.* 3.80–83) (two tetracolons)

> *Consulibus insidiās tendere, parāre incendia, opportūna loca armātīs hominibus obsidēre; ipse cum tēlō esse, item aliōs iubēre, hortārī utī semper intentī parātīque essent; diēs noctēsque festīnāre, vigilāre, neque insomnīīs neque labōre fatigārī.* "He laid traps for the consuls, prepared fires, occupied strategic places with armed men. He himself was armed, ordered others [to do] the same, urged them to be always attentive and prepared. He was in a hurry days and nights, did not sleep, did not become tired from lack of sleep or from hard labor." (Sall. *Cat.* 27.2) (three tricolons)

437. Litotes or **understatement:** the expression of an affirmative by the negative of the opposite. As a result, the affirmative is even more strongly expressed. An understatement is more ironic than a litotes.

> *Sēcūra quiēs et nescia fallere vīta, . . . ōtia . . . , spēluncae vīvīque lacus et frigida Tempē mūgitusque boum mollēsque sub arbore somnī **nōn absunt**.* "The safe quietness and a life that does not know how to cheat you, free time, caves and lakes with sparkling water, and the cool valleys, the lowing of the cows and the soft sleep under a tree are not absent." (Virg. *Geo.* 2.467–71) (*Nōn abesse* 'not be absent' = 'be abundantly present'.)

438. Metaphor: substitution of a word or phrase denoting one kind of object or action for another that has some resemblance or analogy to it. It is an implied comparison without the word *as* or *like*. A stereotyped metaphor becomes a **cliché**.

Rēmigiōque carens nōn ullās percipit aurās. "For lack of oars, he had no grip on the air." (Ovid *Met.* 8.228) (The wings of Icarus are mentioned as oars.)

Terraque marmoreō est candida facta gelū. "And the earth has become white with the marble frost." (Ovid *Tr.* 3.10.10)

439. Metonymy: the substitution of one word for another to which it is closely associated (but not on the basis of a comparison as in a metaphor). For example, *ferrum* 'iron' is used to mean 'sword', *Mars* 'Mars' to mean 'war'. (See also § 444, pars pro toto.)

Miscuerat pūrīs auctōrem mūneris undīs. "He had mixed wine with pure water." (Ovid *Met.* 11.125) (The "author of the gift" is Bacchus, metonymy for wine.)

Venerem certūs repetunt armenta diēbus. "The cattle seek Venus on certain days." (Virg. *Geo.* 2.329) (*Venus* = 'mating')

440. Onomatopoeia: formation of words by imitation of natural sounds (e.g., *cuculus* 'cuckoo', *ululāre* 'howl', *susurrus* 'murmuring'); also the naming of a thing or an action by imitating the sound corresponding with the thing signified.

Nec gemere āēria cessābit turtur ab ulmō. "The turtledoves will not stop cooing from the lofty elm." (Virg. *Buc.* 1.58) (*Turtur* is onomatopoeic, with the elm echoing the cooing doves.)

Illī indignantēs magnō cum murmure montis circum claustra fremunt. "They [the winds] get angry and, with a mighty murmuring of the mountain, grumble around their bars." (Virg. *Aen.* 1.55–56) (onomatopoeia *murmur* + onomatopoeic assonance (m-n-r-u) + three alliterations)

Saepēs Hyblaeīs apibus flōrem dēpasta salictī, saepe levī somnum suadēbit inīre susurrō. "A willow hedge whose catkins have been sucked by the Hybla bees will often invite you, with its soft whispering, to take a siesta." (Virg. *Buc.* 1.53–55)

441. Oxymoron (the term translates 'sharp foolishness'): a combination of contradictory or incongruous words that has great effect.

Speciōsōque ēripe damnō. "Save me from this brilliant harm." (Ovid *Met.* 11.133)

Cum tacent, clamant. "Through their being silent, they cry out." (Cic. *Cat.* 1.21)

[Aedēs] inānūs sunt opplētae atque arāneīs. "The house is filled with emptiness and spider webs." (Plautus *Aul.* 84)

442. Parallelism: similarity of construction in which various (parts of) sentences run parallel to each other in sounds, syntax, and/or semantics. *Parallellismus membrorum*, reiteration of similar phrases with similar or antithetic content, is often a fundamental property of poetry and poetic texts.

> *Multī illum iuvenēs, multae cupiēre puellae . . .*
> *Nullī illum iuvenēs, nullae tetigēre puellae.*
> "Many young boys, many young girls longed for him . . .
> No young boy, no young girl touched him." (Ovid *Met.* 3.353–55)

> *Insere nunc, Meliboee, pirōs! Pōne ordine vītēs!*
> "Now, Meliboeus, graft your pear trees! Plant your vines in rows!"
> (Virgil *Buc.* 1.73)

443. Paronomasia: a play on words in which words similar in sounds are set in opposition so as to give antithetical force.

> *. . . ut **exsul** potius tentāre quam **consul** vexāre rem pūblicam possēs.*
> ". . . so that as an exile you could make an attempt on the state, rather than as a consul scourge it." (Cic. *Cat.* 1.27)
> *Hīc est **sepulcrum** haud **pulchrum pulchrae** fēminae.* "Here is the un-beautiful grave of a beautiful woman." (*C.I.L.* 6.15346, spelling adapted) (The pun on *sepulcrum* 'grave' and *haud pulchrum* 'not beautiful' interprets *sē-* as a prefix of negation [like *haud*] or separation [§ 13]. Etymologically, however, *sepulcrum* does not contain a prefix but is derived from *sepelī-re.*)
> *Quid metuis? — Nē mihi **damnum** in **Epidamnō** duis.* "What do you fear? — That you do damage to me in Epidamnum." (Plautus *Men.* 267)

444. Pars pro toto or **synecdoche**: substitution of a part for the whole. This is a special case of metonymy (§ 439). For example, *tectum* 'roof' is used to mean 'house', *mucrō* 'point' to mean 'sword', *axis* 'axle' to mean 'chariot', *postēs* 'doorposts' to mean 'door'.

445. Periphrasis: the use of a longer phrasing by means of descriptive adjectives or abstract general terms or by referring to the working of somebody or something.

> *Hominum sator atque deōrum* "the father of men and gods . . ." = Jupiter (Virg. *Aen.* 1.254) (This form of naming is also called *antonomasia* 'naming instead of'.)
> *Cereālia dōna* "the gifts of Ceres" = grain = bread. (Ovid *Met.* 11.122)

> See also the examples under "style" and "satire on lofty style" in § 376.

446. Personification: attribution of human qualities to a thing or an abstraction.

> *At tū, quae rāmīs arbor miserābile corpus*
> *nunc tegis ūnius, mox es tectūra duōrum,*
> *signa tenē caedis.*
> "And you, tree who now with your branches cover the pitiable corpse of one and soon are going to cover those of both of us, pre-

serve the tokens of our death." (Ovid *Met.* 4.158–60) (Notice also the parallelism and the antithesis in v. 159.)

447. **Pleonasm**: the use of more words than necessary to denote mere sense, either for emphasis or by negligence.

> ... *quō saepe solēmus*
> *pastōrēs ovium tenerōs dēpellere fētūs.*
> "...where we, shepherds, often used to drive the weak young of our sheep." (Virg. *Buc.* 1.20–21) (This pleonasm is accompanied by alliteration; *solemus, solebam,* and *solent* with an infinitive occur three times within six verses [20–25], probably for lofty style.)

448. **Poetic plural**: the use of the plural in poetry, sometimes to suggest quantity or magnitude.

> *Cērīs alligat īmās [pennās].* "With [a lot of] wax he bound feathers together at the bottom." (Ovid *Met.* 8.193)

449. **Poetic vocabulary**: a special vocabulary, including independent adjectives and neuter plural participles, that poets often use instead of everyday words. Poetic words include *ensis* (= *gladius*) 'sword', *tellūs* (= *terra*) 'earth', *nātus* (= *fīlius*) 'son', *genitor* (= *pater*) 'creator, father', *undae* (= *mare, aqua*) 'waves, water(s)', *lētum* (= *mors*) 'death', *āles* (= *avis*) 'bird', *aequor* (= *mare*) 'a level surface, sea', *geminī* (= *duo*) 'both', and participles such as *iussa* 'the orders' and *coeptum* 'what has been begun, the undertaking'.

450. **Polysyndeton**: repetition of coordinating conjunctions in a series of words or clauses in close succession. Its purpose is to emphasize the close connection or the enumeration of all members.

> *Dīvesque miserque effugere optat opēs.* "Both rich and wretched, he wishes to escape his wealth." (Ovid *Met.* 11.127–28)
> ... *parātōs esse et obsidēs dare et imperāta facere et oppidīs recipere et frūmentō cēterīsque rēbus iuvāre.* "[The Remi said] that they were ready to give hostages and to execute his orders and to receive him in their towns and to help him with grain and other supplies." (Caes. *B.G.* 2.5.3)

451. **Preterition** or **pretermission** or **paralepsis**: a brief mention in which one declares that one is not going to speak about what one is mentioning. Such an "omission" rhetorically emphasizes what is only briefly suggested.

> *Quid loquar ut vincti concrescant frigore rivi?* 'Why should I mention how streams shackled by winter congeal?' (Ovid *Tr.* 2.10.25)

452. Proleptic adjective (not to be confused with prolepsis: see § 389): the anticipative use of an adjective (as attribute or predicativum), whereas it actually only indicates the end of the action.

> *Submersās obrue puppīs.* "Overwhelm the sunken ships." (Virg. *Aen.* 1.69) (The meaning here is "Overwhelm the ships so that they sink.")
>
> *... En quō discordia cīvēs*
> *prōduxit miserōs!*
> "Behold, where has the discord brought our unfortunate citizens!" (Virg. *Buc.* 1.71–72) (*Miserōs* 'unfortunate' here means "so that they became unfortunate." *Miserōs* also stands in a hyperbaton, at the end of the sentence, and in an enjambment.)

453. Repetition: a reuse of the same word(s) for emphasis.

> *Nihil agis, nihil mōlīris, nihil cōgitās.* "You do nothing, you attempt nothing, you ponder nothing." (Cic. *Cat.* 1.8)

454. Rhetorical question (§ 230): a question not intended to elicit an answer but asked for rhetorical effect. For such a question, there is no answer or only one possible, self-evident answer. (In indirect speech, the rhetorical question is considered to be a statement: see § 273c.)

> *Quousque tandem abūtēre, Catilīna, patientiā nostrā? Quam diū etiam furor iste tuus nōs ēlūdet? Quem ad fīnem sēsē effrēnāta iactābit audācia?* "How long, Catiline, will you abuse our patience? And how long will that frenzy of yours escape our grasp? To what lengths will your unbridled audacity go?" (Cic. *Cat.* 1.1)

455. Simplex pro composito: the use in poetry of a non-compound verb instead of a related compound one.

> *Daedalus clausus erat pelagō.* "Daedalus was locked in by the sea." (Ovid *Met.* 8.183–85) (*clausus* instead of *inclusus*)
> *Dulcia linquimus arva.* "We leave our sweet fields." (Virg. *Buc.* 1.3) (*Linquimus = relinquimus*)

456. Symmetry: see parallelism (§ 442).

457. Syncope: the loss of one or more sounds in the interior of a word, as in *perīclum* (= *perīculum*) and *audissem* (= *audīvissem*). See § 81.

458. Synesthesia: combination of words from different senses, as in a reference to "shouting colors."

459. Synizesis: the connection of vowels by a slur so as to form one syllable in metrics. The first vowel usually becomes a semi-vowel. For example, trisyllabic *genua* and *aurea* become disyllabic; disyllabic *prout, mihi, cuī,* and *dehinc* become monosyllabic. **Synaeresis** is sometimes used as a synonym for this stylistic technique but, rather, indicates contraction of two vowels, as in *nēmō* (< *nehemo*) and *cōgō* (< *coagō*).

460. Tautology: repetition of the same idea by other words, usually for emphasis.

> *Monēre, ōrāre Titurium prō hospitiō* . . . "He advised—yes, begged— Titurius in the name of hospitality . . ." (Caes. *B.G.* 5.27.7)
> *Domum meam maiōribus praesidiīs **mūnīvī atque firmāvī.*** "I have secured and fortified my house with greater guards." (Cic. *Cat.* 1.10)

461. Tmesis: the separation of parts of a compound word by intervening words.

> *Cūius reī **lubet** simulātor dissimulātor* "[He was] a pretender and dissembler of anything you want" (Sall. *Cat.* 5.4)
> *Semper honōs nōmenque tuum laudēsque manēbunt, **quae** mē **cumque** vocant terrae.* "Your honor and name and fame will always remain in what lands soever call me." (Virg. *Aen.* 1.609–10)

462. Variation: a change in vocabulary, sounds, syntactic structure, and word order or, more generally, in content or feelings. The grammatical change, frequent in Tacitus, is also called asymmetry.

> *Baucis **anus parilī́que aetāte** Philēmōn.* "The old woman Baucis and Philemon of similar age." (Ovid *Met.* 8.631) [Note also the chiasmus.)
> *Incerta **prō** certīs, bellum **quam** pacem mālēbant.* "They preferred uncertainty to certainty, war over peace." (Sall. *Cat.* 17.6)
> *Nam Tiberius cuncta per consulēs incipiēbat, tamquam **vetere rē pūblicā** et **ambiguus imperandī.*** "For Tiberius started everything through the consuls, as if the old republic still existed and as if [he was] uncertain about his emperorship." (Tac. *Ann.* 1.7.2) (The apparent comparison contains an ablative absolute [§ 349–54] and a predicative apposition [§ 290].)
> *Nec quisquam dēfendere audēbat, **crebrīs multōrum minīs restinguere prōhibentium,** et **quia aliī palam facēs iaciēbant atque esse sibi auctōrem vōciferābantur, sīve ut raptūs licentius exercērent, seu iussū.*** "And nobody dared to fight the fire, because of the frequent threats of the numerous people who were forbidding to extinguish it, and because others were openly throwing torches and shouting that they had instructions, either to plunder more freely, or because [indeed] they had an order." (Tac. *Ann.* 15.38.8) (The first variation involves *crebrīs . . . minīs . . .*, an adverbial modifier, versus *quia . . . iaciēbant atque vociferābantur,* two adverbial clauses. The second variation is in *sīve . . . seu.* The third involves *ut . . . exercērent,* an adverbial clause, versus *iussū,* an adverbial modifier.)

463. Zeugma (cf. *iūgum* 'yoke', *iungere* 'join together'): the incorrect, audacious, or bizarre combination of words, particularly of a verb and two different nouns with which it has different semantic and/or syntactic relations.

> *Vīdit novī generis **faciem**, insolitum **incessum**, **vōcem** nullīus terrestris animālis.* "He saw the face of the new species, the unusual gait, and the voice of no earthly living being." (Seneca *Apoc.* 5.3) (semantic zeugma)
> ***Manūs ac supplicēs vōcēs** ad Tiberium **tendens** excipitur.* "When he stretches out his hands and his suppliant words to Tiberius, he is listened to." (Tac. *Ann.* 2.29.2)
> *Causa praecipua ex formidine, nē Germānicus, in **cūius** manū tot legiōnēs, immensa sociōrum auxilia, mīrus apud populum favor, habēre imperium quam exspectāre mallet.* "The main cause came from his fear that Germanicus, in whose hands were so many legions and immeasurable allied auxiliary troops, and who enjoyed a wonderful popularity with the people, might rather want to be in power than to wait for it." (Tac. *Ann.* 1.7.5) (In this syntactic zeugma, the first relative clause starts with a genitive in *in cūius manū;* the second should have started with *cuī* [dat. of possessor with an elliptic *erat:* see § 138e] before *mīrus favor.*)

20
Metrics

Latin metrical feet

464. A Latin verse consists of measures or feet. Their nature and number vary according to the kind of verse chosen by the poet. The pattern of the verses or versification is studied in metrics. The technique of dividing a verse into feet is called scansion.

A Latin verse is based not on rhyme or on the number of syllables but on the length of the syllables. (For caesural rhyme and homoeoteleuton, see § 417 and 430.)

465. **A measure or foot consists of a number of syllables of a certain length** (long or short). A short or light syllable counts one **mora** (time unit); a long or heavy syllable, two morae. The total length of one foot often consists of three or four morae. (Cf. the bar of three or four counts in music: 3/4 or 4/4 time.)

Frequently used feet of **three morae** are
the **iambus**: ˘ – (short + long: 1 mora + 2 morae);
the **trochee**: – ˘ (long + short: 2 + 1);
the **tribrach**: ˘ ˘ ˘ (short + short + short: 1 + 1 + 1).

Frequently used feet of **four morae** are:
the **dactyl**: – ˘ ˘ (long + short + short: 2 + 1 + 1);
the **spondee**: – – (long + long: 2 + 2);
the **anapest**: ˘ ˘ – (short + short + long: 1 + 1 + 2).

Latin versification schemes

Dactylic hexameter

466. The **dactylic hexameter** or **heroic hexameter** consists of **six feet** that in principle contain a **dactyl** (of **four morae**) each. However, there are some alternatives.

a) The first four feet can contain spondees, whereas the fifth very rarely can. If the fifth foot contains a spondee (for special effects), the verse is called a spondaic verse.
b) The dactyl almost always occurs in the fifth foot, but never in the sixth.
c) The sixth foot consists of a spondee (of four morae) or a trochee (of three morae).

The first long syllable of every foot carries the **verse accent**, or **ictus**, which is indicated by an accent mark (').

The scheme of a dactylic hexameter is thus

$$\acute{–}\,\smile\smile\,/\,\acute{–}\,\smile\smile\,/\,\acute{–}\,\smile\smile\,/\,\acute{–}\,\smile\smile\,/\,\acute{–}\,\smile\smile\,/\,\acute{–}\,\smile$$
$$\quad 1 \qquad 2 \qquad 3 \qquad 4 \qquad 5 \qquad 6$$

467. Caesura. A verse (but never a word) is cut by the **caesura** ($<$ *caedere, caesum*), or breathing pause, indicated in the following examples by two vertical lines (‖). The caesura divides a line into sections that the mind can take in at once without effort. The major caesuras, sometimes accompanied by secondary pauses (not mentioned here), can occur

   a) after the fifth half foot (= after the first long syllable of the third foot), where such pause is called a strong masculine caesura of the third foot, or semiquinaria;
   b) after the first long syllable of the second and/or fourth foot, where such pause is called a masculine caesura, or the semiternaria and/or semiseptenaria;
   c) between the two short syllables of the third foot, where such pause is called a feminine caesura.

468. Elision. If the last syllable of a word ends in a vowel, a diphthong, or an **m** while the next word begins with a vowel, a diphthong, or an **h**, then the last syllable of the first word is **elided**. This means that this syllable does not count in the scansion. It is pronounced lightly together with the initial vowel of the following word. One instance is seen in § 470, three instances in the second example of § 473.

If, however, the second word is *es* or *est,* the initial *e* of this verb is elided. An example is seen in the second line of the epigram in § 410: *Quae ratiō (e)st?*

Elision is applied to avoid the disturbing hitch, the **hiatus**, between two vowels. Exceptionally, the hiatus is allowed under certain conditions (§ 428).

469. Scansion. In order to scan a verse, one uses the following technique, strictly in this order. Do not jump to step c too fast!

   a) Indicate the length of the syllables on the basis of the rules about quantity (§ 7–8).
   b) Use a dictionary to check the length of some syllables if there are many syllables with unknown length.
   c) Separate the feet of the verse with slashes (/). Begin at the end: the sixth and fifth feet together generally occupy the last five syllables. Add the missing length marks.
   d) Place the ictus (') on the first long (heavy) syllable of each foot.
   e) Indicate each caesura with two vertical lines (‖).

470. Example.

$$\underline{\bar{}}' \quad \smile\smile/\underline{\bar{}}' \quad \smile\smile/\underline{\bar{}}' \parallel - /\underline{\bar{}}' - /\underline{\bar{}}' \smile \smile/\underline{\bar{}}' \smile$$

atque_ita compositās parvō curvāmine flectit.

"And he bent the so-composed [wings] with a light curve." (Ovid *Met.* 8.194)

471. **The ictus and the word accent** may or may not coincide in a verse. If they always coincide, there occurs a monotonous jingle, which is not very aesthetic. In the opposite case, when all rhythm disappears, one might have the feeling one is reading prose. Therefore, Latin poets make the ictus and the word accent almost always coincide in the fifth and sixth feet, so that the rhythm is felt. Earlier in the verse, they see to it that the two do not coincide in most feet.

A caveat about this clash of the ictus and the word accent is in order. The Romans may not have felt this problem so strongly, because the word accent in classical Latin was rather downgraded in the **breath group**, or **cursus**. Only the last word accent in the cursus may be audible, as in modern French. In any case, one should read Latin verses aloud and get a feeling of which syllables might or should be accentuated. In the verse in § 470, it seems reasonable that one should stress not all six syllables bearing the ictus but only the following three syllables: *-po-* in the breath group *atque ita compositās* (the end of the direct object), *-va-* in *parvō curvāmine* (the ictus and the word accent coincide at the end of an adverbial phrase), and *-flec-* in *flectit* (the ictus and the word accent coincide at the end of the sentence).

If the ictus and the word accent do not coincide in the fifth and sixth feet, the poet intends something special. The first line of the following example runs as explained earlier in this section (there is strong rhythm through the coincidence of the ictus and the word accent in the fourth, fifth, and sixth feet), but the irregular jolting rhythm of the second line corresponds to the thumping waves. In the example that follows, the ictus is indicated by an accent mark (´), the word accent by an underlined vowel in the stressed syllable.

Fránguntúr rēmí; tum próra āvértit et úndīs
dát latus; ínsequitúr cumuló praerúptus aquáe mons.

"The oars snap; then the prow turns around and exposes its broadside to the waves; there follows in a heap an abrupt mountainous sea." (Virg. *Aen.* 1.104–5)

In verse 105 of this example, a massive steep mountain of water plummets down on the ship in a very rough rhythm, violating the normal cadence of the end of a dactylic hexameter. Moreover, the last five words form an anticlimax (§ 409), going from a four-syllable word to a monosyllabic word at the end of the line: this almost never occurs in an epic dactylic hexameter, but here the poet makes the whole sentence fall down onto the small monosyllabic word.

472. On the average, **a dactylic hexameter contains one verb per line**, as in the example in § 470 and the first example in § 473. More main verbs per line reflect an increased activity, as during the storm in the example in § 471. **Two dactylic hexameters usually form one grammatical sentence.** Deviations from that rule indicate special intentions of the poet: unrest, speed, grandiloquence, and so on.

473. **Dactyls and spondees** usually succeed each other in a verse. When one of the two predominates, a particular mood is created. A preponderance of dactyls gives the verse a certain speed, lightness, hilarity, or unrest. A preponderance of spondees suggests slowness, darkness, melancholy, or stateliness.

$$\acute{-} \; \smile \; \smile / \acute{-} \; \smile \; \smile / \acute{-} \; \| \; \smile \; \smile / \acute{-} \; \smile \; \smile / \acute{-} \; \smile \; \smile / \acute{-} \; \smile$$
Quadrupedante putrem sonitū quatit ungula campum.
"With galloping sound the hoofs strike the loose sand." (Virg. *Aen.* 8.596) (five dactyls for the speed of the quadrupeds; many hard stops and sonorous nasals; two crossed hyperbata forming a golden verse [*abAB:* § 432])

$$\acute{-} \; - / \acute{-} \; - / \acute{-} \; - / \acute{-} \; \| \, - / \acute{-} \; \smile \; \smile / \acute{-} \; \smile$$
Monstrum horrendum, informe, ingens, cuī lūmen ademptum.
"A horrible monster, shapeless, enormous, bereft of light." (Virg. *Aen.* 3.658) (The Cyclops Polyphemus is described in four slow, dark spondees with dark *o*'s and *u*'s, nasals, and *r*'s. *Cuī* forms a synizesis [§ 459].)

Dactylic pentameter

474. A **dactylic pentameter** actually is a dicatalectic hexameter, that is, a dactylic hexameter composed of two catalectic (incomplete) members. **The third and the sixth feet contain only one syllable.** Hence, 2½ + 2½ = 5 feet. The first and second feet of the first **hemistich** (half a verse) can contain either dactyls or spondees. The second hemistich necessarily contains two dactyls and one **syllaba anceps** (long or short syllable). The caesura always falls between the two hemistichs, thus between the third and fourth feet. The scheme is thus

$$\acute{-} \; \overline{\smile \smile} / \acute{-} \; \overline{\smile \smile} / \acute{-} \; \| \, \acute{-} \; \smile \smile / \acute{-} \; \smile \smile / \acute{-}$$
$$\quad 1 \qquad 2 \qquad 3 \;\; 4 \qquad 5 \qquad 6$$

475. The pentameter only occurs in combination with a dactylic hexameter. Together they form an **elegiac distich**. This poetic verse accompanied by the flute is used for various subject matters among the Greeks; the Romans use it chiefly for love poetry (Catullus, Ovid, Tibullus, Sulpicia, etc.) and epigrams (Martial). The two lines of the elegiac distich usually form one grammatical sentence or at least express one coherent thought. The following example contains twice two parallel sentences but a unity of sense.

$$\bar{\text{T}}\acute{\text{e}} \smile \; \smile /\acute{\text{-}} \; - /\acute{\text{-}} \; \| - /\acute{\text{-}} \quad \smile\smile /\acute{\text{-}} \; \smile \smile /\acute{\text{-}} \smile$$

Tē loquor absentem, tē vox mea nōminat ūnam;

$$\acute{\text{-}} \smile \; \smile /\acute{\text{-}} \; \smile \smile /\acute{\text{-}} \| \acute{\text{-}} \quad \smile\smile / \acute{\text{-}} \; \smile \; \smile /\acute{\text{-}}$$

nulla venit sine tē nox mihi, nulla di ēs.

"I mention you in your absence, my voice names only you; not one single night comes to me without you, not one single day." (Ovid *Tr.* 3.3.17–18)

Glossary

ablative absolute Dependent adverbial clause without a conjunction and with the subject and the non-finite predicate in the ablative.

adjectival modifier See **attribute**.

adjective Part of speech. Used as an attribute or as a nominal part of the predicate. Also used independently as a noun.

adverb Part of speech. Determines a verb, an adjective, another adverb, or a whole sentence.

adverbial modifier Non-obligatory constituent in the sentence.

agreement Occurs when an inflectional form is identical or at least somehow corresponds in grammatical categories (e.g., gender, number, case, and person) to the head of a phrase or the subject of a clause.

apposition A noun or noun phrase expanding another noun and agreeing with it in case.

argument See **obligatory** and **predicate frame.**

attribute Non-obligatory immediate constituent of the head in the noun phrase. Does not have the same function as the whole noun phrase. Can be a determiner, adjective, appositive noun, noun in the genitive, participle, gerundive, relative clause, and so on.

circumstantial modifier See **adverbial modifier.**

clause Part of the sentence that has its own kernel. Is either independent or dependent. Has a finite, non-finite, or nominal predicate.

clause marker General term for various words indicating (the beginning of) a dependent clause: relative pronoun, subordinating conjunction, indirect question particle, interrogative pronoun, and interrogative adverb. The accusative ending and the infinitive ending are markers of the infinitive clause; the ablative ending is a marker of the subject and predicate of the ablative absolute.

cluster Group of two or more equivalent elements (conjoined nouns, phrases, etc.).

complement Obligatory constituent in the kernel of the sentence, by which a predication is made complete. See **predicativum** and **infinitive complement.**

constituent Part of a construction on all levels of the grammatical hierarchy.

copula Verb without meaning of its own. Carrier of person, number, tense, and mood of the nominal predicate. Links the nominal part of the predicate to the subject.

deictics   Expressions whose referent can only be understood with respect to the interlocutors. For example, the referent of the pronouns of the first and second person varies according to who is speaking; the same holds for the place indicated by demonstratives.

dependent clause   Clause that depends on a governing clause. Can have a subject, object, adverbial, or attributive function. Its form may vary, including finite clause with conjunction, relative clause, infinitive clause, participial clause, and so on.

determiner   Numeral or demonstrative, possessive, interrogative, or indefinite pronominal adjective determining a noun or noun phrase.

dominating verb   See **governing**.

embedded clause   See **dependent clause**.

enclitic   Monosyllabic word without independent stress, attached in pronunciation to the preceding word.

FAP   Future active participle. Expresses posteriority with respect to the governing verb.

function   Syntactic relation of a sentence constituent to the predicate. More generally, syntactic relation of one constituent to another in a whole.

future perfect   Future perfective tense.

governing   Affecting, conditioning, influencing. Relation of the head of a construction to its modifier (noun to adjective, preposition to noun) or of a higher predicate to a lower one.

Greek accusative   Morphological label for adverbial modifier of respect.

head   Nucleus of a phrase. Can be determined or modified by other attributive constituents.

IAP   Imperfective active participle. Expresses simultaneity with the governing verb.

imperfective   Non-completed aspect of a verb. Characterized by the imperfective stem. Expresses simultaneity with the governing verb.

infinitive clause (or *accusativus cum infinitivo*)   Dependent subject or object clause without a subordinating conjunction; the subject is in the accusative, and the predicate is an infinitive verb. Abbreviated *AcI*.

infinitive complement   Obligatory constituent in the personal passive, or *nominativus cum infinitivo* (*NcI*).

kernel   Nucleus or minimal grammatical clause. Contains at least a predicate and zero, one, two, or three other obligatory constituents (or arguments).

main clause   Clause on the highest level in the grammatical hierarchy in the sentence. Can contain one or more dependent clauses.

matrix clause   See **main clause**.

modifier   Non-obligatory subordinate constituent of a grammatical construction, such as the attribute in the phrase or the adverbial in the sentence.

mood   Semantic component of the verb that expresses whether the action or state it denotes is conceived as fact or in some other manner. Also refers to the corresponding set of inflectional forms.

morpheme   Smallest meaningful unit of a word. Can be a root or a (derivational/inflectional) affix.

NcI   Nominativus cum Infinitivo. Contains a subject, a passive verbal predicate, and an infinitive complement. Also called personal passive.

noun (or **substantive**)   Part of speech. Latin *nomen substantivum*.

noun clause   See **subject** and **object**.

object   Obligatory constituent in the predicate frame of certain verbs. Its case may vary. Can be a noun, a noun phrase, a pronoun, a clause, and so on.

obligatory   Required by the frame of a given verb. Part of the kernel.

perfect   Present perfective tense.

perfective   Completed aspect of a verb. Characterized by the perfective stem in the active voice and by the perfect passive participle in the passive voice. Expresses anteriority to the governing verb.

personal passive   See **NcI**.

phoneme   Smallest meaningful sound unit as distinct from another in a given language.

phrase   Group of words forming a syntactic and semantic sense unit. The term usually occurs with a qualifying term: e.g., noun phrase, prepositional phrase, infinitive phrase, participial phrase, verb phrase, and so on.

pluperfect   Past perfective tense.

PPP   Perfective passive participle. Expresses anteriority with respect to the governing verb.

Pragmatics   Part of linguistics that deals with the relation between linguistic expressions and their users.

predicate   Basis of a kernel (as well as of a clause and a sentence) to which all other sentence constituents are related semantically and syntactically. Mostly a verb (either finite, an infinitive, or a participle); also a noun or an adjective with or without a copula.

predicate frame   Indicates the number of obligatory kernel constituents (also called arguments) required by a given predicate, as well as the semantic roles that the arguments fulfill.

predicativum   Sentence constituent indicating the state or function of (another) sentence constituent in its relation to the predicate. Can be obligatory (predicative complement of the subject or object) with certain verbs, or non-obligatory (predicative apposition).

prefix object   Object called for by a verb compounded with a prefix.

prepositional object   Obligatory constituent with certain verbs. Governed by a preposition.

prepositional phrase   Phrase in which a preposition governs a noun or noun phrase. Most often a non-obligatory constituent in the sentence, but sometimes an obligatory constituent in the kernel or an attribute in a noun phrase.

present stem   See **imperfective**.

rheme   New or important information about the theme in the sentence. A dynamic element in the communication.

semantic role   Meaning relation of a constituent to the predicate or of an attribute to its head.

semantics   Area of linguistics dealing with meaning. Either lexical (vocabulary) or grammatical (semantic role in a construction).

sentence   Major unit of language and grammatical analysis. Consists at least of a predicate and usually of one, two, or three other obligatory constituents (arguments) and one or more non-obligatory constituents. Is itself usually part of a larger unit (a turn in a dialogue, paragraph, chapter, etc.)

sequence of tenses   Anterior, simultaneous, or posterior relation of a subordinate verb to its governing verb. Governs the tense used for expressing such relation. Latin *consecutio temporum*.

shifters   See **deictics**.

simple future   Future imperfective tense.

speech act   Unit of linguistic communication involving spoken or written signs (e.g., words, sentences), a human producer, a human consumer, an intention, and circumstances.

subject   First obligatory constituent required by a predicate in the kernel. Governs agreement of the predicate. Can be a noun, pronoun, phrase, or clause.

subordinate clause   See **dependent clause**.

subordinating conjunction   Part of speech. Marker of a dependent clause with a finite verb.

syntax   Area of grammar dealing with formal relations between constituents.

thematic vowel   Vowel connecting the stem of a noun or a verb with the ending.

theme   Sentence constituent about which something is said. Not a dynamic part of the sentence, but a part providing cohesion between the rheme and the context.

valence (or **valency**)   Relative capacity (based on the predicate frame) of a verb to attract arguments. Valence can vary from 0 to 3.

verb   Part of speech. Usually functions as the predicate of the clause or sentence.

Index

The numbers refer to the paragraphs.